THE PROCESS OF COMMUNICATION

The Process of Communication

[For Degree/P.G. Diploma Courses in Journalism and Media Communication]

By
S. Kundra

ANMOL PUBLICATIONS PVT. LTD.
NEW DELHI - 110 002 (INDIA)

ANMOL PUBLICATIONS PVT. LTD.
4374/4B, Ansari Road, Daryaganj
New Delhi - 110 002
Ph.: 23261597, 23278000
Visit us at: www.anmolpublications.com

The Process of Communication

First Published, 2005

ISBN 81-261-2435-0

PRINTED IN INDIA

Published by J.L. Kumar for Anmol Publications Pvt. Ltd., New Delhi - 110 002 and Printed at Mehra Offset Press, Delhi.

Contents

Preface

"The Process of Communication" as a paper is being taught at the various diploma, graduate and post graduate level in 'Media Communication and Journalism' at various universities and institutions. This book is designed as an introductory text to the above paper, encompassing vital information on all pertinent aspects. Thus the material presented here would be of interest as well as of great use to the students, teachers and professionals of Media Communication and Journalism. This book will provide complete knowledge of the nature, scope, functions and process of communication, intra-personal, inter-personal group, basic models of communication, print media, electronic media, technological developments in communication etc. to the students.

The major topics dealt in this book are—Theory and Fundamentals of Communication; Mass Communication—A Process; Functions of Communication; Impact on Different Sections; Kinds and Theories of Communication; Mass Media Development; Basic Models of Communication; Technological Development in Communication; Mass Media in Practice; Media for Mass Communication.

It is hoped that all those will benefit from the contents of this book for whom it is meant. The author will feel amply rewarded, if motive is achieved.

Author

1

Theory and Fundamentals of Communication

'Communication' (together with its twin 'information') is perhaps one of the most hyped words in contemporary culture. It encompasses a multitude of experiences, actions and events, as well as a whole variety of happenings and meanings, and technologies too. Thus, a conference or a meeting or even a mela or procession is a 'communication event', newspapers, radio, video and television are 'communication media', phones, pagers, and email are 'communication technologies', and journalists, advertisers, public relations personnel, and even camera crew and news-readers are 'communication professionals'.

Further, the contemporary period has come to be labelled variously the 'Information Age', the 'Communication Age', and most recently, the Cyber or Networking Age. The uses and understanding of Communication have come a long way from its original association first with 'means of transport' and later with 'transmission'. The English word 'communication' is derived from the Latin noun 'communis' and the Latin verb 'communicare' which means 'to make common'. Terms closely related to communication and with similar etymological origins include community, communion, commonality, communalism and communism. The closest Indian language equivalent to the original concept of communication is 'sadharanikaran'.

Communication, in its simplest sense, is a human relationship, involving two or more persons who come together to share, to dialogue and to commune, or just to be together say at a festival or a time of mourning. Communication is thus not so much an act or even a process but rather social and cultural 'togetherness'. Communion with oneself, with God, nature, the world of spirits, and with one's ancestors are also forms of communication.

A Social Science

The study of Communication in its multitudinous forms, whether in its human or technological dimensions, has now taken on the characteristics of an interdisciplinary and multi-disciplinary social science. To begin with, Communication Science or Communication Studies was based in university departments of Sociology or Psychology or Political Science, and it borrowed heavily from these social science disciplines. In its turn, Communication Studies has led to a re-orientation in the disciplines themselves, a greater involvement with popular cultures, and with men and women as communicators at home and in the workaday world. Studies of propaganda by social scientists resulted in greater interest among governments and academicians in the 'power' of communication strategies. Government departments of defense provided generous funding for propaganda research, and business and industry promoted media research so as to better exploit communication for advertising and marketing their products and services. The United States' government departments, private companies and the media themselves were the prime supporters of university courses and research in the mass media. Communication Studies was largely influenced by such needs and such research, as well as the rapid growth of the press, and later of the cinema, radio and television. The discipline of Communication owes its origins to the United States of the 1930s, a time when Nazi propaganda was a sotirce of great concern; the US government established an Institute of Propaganda Research to develop techniques for influencing public opinion. In Britain and France, the discipline had its roots in literary and linguistic studies, while in Germany the origins are traceable to the Institute of Social Research (the Frankfurt School) and to Freudian psychoanalysis.

In India, the discipline of Communication came into its own with the Government's need for propagating family planning, social development and national integration throughout the land. The Indian Institute of Mass Communication was established in 1965 by the Ministry of Information and Broadcasting to provide training and conduct research to assist in this effort. University departments of Journalism joined in this effort as well, but continued for the most part to be no more than trade schools for the print media.

Fact of Communication

Communication is a fact in the world of human beings, animals, and plants, and is an ever-continuing process going on all the time. It is as necessary to human, animal and vegetable existence as life itself. Halt communication and the life processes wither and die. The need for communication is as basic as the hunger for food and drink, perhaps even more so. In the beginning after all was 'Aum' or the 'Word', the first sound ever made or heard. In Indian tradition the 'Word' is the Shabda Brahman, the divine word.

'Communication is the name we give to the countless ways that humans have of keeping in touch not just words and music, pictures and print, nods and becks, postures and plumages; to every move that catches someone's eye and every sound that resonates upon another's ear.'

This observation is true also for animals, birds and bees, and other land, sea and air creatures too. The singing and chirping of birds, the croaking of frogs, and the many visual and olfactory signals among bird and beast are forms of communication; some simple, others very highly sophisticated. The dance of the honeybee, for instance, is an advanced means of communication for it conveys to other bees the precise direction and distance of the place where nectar will be found.

Need for Communication

A human being's need for communication is as strong and as basic as the need to eat, sleep and love. It is both an individual and a social need. It is both a natural individual demand and a requirement of social existence to use communication resources in order to engage in the sharing of experiences, through 'symbol-mediated interaction'. The severest punishment for a child is to be isolated, to be left alone, not to be spoken to. North Indian children mete out this punishment when they say'kuttie' to their playmates, holding out their thumb as an accompanying gesture.

Grown-ups too and especially the aged need company, need to communicate. Society punishes criminals by locking them up in solitary cells, thus starving them of the basic need, and indeed the fundamental right to communicate. Communication involves active interaction with our environments-physical, biological and social. Deprived of this interaction we would not be aware of whether we are safe or in danger, whether hated or loved, or satisfied or hungry. However, most of us take this interaction and this relationship for granted, unless we experience some deprivation of it. When that happens we adapt ourselves to the environment so that we don't lose touch, in both the literal and figurative senses. For, to lose touch is to suffer isolation.

The basic human need for communication can perhaps be traced to the process of mankind's evolution from lower species. Animals, for instance, have to be in sensory communication with their physical and biological surroundings to find food, protect themselves and reproduce their species. A loss of sensation the inability to hear a predator, for instance, can mean loss of life. Similarly, to be lost from primitive social communication from the pack, from the herd or the tribe is to be condemned to death. What happens to a person who is 'excommunicated'—literally, cut off from communication by his group or his society? Malcolm X, the Black Muslim leader, described the experience of being expelled from his group as 'a state of emotional shock'. Elaborating, he said that this state was like that of someone who for twelve years had an inseparable, beautiful marriage partner and then suddenly one morning at breakfast the marriage partner had thrust across the table some divorce papers. I felt as though something in nature had failed, like the sun or the stars. It was that incredible a phenomenon to me something too stupendous to conceive.

Others who have been isolated for a period of time from human company are known to have experienced nightmarish hallucinations. Indeed, social isolation can also be hazardous to the heart as much as to the mind. It is estimated that single men without Close friends run two or three times the risk of developing heart disease as their more sociable counterparts.

However, lack of communication can be as disorienting an experience as too much of it. Indeed, the apparent effects of sensory deprivation and sensory overload are frequently similar: anxiety, apathy;. impaired judgement, strange visions, and something akin to schizophrenia. The 'information explosion' brought about by satellite television, the internet and other technologies is an instance of this sensory overload.

Role of Language

But sensory communication alone was not enough for man to survive. Hence the evolution of symbolic communication called language from non-verbal gestures, grunts and grimaces to the verbal, and then to the written and printed word. Language is inseparable from culture which is its very source of sustenance; language embodies and expresses a community's culture. The 'arts' have grown out of this same fundamental desire and need to express oneself and to reach out to others. Cro-Magnon men and women adorned their caves with paintings of animals and hunters; the modern artist shows a preference for the abstract and 'pop', for the electronic and computer arts, for 'virtual reality'. But the human need to communicate has remained the same; only the forms and languages have changed.

Role of Information

Communication and information are not similar concepts or experiences. Communication is not the mere sending ot receiving of information in whatever form. Rather, it is a whole situation and an experience; a human relationship, in sum. Information, on the other hand, is made up of bits of messages, verbal and non-verbal, and is essentially unilinear. Significant information can bring about a communication relationship, but not when the exchange of information is on an unequal or commercial basis. Then information turns into a 'commodity', an item to be bought and sold in the market place. A commodity, by definition, has a price attached to it. Authentic communication is not helped but rather distorted by such 'commodotized' information. Business communication thus, is a contradiction in terms; when communication becomes a business it turns into a commodity with an exchange value.

An Argentinean scholar, Ricardo C. Noseda, distinguishes between communication and information thus: Communication is not an act but a process by which an individuality enters into mental co-operation with another individuality until they come to constitute a common conscience. Information, instead, is just a unilateral translation of a message from an Emitter to a Receiver.

Right to Communicate

The right to information has been declared a fundamental right by a United Nations Charter (and such a right is to recognised in the Freedom of Information Bill introduced in Parliament in May 1997), but what human beings need much more fundamentally is in fact the right to communicate. It is such a right that gives men and women their dignity and their freedom, as well as the ability to participate in the social religious, economic and political life of a nation.

The right to communicate is now seen as a fundamental human right, much more comprehensive than existing freedoms of speech, the press, etc. It is the basic right of an individual and it extends, in some degree at least, to groups, nations and the international community, and to have important legal, economic and technological. implications. It is closely related to the democratisation of communication within and between countries, and to concepts of 'access', 'participation' and the 'two-way' flow.

FUNDAMENTALS OF COMMUNICATION

Every communication order is ultimately conditioned or influenced by the political system and cultural milieu and the ends and purposes for which it is to be used. What could India's freedom mean to the concept of mass communication? What could be the type of new orientation for individual media, their functional roles and dimensions, their goals and priorities?

With the dawn of freedom, the Indian media were delinked from the apron-strings of British political and cultural imperialism. As part of the sovereign national system, they could now be used to serve the people and the nation according to new visions and national goals, policies and targets set by the new architects of the nation, the media managers and experts. However, when the Britishers left, India was emaciated by the Partition and was left at the lowest level, politically, economically, socially and communication wise. There were yawning gaps in the communication infrastructure. India's tryst with its new density was therefore very uncertain.

Politically, the Constitution of India, enforced on 26 January 1950, the first Republic Day, had granted to every citizen and media the freedom of speech and expression and to every adult the right to vote and elect legislators. The establishment of a representative system of government, gave the right to every citizen to be informed, that is to have reasonable access to social, political, aesthetic, normal and other ideas and information vital for the grooming of enlightened voters and inculcation of democratic citizenship. It also implied the right to reasonable access to competitive sources of information and media. These rights which flowed out of democratic citizenship enjoined new obligations on the communication media and government to inform and educate the citizens and children of the country and at the same time stimulate awareness about fundamental and other civic and social duties. It was generally agreed that mass media of communication would have a key role in the building of our democratic polity and illumination of our social fabric.

With the beginning of the era of planned development since 1950-51, another role of the media of mass communication came to the forefront. It would provide communication support to the plans and inform people about the philosophy and objectives of plans, about the targets and benefits accruing to them as also about their responsibilities involved in the planned efforts. The other demand on communicators was to enthuse and involve people by removing ignorance and superstitions, by changing their negative attitudes and motivating them into purposeful action, all through persuasive and two-way communication. The dimension of their task was underlined by the Study Team on Mass communication sponsored by Ford Foundation, which observed that "India's development task is so great and her population so large that only by the most efficient possible programme of public information necessarily emphasising mass communication can communicators hope to reach people often enough and effectively enough to activate, on the needed scale, discussion process and subsequent action in the cities, towns and villages." In this context, the Vidyalankar Committee stated that the principal aim of publicity or communication was to prepare the minds of the people to meet the challenges of these new problems.

On the basis of studies on development and communication done in India, UNESCO and various developing countries, as also on the basis of field-based experience and communication and promotional research studies and surveys, a new professional thinking on the concept, role and process of relevant communication gradually emerged. Broadly speaking, the purpose of communication came to be understood as:

(1) politically to create, inform and enlighten public opinion, the basis of a democratic developing society to create awareness among individuals as also about their fundamental duties and obligations to promote scientific temper and national cohesion in society and inculcate the spirit of cooperative partnership among all sections of people, and to foster the establishment of feedback loops and research methodologies to assess public opinion and interpret it;

(2) economically, to act as an activist in the extension of technology transfer among various sections of farmers, workers and other members of the working force, to provide a supporting pad to efforts at modernization and

economic growth, afford market and tourist information and to stimulate advertising and promotional campaigns; and

(3) culturally to foster individual and community expression, discovery, enrichment, creativity and enlightened reaction.

This type of purposeful and dynamic communication system couldn't grow out of the mass media-oriented Western concepts, models and theories, which were not very relevant to rural areas in India or any other developing country. It had to be evolved out of a process of trial and error, experimentation and deliberation. Conceptually it had to be envisaged and shaped by professional committees or bodies especially to be set up for the purpose and reinforced by the directions and guidelines of intentional, regional, national and local seminars, conferences or memorial lectures. Such a system could not grow it was sustained and nurtured by the committee, trained and socially and professionally oriented practitioners and their managers as also by a competent research base. But above all, none of these things would happen unless the efforts in this direction get the policy backing and financial and administrative support of the government and proper appreciation and cooperation of the media and their organisations and the people.

Challenges and Opportunities

After Independence, challenges and experimental opportunities came in quick succession. Rehabilitation of refugees, the problem of integrating the recognised states, the Kashmir issue, green revolution, communal disturbances, strikes, inflation, abject poverty, colossal unemployment, malpractices in the public distribution system, corruption, shortage of essential commodities and housing facilities, wars, local and general elections, student unrest, gheraos, walkouts and many more problems constituted serious challenges. Fortunately, policy support and communication aid sanctions flowed from the dynamic and supporting leadership of the various Indian Prime Minister's and their governments. New dimensions of importance were given by these personalities. As a supporting measure professional introspection, trend setting and guidelines came from the various mass communication and professional bodies and media commissions and committees set up by the government from time to time. Eminent among the bodies which left their impress on the communication scene of India included the first Press commission, UNESCO sponsored Evalution Study Team on TV, the Study Team on Mass Communication sponsored by the Ford Foundation, the Vidyalankar Committee for the Study of Five Year Plan Publicity, the Chanda Committee on Broadcasting and Information Media. All these bodies were set up or functioned in the sixties and seventies.. The Verghese Committee on Autonomy for Akashvani and Doordarshan, the Kuldip Nayar Committee on News Agencies, the second Press Commission, Satellite Instructional Television Experiment evaluation teams and the Joshi Panel on TV Software deliberated and submitted professional guidance emerged from the numerous UNESCO or international, regional and national communication and media seminars, conferences and evaluation and promotional surveys and reports undertaken by various research teams.

Dynamic Political Support

A look into the visions and dynamic and supporting leadership of the various Indian Prime Ministers and their governments would reveal that without them many Indian communication systems and patterns or strategies of mass communication would have remained still-born. In fact, the individual trend and directional setting in the communication process by each Prime Minister has been pronouncedly significant. For instance, Pandit Jawaharlal Nehru, India's first Prime Minister, sought to make mass communication a process of dialogue more than a merely to and fro communication, and certainly more than downward communication. A builder of modern India, he was also a builder of the communication system and media in our country. His package contribution was the laying of the foundation, securing extension a modernization of media, introducing professionalism, tempering of media freedom with social responsibility and giving a rural and research orientation. The second Prime Minister, Lal Bahadur Shastri, reinforced Pandit Nehru's directional and managerial model by adding a focus on professional integrity and dedicated service. The third Prime Minister, Indira Gandhi and her government have provided a thrust for sophisticated multi-media technology. Blending and balancing with the resurgent indigenous technology, it aimed to ultimately strengthen and streamline the entire communication network to make it more rural service worthy, elastic and effective enough to offer services of international standard to prestigious international meets in India as also to provide communication support to the implementation of the 20-point programme. The new technology helped in rearing the confidence building role of the electronic media which operate in the public sector. Smt. Gandhi's government also recognised the importance of a free press but insisted on its responsible functioning and observance of a code of ethics in the discharge of its professional and social responsibilities. There was a focus on the need of the Indian media and practitioners to play a leading role in the New World Information and Communication Order to seek a balanced and two-way flow of information in the world, so as to contribute to the maximum extent possible to the South to South cooperative communication efforts and programmes. There was an emphasis on using media for national unity and integration. Liberalisation of the import policy for facilitating media machinery and material for faster mechanisation of the media units, ensued while offering encouragement to communication research and training and media development programmes. The fourth Prime Minister, Morarji Desai and his government sought to emphasise on autonomy of media, including that of Akashvani and Doordarshan, austerity and professional integrity. The fifth Prime Minister, Choudhary Charan Singh and his government, during his short tenure, endeavoured to bend the functioning of the media primarily for the benefit of rural areas and agriculturists. The seventh and the present Prime Minister and his government are additionally focusing on the application of computer and other modern technologies and are emphasising on open university educational aspect of mass media and better professionalism and programming.

There is a consensus of media experts, however, that the real architects of India's present modernised, multimedia, integrated, development oriented system of communication were Pandit Nehru and Indira Gandhi—as a matter of coincidence father and daughter. If India has entered the satellite, electronic and modern visual communication age, it is primarily for the vision and dynamic leadership of these two Prime Ministers. If our country has developed and revitalized traditional and other indigenous media, and made them in conjunction with modern mass media as instruments of innovative and development communication, specially in the areas of family welfare, health, agricultural extension and eradication of illiteracy, the credit for this too goes primarily to the incisiveness and initiative of these two leaders and their governments. Apart from bequests of national leaders, there are existent visible and invisible contributions of several other professional and individual entrepreneurs, exponents, trainers and researchers who have helped individually and co-operatively in making our communication system what it is.

New Perspective

Since Independence, the concept of mass communication in India has been transformed. From the Western theories-based hypotheses it has now become most flexible, relevant and development-oriented. Now, a participatory type has been envisaged by the 7th Plan for a decentralised form of planning system at the district level. Four stages have marked this transition in our country:

(1) communication considered as a process of transmitting information, ideas, thoughts, feelings and attitudes to large anonymous audiences with an accompanying hypodermic model of who says what in which channel to whom with what effect;

(2) focus in media strategies shifting from mass media to media mix or relevant communication technologies. Experience and research revealing that with literacy, financial and technical problems rampant in a country, there could be very little success by adopting only big media strategies. Attention thus started being fixed on low cost small media such as low powered radios and indigenous or folk form of channels as well;

(3) a distinction being made between informational communication and persuasive communication seeking to influence the behaviour or attitudes of the respondents;

(4) communication being accepted as a multi-disciplinary science or a distinct discipline supported by its own hypotheses, systematic knowledge, research methodologies and trend and case studies.

This nebulous concept of positive, multi-lateral promotional communication of participatory type came to be known by different names, such as development communication, development support; communication, integrated rural communication, participatory communication and the like. The philosophy behind these themes was to provide a meaningful system in developing countries to harmonise development and communication efforts aimed at giving the rural and urban people a better deal. While the relationship between the two was accepted by all, the issue of cause and effect has remained still unresolved. In other words, which is the mover and which is the moved, remains a chicken and egg question. Whatever the perception, both development and communication are now considered engaged in a reactory system, one helping the other, complementing and supplementing each other in the process of fostering balanced growth and progress. If people have access to mass media, and the messages are segmented and relevant, even rural people with low literacy rates and per capita incomes can be sensitised, motivated and changed.

Being considered different from terms like advertising, public relations, propaganda, agriculture extension, rural communication, promotion, marketing communication and even the Western concept of mass media-oriented communication, the term 'development communication', in the Third World. countries has acquired a more positive and pragmatic role and result-oriented connotation. As explained by Nora Quebral of Indonesia, this brand of communication implies "the art and science of human communication applied to the speedy transformation of a country and the mass of its people from poverty to a dynamic state of economic growth that makes possible greater social equality and the larger fulfilment of human potential." This development support concept of mass communication is thus dynamic, purposive, practical and promotional in approach and nature. It is a new hope for development and social change in the Third World. Though not a panacea for all ills, it is one of the vital components in any development planning and implementation. This science and art of communication views an individual, a society or a nation in its totality, transcending thereby from a piecemeal or a segmented view of rural or urban society, economic and human development. In our country development communication combines in it the philosophy of humanism of Pandit Nehru, intending to achieve a better, richer and fuller way of life, along with the growth and development of the country as a whole. Another strand of the concept which is typically Indian is that development communication should grow mostly out of people's participation and people's satisfaction, the essential ingredients of which are:

(a) a sense of feeling to have actively participated;

(b) a sense of pride in evolving co-operative solutions to the problem in hand;

(c) a sense of achievement, reflected in the concrete betterment of poorer sections of the people and of backward areas.

Research studies based on Western models ascribe to mass communication different roles in development, varying from nil to the enthusiastic, from a cautious to a pragmatic position. Lloyd Sommerlad a UNESCO expert projected a balanced and pragmatic picture about the role which communication can play in national development. In his view "communication is an important element in the matrix of influences which lead to innovation and modernisation of a society. If used constructively, the media can help create an environment favourable for change and development. They can enlarge horizons, bring information about the experience of others, raise aspirations and help to provide the motivation for improved practices and social conditions. They are part of the process of teaching new and better ways of working and living. The extent to which communication, both interpersonal and mediated, contributes to development depends on the policies and strategies adopted and the skill with which the tools are used. Essential will be the planned use of extension services and the media, co-ordination of the parallel channels of communications, co-operation between various government and private agencies involved in the development; a programme appropriate to the cultural background and provision of participation, feedback and a multilateral flow of information."

The communication revolution in India is experiencing the confluence of three stages of technological growth: wire, wireless and integrated. True to its tradition of assimilation of foreign and indigenous elements, India is pressing into service the earlier and modem media and using high cost and low cost communication technologies. Her Song and Drama Division, Field Publicity units and extension agencies, padyatras, folk media and human activist system on the one hand and satellite, colour TV, video, cassette, computer, electronic and digital technologies used in press communications and telecommunications on the other indicate the balance the country holds so as to meet the needs of her mammoth, multi-media mass communication exercises, movements and campaigns. Some of the innovative multi-media programmes involved in the green and white revolutions in the northern states, TV coverage during the course of SITE, Kheda, on-going SITE and INSAT-IB experiments and the 9th Asiad, 7th Non-aligned and recent Commonwealth Summit and Namedia meets are pointers to the evolution of the spirit and urge for innovation and experimentation. Similar trends were visible in the video technology based experiment for intercommunity communication near Delhi, the Farms School programme of All India Radio and the newspaper communication support for Chattera Village initiated by the Hindustan Times, a Delhi English daily.

Apart from these illustrations, the government sector publicity media units provide more robust and wider display of media mix. For instance, outside publicity done through Field Publicity units undertake a variety of publicity programmes like film shows, group discussions, talks, seminars, song and drama programmes and photo displays.

These pertain to major national themes like national integration adult education, child welfare, family welfare, agriculture and agro-based small-scale industries. Similar programmes are also organised to make people aware of social evils like untouchability and drinking. The Song and Drama units utilise live entertainment media to make the masses aware of the various national programmes and objectives. It has a wide range of stage forms like puppet shows, plays, dances, dramas, ballads, harikathas and sound and light shows.

The mix used by the Directorate of Advertising and Visual Publicity is a visual package. It comprises press advertisements, illustrated printed material like posters, folders, leaflets, cinema slides, metallic tablets, radio and television spots and photographic exhibitions.

Another set of print medium mix for mass circulation is brought out by the Publications Division of the Ministry of Information and Broadcasting comprising books, pamphlets and journals in Hindi, English and other Indian languages on a wide range of subjects including art and culture, history and tradition, political evolution, democratic process, economic development and social resurgence.

Thus we see that whether it is the sphere of agriculture, family planning or government publicity India has been pursuing the policy of appropriate mix of media and technologies. This has entailed the use of face to face, group, written, printed, visual, folk, computerized electronic, outdoor or even a mix of them. The approach has been multi-media and crossdisciplinary, goal and result oriented. Centralisation in core programmes have been successful in so far as it has sought to stimulate unity in basic plan programmes or achieving integration in national cultural programmes, but it has equally underlined the importance that at grassroots level the development programmes should be localised and an a specific and implemented as far as possible by the involvement of local people, but you need to support decentralisation which has inherent value, by an integrating system. Here the challenge to media practitioners and managers is in finding ways of making satellite and other big media an integrating force, at the same time making them help to knit together several decentralised activities at the grass roots level.

The family planning communication package is an example. It envisages an all out effort at dovetailing of population education in the formal educational system as also in the non-formal training programmes of functionaries of development departments'. It has centralised programmes integrated with decentralised activities. Its media package is wide complexioned and involves a still more dynamic package comprising radio, TV, colour films in 16mm film strips, cinema slides, exhibitions, tape recorders, newspapers, magazines, posters, folders, brochures, leaflets, hoardings, wall paintings, bus boards, match box labels, dramas, puppet shows and other local folk art media. Its symbols and slogans are splashed all over, from mud walls in villages to telephone and telegraph poles in cities, reminding, people that family planning is an intrinsic part of the environmental scene and an aid to family welfare.

India has made use of another multi-dimensional, multimedia and demonstrational audio-visual aid called exhibition. In size, stature and character it varies from stationary to mobile or even exhibition on wheels; from simple village exhibitions, trade fairs and a seasonal market to very big, modernly designed multi-levelled complexes, known as national and international exhibitions or world trade fairs. These exhibitions use a package of communication media ranging from spoken word exhibits or visuals to video, TV, films, radio, projectile aids, traditional media, promotional literature, outdoor publicity aids, balloons, neon light and sky splashed advertisements. Cumulatively these exhibitions draw large crowds and their impact differ from creating awareness and publicity to more dramatic results in terms of transfer of technology and sale of goods and machinery. Policies and programmes of government are also publicised through photographic exhibitions. Art exhibitions and gallaries promote education about art forms of various kinds.

Whatever form that these innovatory types of communicition strategies may take person-to-person or group, written, printed, visual, folk or electronic, indoor or outdoor, hot or cold, or even a mix of them-the basic feature is that these programmes are goal oriented, research fed, professionally planned and executed and assessed. They are pragmatic and multi-media and disciplinary in approach. They are fairly sensitive and alive to criticism and suggestions and in a sense quite responsive and flexible.

The dimensions of integrated communication system which are found relevant to rural India warrant closer relationship between the administrative and communication agencies; credible and knowledgeable sources; segmentation of messages for different audiences; linkage of information to the felt needs of the people; and projection of timely usable, solution-oriented and people-beneficiary messages. The other requisite preconditions of a successful system of communication are management decentralisation for effective participation of people and, the inculcation of the philosophy of empathy among the media practitioners and managers and policy makers.

Despite a large measure of success in mass communication, one big lesson that emerges out of the Indian scene of communication is that we must continuously rediscover the goals and dimensions of mass communication and its media. To this end, our communication system, our postulates, our media's role and their functions need to be periodically or as a part of inbuilt research, assessed, modified or revamped. This would help us realise our cherished dreams of a sunny future without,being swept off our feet or alienating us from our fundamental values. Here the application of feedback research is significant. So is the contribution of a professionally and media-oriented and socially activising training system, which can strengthen the country's capacity for attracting to the communication, advertising and public relations professions, man of vision, integrity, independent judgement and professional aptitude.

Mass Communication

Every communication order is ultimately conditioned or influenced by the political system and cultural milieu and the ends and purposes for which it is to be used. What could India's freedom mean to the concept of mass communication? What could be the type of new orientation for individual media, their functional roles and dimensions, their goals and priorities?

With the dawn of freedom, the Indian media were delinked from the apron-strings of British political and cultural imperialism. As part of the sovereign national system, they could now be used to serve the people and the nation according to new visions and national goals, policies and targets set by the new architects of the nation, the media managers and experts.

However, when the Britishers left, India was emaciated by the Partition and was left at the lowest level, politically, economically, socially and communication wise. There were yawning gaps in the communication infrastructure. India's tryst with its new density was therefore very uncertain.

Politically, the Constitution of India, enforced. on 26 January 1950, the first Republic Day, had granted to every citizen and media the freedom of speech and expression and to every adult the right to vote and elect legislators. The establishment of a representative system of government, gave the right to every citizen to be informed, that is to have reasonable access to social, political, aesthetic,. normal and other ideas and information vital for the grooming of enlightened voters and inculcation of democratic citizenship. It also implied the right to reasonable access to competitive sources of information and media. These rights which flowed out of democratic citizenship enjoined new obligations on the communication media and government to inform and educate the citizens and children of the country and at the same time stimulate awareness about fundamental and other civic and social duties. It was generally agreed that mass media of communication would have a key role in the building of our democratic polity and illumination of our social fabric.

With the beginning of the era of planned development since 1950-51, another role of the media of mass communication came to the forefront. It would provide communication support to the plans and inform people about the philosophy and objectives of plans, about the targets and benefits accruing to them as also about their responsibilities involved in the planned efforts. The other demand on comunica.tors was to enthuse and involve people by removing ignorance and superstitions, by changing their negative attitudes and motivating them into purposeful action, all through persuasive and two-way communication. The dimension of their task was underlined by the Study Team on Mass communication sponsored by Ford Foundation, which observed that "India's development task is so great and her population so large that only by the most efficient possible programme of public information—necessarily emphasising mass communication-can communicators hope to reach people often enough and effectively enough to activate, on the needed scale, discussion process and subsequent action in the cities, towns and villages." In this context, the Vidyalankar Committee stated that the principal aim of publicity or communication was to prepare the minds of the people to meet the challenges of these new problems.

On the basis of studies on development and communication done in India, UNESCO and various developing countries, as also on the basis of field-based experience and communication and promotional research studies and surveys, a new professional thinking on the concept, role and process of relevant communication gradually emerged. Broadly speaking, the purpose of communication came to be understood as:

(1) politically to create, inform and enlighten public opinion, the basis of a democratic developing society to create awareness among individuals as also about their fundamental duties and obligations, to promote scientific temper and national cohesion in society and inculcate the spirit of cooperative partnership among all sections of people, and to foster the establishment of feedback loops and research methodologies to assess public opinion and interpret it;

(2) economically, to act as an activist in the extension of technology transfer among various sections of farmers, workers and other members of the working force, to provide a supporting pad to efforts at modernization and economic growth, afford market and tourist information and to stimulate advertising and promotional campaigns; and

(3) culturally to foster individual and community expression, discovery, enrichment, creativity and enlightened reaction.

This type of purposeful and dynamic communication system couldn't grow out of the mass media-oriented Western concepts, models and theories, which were not very relevant to rural areas in India or any other developing country. It had to be evolved out of a process of trial and error, experimentation and deliberation. Conceptually it had to be envisaged and shaped by professional committees or bodies especially to be set up for the purpose and reinforced by the directions and guidelines of intentional, regional, national and local seminars, conferences or memorial lectures. Such a system could not grow it was sustained and nurtured by the committee, trained and socially and professionally oriented practitioners and their managers as also by a competent research base. But above all, none of these things would happen unless the efforts in this direction get the policy backing and financial and administrative support of the government and proper appreciation and cooperation of the media and their organisations and the people.

Post-independence Challenges and Opportunities

After Independence, challenges and experimental opportunities came in quick succession. Rehabilitation of refugees, the problem of integrating the recognised states, the Kashmir issue, green revolution, communal disturbances, strikes, inflation, abject poverty, colossal unemployment, malpractices in the public distribution system, corruption, shortage of essential commodities and housing facilities, wars, local and general elections, student unrest, gheraos, walkouts and many more problems constituted serious challenges. Fortunately, policy support and communication aid sanctions flowed from the dynamic and supporting leadership of the various Indian Prime Minister and the governments. New dimensions of importance were given by these personalities. As a supporting measure professional introspection, trend setting and guidelines came from the various mass communication and professional bodies and media commissions and committees set up by the government from time to time. Eminent among "the bodies which left their impress on the communication scene of India included the first Press commission, UNESCO sponsored Evaluation Study Team on TV, the Study Team on Mass Communication sponsored by the Ford Foundation, the Vidyalankar Committee for the Study of Five Year Plan Publicity, the Chanda Committee on Broadcasting and Information Media. All these bodies were set up or functioned in the sixties and seventies. The Verghese Committee on Autonomy for Akashvani and Doordarshan, the Kuldip Nayar Committee on News Agencies, the second Press Commission, Satellite Instructional Television Experiment evaluation teams and the Joshi Panel on TV Software deliberated and submitted professional guidance emerged from the numerous UNESCO or international, regional and national communication and media seminars, conferences and evaluation and promotional surveys and reports undertaken by various research teams.

Dynamic Political Support

A look into the visions and dynamic and supporting leadership of the various Indian Prime Ministers and their governments would reveal that without them many Indian communication systems and patterns or strategies of mass communication would have remained still-born. In fact, the individual trend and directional setting in the communication process by each Prime Minister has been pronouncedly significant. For instance, Pandit Jawaharlal Nehru, India's first Prime Minister, sought to make mass communication a process of dialogue more than a merely to and fro communication, and certainly more than downward communication. A builder of modern India, he was also a builder of the communication system and media in our country. His package contribution was the laying of the foundation, securing extension a modernization of media, introducing professionalism, tempering of media freedom with social responsibility and giving a rural and research orientation. The second Prime Minister, Lal Bahadur Shastri, reinforced Pandit Nehru's directional and managerial model by adding a focus on professional integrity and dedicated service. The third Prime Minister, Indira Gandhi and her government have provided a thrust for sophisticated multi-media technology. Blending and balancing with the resurgent indigenous-technology, it aimed to ultimately strengthen and streamline the entire communication network to make it more rural service worthy, elastic and effective enough to offer services of international standard to prestigious international meets in India as also to provide communication support to the implementation of the 20point programme. The new technology helped in rearing the confidence building role of the electronic media which operate in the public sector. Smt. Gandhi's, government also recognised the importance of a free press but insisted on its responsible functioning and observance of a code of ethics in the discharge of its professional and social responsibilities. There was a focus on the need of the Indian media and practitioners to play a leading role in the New World Information and Communication Order to seek a balanced and two-way flow of information in the world, so as to contribute to the maximum extent possible to the South to South cooperative communication efforts and programmes. There was an emphasis on using media for national unity and integration. Liberalisation of the import policy for facilitating media machinery and material for faster mechanisation of the media units, ensued while offering encouragement to communication research and training and media development programmes. The fourth Prime Minister, Morarji Desai and his government sought to emphasise on autonomy of media, including that of Akashvani and Doordarshan, austerity and professional integrity. The fifth Prime Minister, Choudhary Charan Singh and his government, during his short tenure, endeavoured to bend the functioning of the media primarily for the benefit of rural areas and agriculturists. The seventh and the present Prime Minister and his government are additionally focusing on the application of computer and other modern technologies and are emphasising on open university educational aspect of mass media and better professionalism and programming.

There is a consensus of media experts, however, that the real architects of India's present modernised, multi-media, integrated, development oriented system of communication were Pandit Nehru and Indira Gandhi as a matter of coincidence father and daughter. If India has entered the satellite, electronic and modern visual communication age, it is primarily for the vision and dynamic leadership of these two Prime Ministers. If our country has developed and revitalized traditional and other indigenous media, and made them in conjunction with modern mass media as instruments of innovative and development communication, specially in the areas of family welfare, health, agricultural extension and eradication of illiteracy, the credit for this too goes primarily to the incisiveness and initiative of these two leaders and their governments.

Apart from bequests of national leaders, there are existent visible and invisible contributions of several other professional and individual entrepreneurs, exponents, trainers and researchers who have helped individually and co-operatively in making our communication system what it is.

New Perspective on Mass Communication

Since Independence, the concept of mass communication in India has been transformed. From the Western theories-based hypotheses it has now become most flexible, relevant and development-oriented. Now, a participatory type has been envisaged by the 7th Plan for a decentralised form of planning system at the district level. Four stages have marked this transition in our country:

(1) Communication considered as a process of transmitting information, ideas, thoughts, feelings and attitudes to large anonymous audiences with an accompaying hypodemic model of who says what in which channel to whom with what effect;

(2) a distinction being made between informational communication and persuasive communication seeking to influence the behaviour or attitudes of the respondents;

(3) focus in media strategies shifting from mass media to media mix or relevant communication technologies. Experience and research revealing that with literacy, financial and technical problems rampant in a comuntry, there could be very little success by adopting only big media strategies. Attention thus started being fixed on low cost small media

such as low powered radios and indigenous or folk form of channels as well;

(4) communication being accepted as a multi-disciplinary science or a distinct discipline supported by its own hypotheses, systematic knowledge, research methodologies and trend and case studies.

This nebulous concept of positive, multi-lateral promotional communication of participatory type came to be known by different names, such as development communication, development support communication, integrated rural communication, participatory communication and the like. The philosophy behind these themes was to provide a meaningful system in developing countries to harmonise development and communication efforts aimed at giving the rural and urban people a better deal. While the relationship between the two was accepted by all, the issue of cause and effect has remained still unresolved. In other words, which is the mover and which is the moved, remains a chicken and egg question. Whatever the perception, both development and communication are now considered engaged in a reactory system, one helping the other, complementing and supplementing each other in the process of fostering balanced growth and progress. If people have access to mass media, and the messages are segmented and relevant, even rural people with low literacy rates and per capita incomes can be sensitised, motivated and changed.

Being considered different from terms like advertising, public relations, propaganda, agriculture extension, rural communication, promotion, marketing communication and even the Western concept of mass media-oriented communication, the term 'development communication' in the Third World countries has acquired a more positive and pragmatic role and result-oriented connotation. As explained by Nora Quebral of Indonesia, this brand of communication implies "the art and science of human communication applied to the speedy transformation of a country and the mass of its people from poverty to a dynamic state of economic growth that makes possible greater social equality and the larger fulfilment of human potential".

This development support concept of mass communication is thus dynanamic, purposive, practical and promotional in approach and nature. It is a new hope for development and social change in the Third World. Though not a panacea for all ills, it is one of the vital components in any development planning and implementation. This science and art of communication views an individual, a society or a nation in its totality, transcending thereby from a piecemeal or a segmented view of rural or urban society, economic and human development. In our country development communication combines in it the philosophy of humanism of Pandit Nehru, intending to achieve a better, richer and fuller way of life, along with the growth and development of the country as a whole. Another strand of the concept which is typically Indian is that development communication should grow mostly out of people's participation and people's satisfaction, the essential ingredients of which are:

(a) a sense of feeling to have actively participated;

(b) a sense of pride in evolving co-operative solutions to the problem in hand;

(c) a sense of achievement, reflected in the concrete betterment of poorer sections of the people and of backward areas.

Research studies based on Western models ascribe to mass communication different roles in development, varying from nil to the enthusiastic, from a cautious to a pragmatic position. Lloyd Sommerlad a UNESCO expert projected a balanced and pragmatic picture about the role which communication can play in national development. In his view communication is an important element in the matrix of influences which lead to innovation and modernisation of a society. If used constructively, the media can help create an environment favourable for change and development. They can enlarge horizons, bring information about the experience of others, raise aspirations and help to provide the motivation for improved practices and social conditions. They are part of the process of teaching new and better ways of working and living. The extent to which communication, both interpersonal and mediated, contributes to development depends on the policies and strategies adopted and the skill with which the tools are used. Essential will be the planned use of extension services and the media, co-ordination of the parallel channels of communications, co-operation between various government and private agencies involved in the development; a programme appropriate to the cultural background and provision of participation, feedback and a multilateral flow of information."

The communication revolution in India is experiencing the confluence of three stages of technological growth: wire, wireless and integrated. True to its tradition of assimilation of foreign and indigenous elements, India is pressing into service the earlier and modern media and using high cost and low cost communication technologies. Her Song and Drama Division, Field Publicity units and extension agencies, padyatras, folk media and human activist system on the one hand and satellite, colour TV, video, cassette, computer, electronic and digital technologies used in press communications and telecommunications on the other indicate the balance the country holds so as to meet the needs of her mammoth, multi-media mass communication exercises, movements and campaigns. Some of the innovative multi-media programmes involved in the green and white revolutions in the northern states, TV coverage during the course of SITE, Kheda, on-going SITE and INSAT-IB experiments and the 9th Asiad, 7th Non-aligned and recent Commonwealth Summit and Namedia meets are pointers to the evolution of the spirit and urge for innovation and experimentation. Similar trends were visible in the video technology based experiment for intercommunity communication near Delhi, the Farms School programme of All India Radio and the newspaper communication support for Chattera Village initiated by the Hindustan Times, a Delhi English daily.

Apart from these illustrations, the government sector publicity media units provide more robust and wider display of media mix. For instance, outside publicity done through Field Publicity units undertake a variety of publicity programmes like film shows, group discussions, talks, seminars, song and drama programmes and photo displays. These pertain to major national themes like national integration adult education, child welfare, family welfare, agriculture and agro-based small-scale industries. Similar programmes are also organised to make people aware of social evils like untouchability and drinking. The Song and Drama units utilise live entertainment media to make the masses aware of the various national programmes and objectives. It has a wide range of stage forms like puppet shows, plays, dances, dramas, ballads, harikathas and sound and light shows.

The mix used by the Directorate of Advertising and Visual Publicity is a visual package. It comprises press advertisements, illustrated printed material like posters, folders, leaflets, cinema slides, metallic tablets, radio and television spots and photographic exhibitions.

Another set of print medium mix for mass circulation is brought out by the Publications Division of the Miriistry of Information and Broadcasting comprising books, pamphlets and journals in Hindi, English and other Indian languages on a wide range of subjects including art and culture, history and tradition, political evolution, democratic process, economic development and social resurgence.

Thus we see that whether it is the sphere of agriculture, family planning or government publicity India has been pursuing the policy of appropriate mix of media and technologies. This has entailed the use of face to face, group, written, printed, visual, folk, computerised electronic, outdoor or even a mix of them. The approach has been multi-media and cross-disciplinary, goal and result oriented. Centralisation in core programmes have been successful in so far as it has sought'to stimulate unity in basic plann programmes or achieving integration in national cultural programmes, but it has equally underlined the importance that at grassroots level the development programmes should be localised and area specific and implemented as far as possible by the involvement of local people. but you need to support decentralisation which has inherent value, by an integrating system. Here the challenge to media practitioners and managers is in finding ways of making satellite and other big media an integrating force, at the same time making them help to knit together several decentralised activities at the grassroots level.

The family planning communication package is an example. It envisages an all out effort at dovetailing of population education in the formal educational system as also in the non-formal training programmes of functionaries of development departments. It has centralised programmes integrated with decentralised activities. Its media package is wide complexioned and involves a still more dynamic package comprising radio, TV, colour films in 16 mm film strips, cinema slides, exhibitions, tape recorders, newspapers, magazines, posters, folders, brochures, leaflets, hoardings, wall paintings, bus boards, match box labels, dramas, puppet shows and other local folk art media. Its symbols and slogans are splashed all over, from mud walls in villages to telephone and telegraph poles in cities, reminding people that family planning is an intrinsic part of the environmental scene and an aid to family welfare.

Alongwith discovering new media mixes, strategy of field publicity or extension is also changing. The necessity of people's involvement and obtaining their feedback is calling for modification in the strategies known by various names as area approach, pooling plans or district-level decentralised plans.

India has made use of another multi-dimensional, multi-media and demonstrational audio-visual aid called exhibition. In size, stature and character it varies from stationary to mobile or even exhibition on wheels; from simple village exhibitions, trade fairs and a seasonal market to very big, modernly designed multi-levelled complexes, known as national and international exhibitions or world trade fairs. These exhibitions use a package of communication media ranging from spoken word, exhibits or visuals to video, TV, films, radio, projectile aids, traditional media, promotional literature, outdoor publicity aids, balloons, neon light and sky splashed advertisements. Cumulatively these exhibitions draw large crowds and their impact differ from creating awareness and publicity to more dramatic results in terms of transfer of technology and sale of goods and machinery. Policies and programmes of government are also publicised through photographic exhibitions. Art exhibitions and gallaries promote education about art forms of various kinds.

Whatever form that these innovatory types of communication strategies may take-person-to-person or group, written, printed, visual, folk or electronic, indoor or outdoor, hot or cold, or even a mix of them the basic feature is that these p.ogrammes are goal oriented, research fed, professionally planned and executed and assessed. They are pragmatic and multi-media and disciplinary in approach. They are fairly sensitive and alive to criticism and suggestions and in a sense quite responsive and flexible.

The dimensions of integrated communication system which are found relevant to rural India warrant closer relationship between the administrative and communication agencies; credible and knowledgeable sources; segmentation of messages for different audiences; linkage of information to the felt needs of the people; and projection of timely usable, solution-oriented and people-beneficiary messages. The other requisite preconditions of a successful system of communication are management decentralisation for effective participation of people and the inculcation of the philosophy of empathy among the media practitioners and managers and policy makers.

Despite a large measure of success in mass communication, one big lesson that emerges out of the Indian scene of communication is that we must continuously rediscover the goals and dimensions of mass communication and its media. To this end, our communication system, our postulates, our media's role and their functions need to be periodically or as a part of inbuilt research, assessed, modified or revamped. This would help us realise our cherished dreams of a sunny future without being swept off our feet or alienating us from our fundamental values. Here the application of feedback research is significant. So is the contribution of a professionally and media-oriented and socially activising training system, which can strengthen the country's capacity for attracting to the communication, advertising and public relations p;ofessions men of vision, integrity, independent judgement and professional aptitude. This would help equip them with media climated and field based knowledge and skill to serve our society.

India has more than 22 states and the population of the country exceeding 850 million. By and large, our society is rural based as people, majority of them, live in villages. The villages number about 600,000 and the economy is mixed *i.e.*, we have both public and private sector. We have annual plans and five years plans in our country. The government is elected to power once in every five years.

India is a country with many languages and dialects. People generally speak them and in officials circles the widely accepted language is English. Hindi is also spoken in northern states and it is also being used as an official language. The State and the people of Tamil Nadu do not know Hindi and instead speak English. These are some of the facts regarding the India today.

Role of Mass Media in Changing Indian Society

Mass media playa crucial role in changing Indian society. It is one of moulding people's opinion on various causes and events. People come to know about their cultural heritage only through mass media. On science and technology, mass media lets us know about where are the scientific institutions are located and what is the contribution being made by each one of them. Also as scientific literature is prepared to us by the mass media. Eminent scientists and technologists write about the scientific progress being made plus publish information on science related topics and we come to know of them. Mass media also playa crucial role as far as data dissemination among scientific segment of the society are concerned. The arts knowledge is promoted by the news media to us and we know about art and artists only through mass media. Apart from reporting on day to day news, mass media also report on various special themes such as history, archaeology etc. These things go into building knowledge of the individual in a given society. Hence, these build up our knowledge and generally, form of mass media or from authorities or they learn from newspapers and magazines in which these things appear. Also on subjects such as engineering media report to the people. In the case of topics like animal welfare, news media keeps as informed on the developments taking place.

Marshall McLuhan, the well known media theorist says advertisements are the best part of any newspaper. The advertisements are read by people with interest. These are also part of mass media since mass media carry them. The function of advertising into inform when *i.e.*, the people about availability of products and services in the market place. Advertisements are various kinds and each one of it is useful to specific segment of the society. Advertisements for company products are different from advts. for industrial products. These are part and parcel of mass media in a changing society.

Yet another role of mass media has been to awake people and inform them about imminent dangers to their health and well being. Mass media keeps us informed during war times and situations. It also inform us about dangers to our physical health such as heart and cancer disease etc. We know what are the causes and which one and how to lead our lives without diseases and health problems. While it informs about threats to our health it also carries advts. for and against them. It serves as a middle man as far as questionable advertisements are concerned.

Mass media also informs about latest trends in different fields for the benefit of the public. They inform us about the latest trends in fashion and life style related information. People change accordingly or make them receive suitable messages from the mass media. Mass media often criticizes and citizens also affect mass media likewise. The relationship is mutual between them.

Mass media play a crucial and very important role as far as the politics in a changing democratic society are concerned, and we know about political events and candidates only through mass media and our decision making process is done only through mass media. We are living in a modern world of reality. The influence of cinema on politics in a changing society such as India is worth mentioning. There is a close relationship between the crime and politics. Film stars make use of their popularity in the politics and come to power and we have had three or four chief ministers from the world of cinema.

In the field of sports also, the influence of mass media cannot be denied. We know about sports and sports persons only through mass media and sports is very popular with young and old alike. The prominence given to sports as far as media are concerned is really too much. True, mass media provide wide coverage to sports and sporting events and persons. In every day newspapers, there is a column allotted separately for sports.

Mass media also play powerful role as far as bringing and promoting one culture in another cultural setting. Both the print and electronic media cover western culture' and parts of eastern. culture which is different from ours. It also promotes international understanding as well.

These are the different role played by mass media as far as a chaning society are concerned. More can be added to the must on the role of mass media in our society which is changing slowly. Mass media need changing society as much as the society needs mass media. Both are independent and can't be separated from each other. We will see the mass communication playing a crucial role in the changing society in the days to come and the society too will have great expectations from the mass media in the upcoming days. As we go further in technology, we need advanced mass media and communication to prepare us to face the challenges of the 20th and 21st centuries. In conclusion, we can say that people need mass media as much as mass media need the people in the coming days.

ORGANISATIONAL COMMUNICATION

One of the most important recent developments in the way people look at organisations has been the increasing amount of attention paid to different aspects of communication. Managers and researchers alike have recognised that businesses must maintain at least an adequate level of communication in order to survive, that increasing the effectiveness of communication within a firm contributes to the efficiency of its operation, and that in some cases highly effective communication can increase productivity and eventually profitability. Perhaps more important has been the realisation that people who understand how communication functions in a business, who have developed a wide repertory of written and oral communicative skills, and who have learned when and how to use those skills seem to advance more rapidly and contribute more fully to their organisations than people who have not done so. As a result the number of college courses and professional training programmes concerned with organisational communication has mushroomed. Of course employees cannot function effectively unless they possess the technical skills that their positions require. But more and more it appears that being also able to recognise, diagnose, land solve communication related problems is vital to the success of people in even the most technical occupations. Accountants must be able to gain complete, accurate, and sometimes sensitive information from their clients, supervisors of production lines must be able to obtain adequate and timely information on which to base their decisions, managers of different divisions must be able to give their subordinates clear instructions, make sure those instructions are understood, create .conditions in which their commands will be carried out, and obtain reliable feedback about the completion of the tasks that they have assigned. In a recent survey of 700 middle managers, almost 85 percent of the respondents reported that it was their subordinates' communication skills (or lack or them) which determined their success or failure in critical situations. Although these managers also noted that factors like their subordinates' job-related expertise and loyalty to their supervisor and organisation also had an important impact on their effectiveness, it was their ability to communicate effectively that was crucial in most cases.

However, being able to communicate effectively at work requires two kinds of knowledge. First, it requires an understanding of the relationships that exit between communication and the operation of organisations. Since communication processes influence the way an organisation operates and are simultaneously influenced by key characteristics of the organisation, neither organisations nor organisational communication can be understood adequately if they are examined in isolation of each other. Second, effective communication depends on employees' understanding how to choose appropriate communication strategies in different situations. This book intends to provide readers with an understanding of strategic communication skills, the ability to analyse a situation, select an appropriate communication strategy from a number of available options, and employ that strategy in an optimal way. However understanding strategic communication demands that an individual understand how communication functions in organisations, how it creates and solves problems, how it makes some situations occur and how it prevents others, how it makes some outcomes more probable and others improbable. This chapter will introduce these two most important concepts: the role of communication in organisations and the characteristics of strategic organisational communication. Subsequent chapters will expand each of these concepts and explain how they contribute to the success of complex organisations and their members.

Role of Communication

Historically, formal organisations have been examined from two very different perspectives. One view has depicted them as the combination of a number of different components, each of which. is linked to each other on the basis of some carefully planned and clearly articulated design. People who accept this perspective believe that organisation are designed in three distinct steps. Designing an organisation begins with an analysised a potential market and a decision about what products-goods or services the organisation should produce. Designers then decide which tasks must be performed in order to produce the desired output and determine how each of these tasks can be completed most efficient. Finally, designers organise the various tasks into structures and sequences which are intended to maximise the efficiency of the total operation. Since many of the component of the organisation are people, someone must be assigned the job of seeing that all who are involved in each part of the production process understand the tasks they are to perform how they are to accomplish those tasks, the fact that they must accomplish them in a timely and efficient manner if the organisation is to function properly. In this perspective, communication is important for instrumental reasons. It functions in wars which allow members to share the information necessary for the successful completion of a complex array of interdependent tasks. Although the end products, task requirements, employee skills, or relationships among these components may change when market conditions or technologies change, this perspective assumes that the rational design of an organisation will stay relatively constant. At least, the organisation will stay stable enough so that the designers can draw a picture, usually in the form of an "organisational chart," which accurately reflects its operation.

Another viewpoint describes organisations as complex, interdependent matrices of ongoing process, not as a rational, carefully planned combination of interrelated static components. This distinction is important for two reasons. First, it leads to a view of the members of an organisation as actors, not as relatively inert components of the organisation. Employees constantly are making choices about how they'will act in the variety of situations they face. Second, organisations are networks of interdependent human actors whose actions both create situations they face allow them to respond to those situations. Although organisations can be designed by objective, outside planners, their designs constantly are in a state of change. Businesses are composed of large numbers of people who constantly are monitoring their own actions and the actions of others, processing that information, and choosing those courses of action that they think are appropriate. This description of organisations does not imply that their members are either manipulative or Machiavellian although it would admit that some of them are. Instead, it suggests that people are active agents who have their own reasons for acting as they do. They are not mechanical components of the production process, doing only what they are designed to do in precisely that way in which they are designed to do it. They are choice-making members whose actions are part of a complicated array of ongoing processes.

Within this perspective, communication is important to an organisation for two reasons. First, communication is the means through which people acquire the information and develop the criteria by which they decide how to act. Second, communication is the process through which they put their choices into practice. That is, through communication members of organisations learn that there are precedents in their organisation which constrain their choices, and they learn what those precedents are. Through communication with others, they develop and express the purposes which guide their actions. They are able to consider the potential effects of different actions only because they are capable of communicating. In addition, it is through communication that members of an organisation are able to coordinate their actions with other members of the organisation. Because the complex array of tasks that must be performed in an organisation are independent, each member of the organisation can perform only if other members do also. In almost situations, only a small proportion of the activities of anyone employees will be necessary preconditions for the successful action of other employees. However, for each member of the organisation, there are some actions that must be taken if the organisation is to operate. And, because all members must depend on the actions of some other member(s) in order to do their jobs, they must be able to predict accurately what those other people will do in different situations. Being able to do so requires 'employees to understand why they act as they do and to recognise that they regularly respond to certain situations in prodictable ways. Communications is the process through which people make sense out of the actions of other people, it is the means by which they are able to understand how they can coordinate their actions with the actions of others. Human action is contextual, it is the result of the choices people make within the situations they perceive themselves to be.

Unfortunately, these two views of organisations and communication often are seen as being mutually exclusive. Scholars who focus their attention on the design or structure of organisations and the functions of communication in organisation that have been described in this chapter often overlook the complex processes through which people decide how to act at work. Conversely, when scholars concentrates on understanding the relationships between processes of communication and processes of organising, they often deemphasise the tasks people perform at work and the function communication plays in the completion of those tasks. Understanding strategic organisational communication requires an analysis of both the functions of communication in organisations and the processes through which communication guides the actions of members.

Functions of Organisational Communication

In some important ways communication functions as a tool for members of organisations: It allows them to issue, receive, interpret, and act on commands; it allows them to create and maintain productive business and personal relationships with other members of the organisations; and it allows them to manage ambiguity and uncertainty.

Command Function

Two types of communication make up the "command" function: direction and feedback. People perform necessary task effectively only when they choose both to initiate action and to limit their actions in clearly prescribed ways. Some members of organisations, usually those given the formal titles of supervisor or manager, issue messages which tell other members to take action and to limit that action to a particular series to be taken at a specified time and at a specified place. If the person to whom the message is directed does not act, or if the person acts inappropriately, the command function will not be wholly successful. It is inevitable that people will resist commands to some degree. In order to function organisations must influence people to act in ways in which they otherwise would not act. For instance, few humans would choose on their own to perform seemingly minor, repetitive tasks hour after hour, day after day. But a large proportion of production-oriented, organisations could not exist if it was not possible for some people to persuade other people to perform these tasks at a predetermined rate for a predetermined period of time with a minimal amount of creativity. Assembly lines operate successfully only because a complex array of very specific commands are communicated to a large number of people in a way that somehow persuade them to follow those commands exactly. If any worker a does a job in a new, varied unanticipated or creative way, the productivity of the assembly line is reduced. When automobile workers respond to the boredom of their jobs by choosing to install parts backward, upside down, or not at all, the quality of the final product usually us reduced. When they respond by celebrating the end of monotonous week with a Thursday afternoon or Thursday through Sunday visit to a local bar, their ability to follow commands exactly on subsequent days usually is reduced. Although these deviations from expected behaviour often do little damage, they create enough problems that most Americans learn at an early age "not to buy a car which was built in Friday." Other types of organisations involve even larger numbers of people whose actions must be initiated and controlled if the organisation is to function. Consequently, the command function of communication relies on process of persuasion and influence. Its effectiveness depends on the availability of some form of influence and some communication strategies through which some members organisations can persuade other members to act in specific and unnatural ways.

The command function also involves the production of adequate feedback about the actions that actually are taken by people who have been issued commands. Supervisors often assume that their subordinates will carry out their commands. This assumption is especially strong when the supervisor has issued a set of routine instructions. Comfortable in the knowledge that their commands will be carried out, supervisors instruct other people to take actions which, when completed, will allow the task that the unit has taken on to be accomplished. If any of the people who are involved in the command process fail to carry out the commands they were given properly or promptly, the supervisors will need to modify the commands that were given to the other people and accurate feedback about the extent to which each of their commands has been carried out.

Almost all people who have worked in organisations which produce tangible products can remember instances in which they found themselves surrounded by piles and piles of partially finished products because some person or group of people failed to receive, understand, or carry out commands. These situations usually strike the workers who are gazing at the piles as being terribly funny, both because they know that the error is someone else's headache and because they have been allowed to take a lengthy break while waiting lor the bottleneck to be eliminated and the unfinished products to reach their stations. Rarely does the supervisor who issued the commands find the situation quite as humorous. The piles of unfinished products do, however, give this supervisor feedback about the effects of the commands. Organisations do seem to function more efficiently when supervisors have access to more timely and less tangible command-related feedback.

Command related communication typically comes in one of two forms: publications and instructions. The differences between the two forms are important because employees' reactions to a command are related in part to the form in which it is issued. Organisations produce a variety of formal written policies and procedures. The published communications have three important characteristics. First, they create the impression that the commands is directed to a general audience. No one has been picked out as the recipient; the message seems to be addressed to anyone. Second, they create the impression that .the command is official; that is, it is written by the organisation or by someone who represents the organisation rather than by anyone individual. Finally, they suggest, both that the command is a relatively permanent injunction and, indirectly, that the problem it addresses is important and recurring.

In contrast, instructions are oral commands, generally given in a face-to-face encounter and addressed to a single person or clearly defined group of persons. Instructions are highly flexible commands which seem to be transient rather than permanent. They are viewed as being linked to a specific problem which is relatively new, rare, or unprecedented and are from an individual rather than from the organisation. Because publications and instructions are different forms of commands, they are appropriate to different kinds of situations. The success of any command depends on part being issued in the proper form.

One function of communication in formal organisations is the command function. Because organisations are composed of large numbers of people who play interdependent roles, their actions must be coordinated effectively. Successful coordination is achieved when members initiate the actions they have been directed to undertake. It occurs when some members of the organisation communicate in ways that create the kind of situations in which other members of the organisation will choose to take the precise actions that are envisioned in the commands. Both the process of creating a appropriate situation and the creation of clear and influential command messages depend on the strategic competence and communication skills of the participants. The command function of organisational communication relies totally on complex processes of constructing, interpreting, and choosing actions in response to a particular type of communication.

Relational Function

Organisational communication also fulfils a relational function, businesses are composed of human beings who are involved in interpersonal relationships with other human beings. Unlike non-work relationships, in which people have a relatively wide degree of freedom in deciding who to form relationships with, the structure of formal organisations dictates that each employee must form relationships with a dearly defined group of people. Sometimes, perhaps most of the time, members of organisations are required to form effective "working relationships" with people with whom they never would choose to form personal relationships. For a number of reasons, imposed relationships are less stable and more prone to friction than are "natural" ones.

Like natural relationships, working relationships can succeed only if the parties involved can achieve at least a minimal degree of understanding and cooperation. To do so they must be able to comprehend the meaning of the messages they exchanges with each other, assess each others' motivations with some degree of accuracy, and negotiate some agreements about how they will act toward one another. Unless these minimal requirements are met, the development of effective working relationships is impossible. Like all relationships, working relationships inevitably will involve some friction, misunderstanding, and conflict about the proper nature of the relationship. However, in non-working relationships the parties usually develop a degree of commitment to each other and to the continuation of the reiationship. Typically they will have voluntary started relationship and will made a number of decisions to continue it in spite of conflicts and frictions because they continue to receive benefits from it. To some degree at least, their commitment is mutual and intrinsic to the relationship. In working relationships, the parties may have very little commitment to the relationship itself. Someone or something else, a supervisor of the organisation-initiated the relationship, the parties stay in it because their roles in the organisation seem to demand that they continue to work together, and the benefits they receive from it are derived from their place in the organisation rather than from the relationship itself.

When people lack an intrinsic commitment to a relationship, it is more difficult to resolve their differences and the degree of communication skills necessary to maintain it is greater. Minor irritations are not overlooked, minor conflicts are not easily resolved, and major disagreements erupt into open confrontation because neither party is as concerned that an open conflict might threaten the continuation of the relationship. Fortunately, and almost inevitably, people do form close personal relationships with some of those with whom they have effective working relationships. Although this means that their work situations will be more pleasant than otherwise would be the case, it also adds a number of complicating factors to the relationship. They must negotiate boundaries the two dimensions of their relationship, arriving at some mutual agreement that they will communicate differently with each other while at work than they will while in other contexts. In addition, they must cope with the fact that their personal relationship is being observed by a large number of people with whom they have working relationships and that the existence of the personal relationship may further complicate some of their working relationships. "Don't have an affair with your boss, or at least don't let anyone know you are" really is very good advice.

Through processes of communication, working relationships are formed, maintained, and in some cases, transformed into personal relationships. As these relationships begin and develop, the participants in them begin to perceive their jobs, their organisation, and their roles in that organisation differently. These perceptions combine to define the situations that each individual believes one faces at work. Perceptions provide the parameters and guidelines within which each individual makes decisions about how to act. These choices influence the character of the relationships with other members of the organisation, and these changed relationships influence other members' perceptions of their organisation and thus influence their actions. Other members' actions in turn alter the character of their relationship and consequently influence the parameters and guidelines within which other members make their choices. In a complex matrix of processes, communication, relationships, perceptions, and choices, the "situations" in which people find themselves at work are created.

In addition, the relationships that people form at work influence their performance in complicated and important ways. Employees' perceptions of and satisfaction with the tasks they are asked to perform are affected by the quality of the relationships they form with the people around them. Similarly, their satisfaction with their jobs will influence their ability to form valued and stable relationships with their co-workers. The quality of employees' relationships with their co-workers influences their ability to gain the information and support they need in order to perform their job and influences their willingness to provide the information and support their co-workers need. The nature of supervisors' relationships with subordinates influences their ability to understand the messages they exchange and the probability that any particular command will be carried out. For all these reasons, the relational and command functions of organisational communication are interdependent and interactive. The success of one depends largely on the success of the other.

Ambiguity-management Function

The third major function of communication in organisations is the management of ambiguity. Humans are essentially choice-making beings, and their activities at work are essentially choice-making activities. Each day they face a series of decision-making situations, In some of these situations they make choices for the organisation; in others their decisions are more personal. Their choice making is complicated by two factors. The first involves the multitude of motivations an individual generally incorporates into decision making. In each organisational choice-making situation, a person simultaneously must consider the effects selecting one of a number of available options will have on one, one's co-workers, and one's organisation. In some situations the personal concern will be more important than the relational or organisational ones; in others, the decision maker will be concerned primarily with the interests of the organisation and only indirectly concerned with one's own interests. Some different situations will involve different combinations of self, relationship, and organisational interest, organisational choice-making is a complex and potentially confusing process. If the individual faces a situation which provides clear and explicit guidelines for determining how these interests should be balanced, it is relatively easy to make effective choices. However, choice making typically takes place in situations in which the guidelines for action are either unclear or contradictory. Communication then becomes the process through which an actor manages an ambiguous situation.

Second, organisational choice making is complicated by the ambiguity of the organisations themselves. The objectives of an organisation at a particular time often are not clear to its members. In addition, the objectives of a particular unit in the organisation or of particular members also may be ambiguous. In organisations which are undergoing rapid change or which exist in rapidly changing environments, these objectives may be particularly confused.

Also, the complex histories of modern organisations complicate the choice making of their individual members. Most situations are not completely unprecedented. The people involved have faced similar situations in the past and can draw on those experiences to help them make effective choices in the new situation. But precedents sometimes hurt choice making more than they help it. Individuals will recall that in similar situations in the past they made a certain choice. They also remember that their choice was followed by a certain good or bad result. They will tend to believe that it was their decision that led to the result all the outcome was favourable, they will tend to repeat the decision. If the outcome was negative, they will tend to avoid taking any similar course of action. But in most cases, choices made by a single individual are only one part of a complicated series of events and decisions which lead to an observed outcome. Not realising this, individual tend to make subsequent choices based on the mistaken belief that it was their choice that cause a particular outcome to occur in the past. In this way the availability of precedents can reduce the quality of the choices that are made.

Precedents complicate choice making in another way. When faced with a decision people tend to search their memories for similar situations. When they discover a precedent they feel a great sense of relief because the new situation suddenly becomes clearer and easier to manage. However, people often discover precedents which really are not precedents It all. They recall past situations that they were able to manage and then define the new situation in a way which makes it seems similar to the past, comfortable situation. Through this process they often overlook important differences between the two.

Organisational choice-making situations are inherently complex and almost always ambiguous. They are simplified and sometimes distorted by characteristically human thought processes. They also are simplified and sometimes distorted by typical communication process. Members of organisations use communication in two primary ways in their attempts to manage ambiguity. First, they communicate. to each other in ordep to structure, make sense out of, new situations. They seek out information which will help them gain perspective on the problem, and they seek out support from others which will confirm interpretation, of the problem and strengthen their commitment to a particular course. addition, they use communication in favour of a particular way of looking at the problem in support of a preferred option. Through communication with other members of the organisation they are able to create a shared mutual understanding of what a problem is and it should be addressed. If the information they gain through communication has been, sufficient, relevant, and accurate, and if the shared perspective that th~y have created has appropriate to the problem, communication will have improved their decision making.

But if the information gained has been inadequate in any significant way, or if the perspective that has been adopted by the people who were involved in the communication is flawed in any important respect, the availability of communication will have reduced the quality of the decision and further complicated choice making in the future. In the latter case, organisational communication has been used to reduce ambiguity artificially; it has not been used to manage ambiguity successfully. Sometimes processes of communication allow members of organisations to make foolish decisions and become comfortable with and strongly committed to them. In other instances communication allows members to make choices which satisfy their needs and the needs of their organisations. In some cases, organisational communication even may provide the basis for making the best possible decisions. A variety of processes inevitably influences the potential effectiveness of the ambiguity-management function of organisational communication.

Communication fulfils three major functions in formal organisations—a command function, a relational function, and an ambiguity—management function. For any organisation to succeed, each of these functions must operate at or above some minimal level of effectiveness. For any individual members of an organisation to perform their roles successfully, they must be capable of using a variety of communication skills to issue effective commands and respond adequately to commands issued by others, to develop and sustain efficient working relationships, and to manage ambiguity strategically. However, some kinds of organisations are designed in ways which lead their members to rely most heavily on one of these three communication functions. Some organisations rely most heavily on the command function, others on the role of communication in the management of relationships, and others on the effective management of ambiguity.

Every organisation must have adequate command, relational and ambiguity managing communication. However, the relative importance of these three functions varies in the three different types of organisations. "Traditional" organisations, rely most heavily on the command function af communication and less heavily on the other two. Human relations and resources organisations depend on effective relational communication. Some versions of this type also rely heavily on the cammand function. In most versions the ambiguity managing function has a limited role.

The final type, "systems-contingency" organisations, relies heavily on ambiguity managing cammunication. In this type, relational and command functions, are important in some situations and less important to' others. In fact, it is the assumption that command and relational communication must be combined in different proportions in different situations that distinguishes the systems-contingency type from the traditional and human relations and resources type.

Theory of Ideal Types

The ideas of the German sociologist Max Weber have been an important part of the study of organisations for decades. In America Weber is best known for his analysis of bureaucracy and bureaucratic orgartisations and for his discussion of the relationships traditional, rational-legal, and charismatic authority. An equally important but less wellknown component of Weber's work is the overall perspective that he took in studying organisations, the theory of "ideal types." This perspective rests on a particular set of assumptions about the nature of organisations and the appropriate means of studying them. His ideas provide a method through which employees can understand their organisations and make effective decisions about how to act on them. Weber's primary assumption was that organisations are composed of human activity and who are enmeshed in independent activities and who continually are making decisions about how to act. Their choices are based on the meanings they attribute to the actions of others and on their interpretations of the organisational situations in which they are involved. When people enter formal organisations they bring with them a long history of monitoring their actions and the actions of others, of processing the information they obtain, and of choosing from among a number of options. People from a particular culture develop ways of monitoring perceiving, and acting which are very much like another. These perceptual "filters" are not identical, of course, because every individual has had unique experiences and has been part of a particular group of relationships with others. To some extent all members of a culture will have developed their own beliefs about what actions are "normal" and proper and about what meanings can be attached to different messages. However, within all this diversity and individuality lies a common core, a culture-bound framework for making sense out of people's actions and of deciding how to act in response. It is this common interpretive scheme that defines a culture and distinguishes it from other cultures.

When employees from a particular culture come together within a formal organisation they bring with them a common way of interpreting and responding to one another. But once they come together, their interpretive frameworks begin to change in subtle but important ways. Human develop their interpretive frameworks through their experiences with other people. Relationships formed with people at work provide us with additional experience communicating with and making sense out of the communication of others. As a result, people drawn together in a formal organisation begin to form new "mini-cultures" at work. These new ways of interpreting and acting both retain the basic frame-work of the employees' general culture and reflect the more specific frameworks that develop through working relationships. The complicated interrelationship that exists between the broad patterns of action that characterise a society and the patterns that develop within an organisational "culture" was the basis of Weber's theory of ideal types.

Weber argued that researchers can understand organisations if they can understand how actors (employees) in them interpret their surroundings and choose among the wide variety of different courses of action that are available to them. The study of organisations should begin with careful observations of the choices that employees make. Eventually these observations will reveal that different groups of employees use different sense-making schemes. Researchers will begin to recognise that members of some organisations typically interpret and act in ways which are different from those in which people act in other organisations. At some point these observers will begin to construct mental images of organisations whose employees share the same basic interpretive frameworks.

For example, employees may perceive that their organisation is like an army—a formal structure with a clearly defined administrative staff which, for some as yet unexplained reasons, is obedient to commands issues by superiors. This type of organisation would function properly if it exhibited a number of necessary characteristics: each member of the staff occupies a specific position in the organisation which has been clearly defined, written duties and a clear place in the hierarchy of the organisation: each person knows who the supervisor is? who the subordinates are? and how each of them fits into the hierarchy of the organisation: each employee is selected on the basis of qualifications for the job, determined by some "objective" measure like educational background or a score on an examination; works under a contract which can be terminated if performance is inadequate; and can be promoted to a more responsible or higher paying position only on the basis of performance or seniority.

Of course, there may be no "real" organisation anywhere which has all these characteristics. Because this type of organisation is an abstraction, which represents the perceptions of a number of different groups of employees, it exists only in the mind of the observer; it is an "idealised" example of a particular "type" of organisation. It is an image of how a certain type of organisation should be designed and how it ought to operate, note a summary of the characteristics and operations of a group of real organisations. But these mental conceptions of ideal types can be useful for researchers. If researchers or managers or any other members of a real organisation understand how different types of organisations should be designed and operated, they can use that knowledge to detect and solve problems in their own organisation. To do so, they would examine their organisation, looking for features of its design or operation which do not correspond to the necessary features of the most relevant ideal type. Armed with perceptions of the essential features of a number of different types, the researcher or manager can discover cases in which the members of the organisation do not choose to act in the ways that are necessary for the organisation to function efficiently. Once these discrepancies are discovered the observer can make careful decisions about how to alter the organisation or change the conditions under which the members make decisions about how to act. When these changes are implemented, the real organisation will begin to operate more like the ideal type to which it is most closely related.

Unfortunately, these are very abstract ideas. A summary of them might increase their clarity. Weber's approach to the study of organisations rests on his theory of ideal types. It suggest that an observer can begin to understand how an organisation operates by attempting to understand how its members interpret and respond to the situations they face in the organisation. The observer then can design the organisation to increase the probability that its members will choose to act in precisely those ways that are in its best interests. Employees always will make their own decisions about how to act. They are human, and consequently they will continually be involved in observing, processing, and responding to their surroundings. But they make their choices based on their interpretations of the situations they face. Both their perceptions and many of the key characteristics of the situations they face can be created strategically through communication. However, appropriate situations can be created only if the people who design organisations know the elements that must be included. The search for these necessary features begins with the construction of a group of ideal types of organisations. Observers ask "What kinds of organisations do employees' interpretive frameworks suggest are possible?" and construct a list of features necessary for each of these "mythical" organisations to operate most efficiently. The most important features will involve the condition under which employees will choose to initiate and limit their actions in desired ways. Among these necessary features will be certain characteristics of organisational communication. After observers have delineated the features of each ideal type of organisation, they can begin to examine existing organisations, searching for points at which the real organisations differ from the ideal type. If they can detect important differences and determine the reasons for them, they can begin to isolate problems in the real organisation and develop strategies for reducing them.

Of course, Weber assumed that most of the "observers" would be scholars involved in academic research. But his perspective can just as readily be used by employees. The social psychologist Fritz Heider once argued that human beings think like researchers think, that the same analytical tools that theorists use to understand the world around them can be used by other people to understand their environment and to decide how to act in the situations they face. Heider's notion that people are "naive theorists" suggest that all theoretical perspectives, of which Weber's of ideal types is one, are based on our interpretations of reality and can be used by us to understand the realities that surround us. This assumption underlies the ideas that will be presented throughout the book. If readers can understand how communication functions in different types of organisations, they can examine their own organisations, determine how communication functions there, and choose the best communicative strategies for responding to the situations they face. Equipped with an understanding of how communication functions in different types of organisations and explanations of why communication functions differently in real organisations, readers can intelligently observe their own organisations and ask themselves these questions: how does communication operate in any organisation? How must people, including myself, act in order for this organisation to operate successfully? Why do they sometimes act in those ways and sometimes act differently? How can I act in order to make the organisation work more effectively and to make the greatest contribution to its success and to my advancement?

These are the kinds of questions. Weber suggested that researchers must ask; the questions provide the kind of information from organisational theory has made. More important, they are the kinds of questions that members of organisations must ask themselves before they can choose the best communicahon strategies to use in different organisational situations. Through understanding how different types of organisations operate and why a particular organisation functions differently, the "naive theorists" who make up an organisation can adopt the best available communication strategies.

Strategic Organisational Communication

For more than two thousand years communication scholars have argued that people communicate most effectively if they adopt the communication strategies that are most appropriate to the situations they face. Plato's intellectual rival, Gorgias, argued that knowing how to adapt to different situations was the only kind of knowledge that was available to human beings and, consequently, should be the focus of education. Some equivalent to Gorgias' concept of adaptation, an idea he labelled Kairos, has been important to the study of human communication since his time. Historically, training students in the art of adapting their communication to different situations has involved two steps: (1) teaching them to analyse the situations they face and choose the best strategies for those situations, and (2) equipping them with the repertoire of communication skills needed to implement those strategies. This book will concentrate on providing readers with the first kind of knowledge. It will examine the myriad of features which make up organisational situations, plan the kinds of communication in which employees must be competent, they and their organisations are to function effectively, describe the strategic through which they can gain the information necessary for them to adapt intelligently to the situation they face at work, and provide guidelines for choosing the optional communication strategies to use in those situation. Although it will discuss a variety of communication skills and suggest when and how those skills might be used by members of organisations, it will make no attempt to provide detailed training in the skills themselves.

SOCIAL RELEVANCE

Long before the mass media were invented, Plato may have provided the opening round in the controversy over the social costs and benefits of mass culture. In his commentary on the training of the children who were to become the leaders of his ideal Republic, he saw the mass culture of his day as posing a threat to the minds of the young:

Then shall we simply allow our children to listen to any stories that anyone happens to make up, and so receive into their minds ideas often the very opposite of those we shall think they ought to have when they are grown up?

No, certainly not [replies, Glaucon].

It seems, then, our first business will be to supervise the making of fables and legends, rejecting all which are unsatisfactory; and we shall induce nurses and mothers to tell their children only those which we have approved. Most of the stories now in use must be discarded.

This theme popular entertainment is harmful to the minds of the young has been a consistent one from the beginnings of mass communication. It has been claimed from time 10 time that such charges can be validated by scientific evidence, but repeatedly this evidence has turned out to be difficult to interpret and therefore controversial. Social sciences insist that any important conclusions about the effects of the media be supported solid evidence. Because of such insistence upon data rather than emotion, they sometimes find themselves in the awkward position of seeming to defend the media when actually they are simply refusing to accept the inadequately supported claims of critics.

Nevertheless, the insistence that conclusions be based on adequate evidence has never deterred the literacy critic from charging the media with a deep responsibility for society's problems. Most nineteenth-century American writers at some point in their careers took time to criticize and condemn the newspaper for superficiality and distortion. The following excerpts from the pens of well-known and influential literacy figures are samples of the climate of opinion prevailing among the literary during the time when the mass newspaper was diffusing through the American society:

Henry David

The penny-post is, commonly, an institution through which you seriously offer a man that penny for his thoughts which is so safely offered in jest. And I am sure that I have never read any memorable news in a newspaper. If we read of one man robbed, or murdered, or killed by accident, or one house burned, or one vessel wrecked, or one steamboat blown up, or one cow run over on the Western Railroad, or one mad dog killed, or one lot of grasshoppers in the winter we never need read of another. If you are acquainted with the principle, what do you care for a myriad instances and applications? To a philosopher all news, as it is called, is gossip, and they who read it and edit it are old women over their tea.

Samuel Clemens

That awful power, the public opinion of this nation is formed and modelled by a horde of ignorant self-complacent simpletons who failed at ditching and shoemaking and fetched up in journalism on their way to the poorhouse.

Stephen Crane

A newspaper is a collection of half-injustices which bawled by boys from mile to mile, Spreads its curious opinion to a million merciful and sneering men, while families cuddle the joys of the fireside when spurred by tale of lone agony. A newspaper is a court where everyone is kindly and unfairly tried by a squalor of honest men. A newspaper is a market where wisdom sells it freedom and melons are crowned by the crowd.

A newspaper is a game where his error scores the player victory, while another's skill wins death.

A newspaper is a symbol; it is a feckless life's chronicle, a collection of loud tales concentrating eternal stupidities, that in remote ages lived unhaltered, roaming through a fenceless world.

One remarkable aspect of these statements is that you could simply substitute the word "television" for "newspaper" and obtain a rather parallel version of the hostility and attacks primarily directed at television by critics, today.

The Basics of Functional Analysis

The tenacity and stability of the mass media generally in the face of such a long history of criticism by powerful voices needs explanation. The problem at first seems deceptively simple: the media appeal to the masses and the masses want the kind of content they get and so the media continue to give it to them.

Many social scientists, such as Skornia, have exposed the inadequacy of this explanation by nothing the old chicken-and-egg problem. It is difficult at best to know if the public taste determines the media fare or if the media fare determines public taste. The answer probably lies somewhere in between with public taste being both a cause and effect of media fare. The relationship between public taste and media fare thus becomes a circular one which, in terms of the chicken-egg analogy, is an ongoing process of chickens producing eggs and eggs producing chickens.

The structural functional analysis of social systems (or "functional analysis" for short) concerns itself with the patterns of action exhibited by individuals or sub-groups who relate themselves to one another within such systems. A social system is, for this reason, an abstraction but one not too far removed from the observable and empirically verifiable behaviours of the persons who are doing the acting. The social system, then, is a complex of stable, repetitive, and patterned action that is in part a manifestation of the culture shared by the actors, and in part a manifestation of the psychological orientations of the actors (which are in turn derived from that culture). The cultural system, the social system, and the personality systems (of the individual actors), therefore, are different kinds of abstractions made from the same basic data, namely, the overt and symbolic behaviours of individual human beings. They are equally legitimate abstractions, each providing in its own right a basis for various kinds of explanations and predictions. Generally speaking, it may be difficult or nearly impossible to analyse or understand fully one such abstraction without some reference to the others.

But, granted that the term "social system" is a legitimate scientific abstraction, how does this general conceptual strategy help in understanding the mass media of communication? To answer this question, we need to set forth in greater detail exactly what is meant by the term social system, and what type of analysis it provides. To aid in providing such an explanation we turn briefly to several ideas that are important aspects of the study of social systems. One of the most important of these ideas is the concept of the "function" of some particular repetitive phenomenon (set of actions) within such a system. The fact that such content has long survived the jibes of influential critics was said to require explanation. One form of explanation will be provided by noting the function of such a repetitive phenomenon within some stable system of action. The term "function" in the present context means little more than "consequence.'" To illustrate briefly, we might hypothesize that the repetitive practice of wearing wedding rings on the part of a given married couple has the function (consequence) of reminding, them as well as others that the two are bound together by the obligations and ties that matrimony implies. This practice thereby contributes indirectly to maintaining the permanence of the marriage, the stabiiity of that particular social system. The practice is in a sense "explained" by noting its contribution to the context within which it occurs. A comparison of a number of such systems with and without this particular item (but in other respects matched) would test the assertion.

In the above example, the social system is a relatively simple one. There are only two "components," and each of these happen to be the behaviour pattern of an individual their patterns are derived both from the individual psychological makeup of the partners and from the cultural norms concerning marriage prevailing in their community, social class, and society. It is a miniature system whose stability is dependent upon satisfaction of its "needs," For example, such a system requires that the parmers perform roles that meet the expectations, each has of the other and the expectations the community has of married couples. This can be thought of as a "need" for adequate role performance, without which the stability of the system would be endangered. Other "needs," related to economic matters and emotional satisfactions, could be cited.

More complex illustrations of social systems can easily be pointed to, where the "components" of the system are not the actions of individual persons but subsystems. A department store, for example, is a complex social system consisting of the actions of managerial personnel, buyers, salespersons, the clerical staff, customers, transportation workers, a janitorial team, and security employees. Each of these components is a smaller system of action within the broader system of the store itself, and it in turn is a complex system of action carried out within the context of the external social conditions of the community. In spite of the complexity, any given set of repetitive actions might be analysed in terms of their contribution to maintaining or undermining the system's stability. Granting to employees the right to buy merchandise at cost could have the function (consequence) of maintaining their morale and loyalty, and thus would contribute fairly directly to the maintenance of the system. Rigid insistence on the observance of petty rules, such as docking the pay of an employee who on rare occasions was late for work, might be disruptive of morale and loyalty, and by contributing to labour turnover it could be dysfunctional. Instead of contributing to the maintenance of the system, it could cause disruptions and instability. Such inductively derived conclusions would be subject to testing for validity, of course, but the functional analysis would have generated the hypothesis to be tested (an important role of theory).

Structure and Function in Media Systems

A "functional analysis," then, focuses on some specific phenomenon occurring within a social system. It then attempts to show how this phenomenon has consequences that contribute to the stability and permanence of the system as, a whole. The phenomenon may, of course, have a negative influence, and if so, it would be said to have "dysfunctions" rather than "functions." The analysis is a strategy for inducing or locating hypotheses that can be tested empirically by comparative studies or other appropriate research methods.

The analysis of social system is extremely difficult, No infallible rules specify precisely how to locate and define the exact boundaries of a given social system, particularly if it is relatively complex. As yet, no completely agreed upon criteria exist for establishing linkages between the components of a system, and no standard formulas can uncover the precise contribution that a given repetitive form of action makes to the stability of a system. A functional analysis of the contribution of some item to the stability of a system, then, is a procedure that is somewhat less than rigorous. But in spite of this source of potential criticism, this strategy has proved useful in our attempts to understand complex social phenomena, such as the mass media.

How can this type of analysis be applied to the mass media? First, we can identify that portion of the content of the mass media that is in "low" cultural taste or provides gratifications to the mass audience in such a manner that it is widely held to be potentially debasing as the "relatively persistent trait or disposition" of the mass media, the seek to explain. It would be difficult in practice to construct a set of categores under which to analyse the content of the media so that material of "low" cultural taste can be identified readily. It would be difficult, but actually it would not be impossible. Excessive violence, the portrayal of criminal techniques, horror and monster themes, open pornography, suggestive music, and dreary formula melodramas are typical categories of content that arouse the ire of critics. Considerable disagreement would probably occur as to the exact content that should be included in any given category. There would also be debates over the number of categories used. Nevertheless, is theoretically possible to identify the content of any given medium that is most objected to by the largest number of critics. We will assume that given sufficient time and resources, and using survey techniques, preference scales, attitude measuring instruments, and other research procedures now available that the content of any given medium could the divided roughly into something like the following three categories:

Low-taste Content. This would be media content widely distributed and attended to by the mass audience, but which has consistently aroused the ire of critics. Examples would be crime dramas on television that emphasize violence, openly pornographic motion pictures, day lime, confession magazines, crime comics, suggestive music, or other content that has been widely held to contribute to a lowering of taste, disruption of morals, or stimulation toward socially unacceptable conduct. Whether or not such charges are true.

Non-debated Content. This would be media content, widely distributed and attended to, about which media critics have said very little. It is not an issue in the debate over the impact of the media on the masses. Examples would be television weather reports, some news content, music that is neither symphonic nor popular, magazines devoted to specialized interests, motion pictures using "wholesome" themes; and many others. Such content is not believed either to elevate or lower taste, and it is not seen as a threat to moral standards.

High-taste Content. This would be media content sometimes widely distributed but not necessarily widely attended to. It is content that media critics feel is in better taste, morally uplifting, educational, or in some way inspiring. Examples would be serious music, sophisticated, drama, political discussions, art films, or magazines devoted to political commentary. Such content is championed by critics as the opposite of the low-taste matarial, which they see as distinctly objectionable.

Of course, the first of the above categories is the one to which we wish to direct most of our attention. It is the repetitive phenomenon whose contribution to the media (as a social system) needs analysis. Nevertheless, it would also be possible to study the other two categories with somewhat parallel perspectives, but this will receive relatively little attention in the present discussion.

Components and Boundaries of the System

We need now to begin to identify the components and boundaries of the social system within which low-taste content occurs so that eventually the contribution it makes to the system can be inductively hypothesized.

Rather than develop a purely descriptively scheme that will apply only to a single medium, it will be more fruitful to attempt to develop a general conceptual scheme into which any or all media could be placed, with suitable minor modifications in details. Such a general scheme will emphasize the similarities between media, particularly in terms of relationships between the components in the system.

Audience. The first major component of the social system of mass communication is the audience. This is an exceedingly complex component. The audience is stratified, differentiated, and interrelated in the many ways that social scientists have studied for years. Some of the major variables that play a part in determining how this component will operate within the system are the major needs and interests of audience members, the various social categories represented in an audience, and the nature of the social relationships between audience members. These variables point to behavioural mechanisms that determine the patterns of attention, interpretation, and response of an audience with respect to content of a given type.

Research Organisations. The rough typology of content suggested is in some degree related to the characteristics of the audience. Organizations devoted to research, to measuring the performances of media audiences, or to various forms of market research provide information to those responsible for selecting the categories of content that will be distributed to the audience. There is a link, then, between the audience as a component in the system and the market research-rating service organizations as a second component. In purely theoretical terms, both components are role system themselves and are thus actually sub-systems. This is in a sense a one-way link. For very minor (or usually no) personal reward, audience members selected for study provide data about themselves to such an agency, but very little flows back. This linkage between components is by comparison relatively simple.

Distributors. The content itself, of whatever type, flows from some distributor to the audience. The role system of the distributor component varies in detail from one medium to another. In addition, several somewhat distinct sub-systems exist within this general. component. First, there are local outlets, which are likely to be in the most immediate contact with the audience. The local newspaper, the local theatre, the local broadcasting station play the most immediate part in placing messages before their respective audiences. But inseparably tied to them are other sub-systems of this general component. Newspaper syndicates, broadcasting networks, or chains of movie theatres pass content on to their local outlets. The link between these two sub-systems is a two-way one. The local outlet provides money, and the larger distributor supplies content. Or the link age may be that the local outlet.provides, a service, and the distributor (who is paid elsewhere) provides money.

The relationship between audience and distributor seems at first to be mostly a one way link. The distributor provides entertainment content (and often advertising), but the audience provides little back in a direct sense. However, it does provide its attention. In fact, it is precisely the attention of the audience that distributors are attempting to solicit. They sell this "commodity" directly to their financial backer or sponsor. In addition, the audience supplies information to the research component and this is indirectly supplied to distributors in the form of feedback so that they may gauge the amount of attention they are eliciting. The linkages between components grow more complex as we seek the boundaries of the system.

Producers and their Sponsors. To the audience, the research, and the distributing component, we may add the role system of the producer of content. This component's primary link is with the financial backer (or sponsor) component and with the distributor, from whom money is obtained and for whom various forms of entertainment content are manufactured. A host of sub-systems are included in this producer component, depending upon the particular medium. Examples are actors, directors, television producers, technicians, foreign correspondents, wire-service editors, film producers, labour union leaders, publishers, copyeditors, clerical staff, and many, many more.

Advertising Agencies. Linking the sponsor, distributor, producer, and research organization are the advertising agencies. Paid primarily by the sponsor, this component provides (in return) certain ideas and services. For the most part, it provides the distributor with advertising messages. It may have links with the research component as well.

Sub-systems of Control. Over .this complex set of interrelated components, there are other sub-systems that exert control. The legislative bodies, at both the state and national level, which enact regulative statutes concerning the media, constitute an important part of such a control component. Another important part of this role sub-system is the official regulative agencies, which implement the policies that have been legislated. The link between the legislative body (control component) and the audience is, course, one of votes and public opinion, to which the component is presumably sensitive and dependent. Information lines between audience, legislative bodies, and regulatory agencies are more or less open.

To the regulatory components whose role definitions are found in legal statute can be added the private voluntary associations that develop "codes" and to some degree serve as a control over the distributors. Such distributors provide them with money, and they in turn provide surveillance and other services.

The regulatory sub-systems draw definitions of permissible and non-permissible content from the general set of external conditions within which this extremely complicated system operates. Surrounding the entire structure as an external condition are our society's general norms concerning morality, and the expressions that these find in formal law. Similar, although less likely to be incorporated into law, are our general cultural norms and beliefs regarding what will be likely to entertain or otherwise gratify Americans. Thus, we seldom see traditional Chinese opera but frequently see. western horse opera. We seldom hear the strains of Hindu temple music but frequently hear the "strains" and other noises of the latest singer whom teenagers admire. If our interests run to more serious fare, we are likely to hear the music of a relatively small list of European or American composers who created their works within a span of about three centuries. Or we are likely to view ballet; opera, drama, and so on, of a fairly limited of artists whose products are defined by our society as classics or as innovative new approaches.

Each of the several media will fit into this general model of a social system in slightly different ways. A complete description of each of the media separately would be tedious. Indeed, each could well occupy the contents of an entire book. Two decades ago, Opotowsky attempted just such a detailed analysis of the television industry, although he did not use the social system concept.

To add to the complexity of this conceptual scheme, it must be remembered that although each medium constitutes a somewhat separate social system in itself, the media are also related to one another in systematic ways. Thus, we may speak of the entire set of communication media, including those which have not been specifically analysed in the present volume, as the mass communication system of the United States.

The structure of this mass communication system has been heavily influenced by the general social, political, economic, and cultural conditions that were current during the period when our mass media were developing and remain as important socio-cultural forces in the society within which they operate. Because of their importance for understanding our mass media as"vhgy are today. Our free enterprise beliefs, our views of the legitimacy of the profit motive the virtues of controlled capitalism, and our general values concerning freedom of speech constitute further external conditions (in addition to those related to moral limits and cultural tastes) within which the American mass communication system operates.

Maintaining Systems Stability

Within the system itself, the principal internal condition is, of course, a financial one. Most of the components in the system are occupational role structures, which motivate their incumbent personnel primarily through money. To obtain money, they are all ultimately dependent upon the most central component of all—the audience. Unless its decisions to give attention, to purchase, to vote, and the like, are made in favourable ways, the system would undergo service strain and would eventually collapse.

Almost any dramatic change in the behaviour of the audience would cause the most severe disruption in the system for any given medium. The consequences of attention loss to the motion picture theatre as a mass medium was shown to be severe.

Such disruptions are infrequent, but they do occur. The key to heading off dramatic changes in audience behaviour, of course, is to provide entertainment content that will satisfy and motivate the largest possible number of audience members to carry out their roles in accord with the needs of the system. Such content will, in other words, maintain the stability of the system. The ideal, from the standpoint of the system, is content that will capture audience members' attention, persuade them to purchase goods, and at the same time be sufficiently within the bounds of moral norms and standards are not provoked.

The entertainment content that seems most capable of eliciting the attention of the largest number of audience members is the more dramatic, low-taste content. Since the most central media system goal is economic profit, sex and violence or any other attention-getting and attention-maintaining content is functional in the sense that even though it may be of low-taste, it maximizes the size of the audience exposed to advertisements. In general, the larger the audience, the more the distributor and producer can charge for advertising. For example, ads in prime-time television periods cost substantially more than those aired during relatively low-audience-size periods, such as early in the. morning.

The assumption made by many media personnel and advertisers that low-taste content appeals primarily to the relatively uneducated, who still constitute a majority of the potential audience, may be false. In an eariy study Wilensky found that educated people said that they preferred and exposed themselves to high-taste content more often than did the relatively uneducated. But when observations were made of what the educated and educated actually aid, there was little difference between their levels of exposure to lowtaste media content.

There is a great deal of evidence to show that the relatively uneducated spend more time than the educated being exposed to the mass media. It may be misleading to conclude that they do so only because the uneducated relish low-taste content. The relatively uneducated majority also have relatively low incomes, which probably means they have less choice than their more educated and wealthier counterparts in how they spend their nonworking hours. The mass media may be more appealing to the relatively uneducated and poor in large part because the media are relatively inexpensive forms of leisure. Moreover, as Baker and Ball point out, it is probably superficial to think that the only reason people in general spend time with the media is because of the inherent appeal of their content. Any number of need-fulfilments and gratifications, over and above tho e related to entertainment or staying informed, are provided by the media. Babysitting and companionship (even when it is electronic companionship) are examples.

When all is said and done, however, it is still true that low-taste content sells and sells' big. This fact establishes it as the key element in the social system of the media. It keeps the entire complex together by maintaining the financial stability of the system. Critics who provoke public attention by denouncing media content or by proclaiming that a casual connection exists between media content and socially undesirable behaviour may temporarily receive some recognition, they may also achieve some temporary disturbance in the system, or if they are persistent enough, they may ultimately even displace some specific from of low-taste content from a given medium altogether, Examples from the past are quiz shows that were found to be "rigged," and popular disc jockeys who were receiving "payola" (a fee for repeatedly playing a song to make it popular). In such cases the audience may be temporarily disaffected, low-taste content comes in such a variety of forms that the temporary or even permanent absence of one minor form does not alter the major picture. Critics have been complaining about newspaper concentration on crime news for a century, yet there has been no noticeable abatement in the reporting of such stories. Critics of the soap opera may have breathed a sigh of relief several years ago when these programs at last disappeared from radio. Their joy must have been short-lived when such daytime serials turned out to be quite popular with television viewers, so popular in fact that soap operas now appear during prime evening hours. Analyses of the level of violent television content show that it goes down slightly after federal government investigations on the effects of television violence or widespread campaigns by voluntary associations (*e.g.*, the P.T.A.), only to returnshortly after the public outcry has subsided.

When a formula is discovered for eliciting attention and influencing purchasing decisions from any large segment of the audience, it will be abandoned by the media only with great reluctance, if at all. The broadcast ballgame, the war movie, the star comedian, the family situation comedy, the western thriller, the detective story, the adventures of the secret agent, the drama of the courtroom—all are beginning to rank with such time-honoured formulas as the sob story, the funnies, the sex-murder account, the sports page, and disclosure of corruption in high places as attention-getting devices that can bring the eye or ear of the consumer nearer to the advertising message.

In short, the social system of the mass media in the United States is becoming more and more deeply established. Some future change can be expected in the kind of content it will produce to maintain its own stability. At present, however, the function of what we have called low-taste content is to maintain the financial stability of a deeply institutionalized social system that is tightly integrated with the whole of the American economic institution, the probability that our system of mass communication in this respect can be drastically altered by the occasional outbursts of critics seems small indeed.

Far more likely than media system change brought about by periodic attacks on low taste media content is media system change brought about by trends in the economic system such as the emergence of a "post-industrial" society. Because the media system is also a sub-system in the larger economic system, it will have to adapt to such changes if it is to survive. If Bell's forecast that systems in the business of producing, processing, and transmitting information will become increasingly involved in key economic sectors of our society is valid, then we would expect significant changes in the nature of the mass media system. One change would surely be a marked increase in the knowledge and technical information of "non-debated" media content will rise sharply with a corresponding decline in low-taste media content.

But as is usually the case when talking about changes in social systems, such future developments in the nature of the mass media are not likely to by that simple. Recall Durkheim's basic principle that as organisms or systems grow, they are likely to become more differentiated or complex. Taking this assumption and combining it with the enormous technological advances in electronic communications' technology witnessed in recent years, it may be hypothesized that media systems will become more specialized. Some media organizations, for example, might specialize in low-taste content, others in knowledge and technical information, others in news content, and still others in high-taste content. Such technological developments as closed-circuit and cable television already are making such specialization possible.

❐

2

Mass Communication—A Process

Communiçation is the process by which two or more people exchange ideas, facts, feelings, or impressions in ways that each gains a common understanding of the meaning, intent, and use of messages. The term "communication" stems from the Latin word "communis" —meaning common. Thus, communication is a cpnscious attempt to share information, ideas, attitudes, and the like with others. In short, It is the act of getting a sender of the message and a receiver of the message tuned together for a particular message, or a series of messages. For two or more people to engage in a common, co-operative effort, they must be able to communicate with each other. Thus, good communication consists of creating understanding of the message.

According to McQuail, "Communication is a process which. increases commonality and also requires elements of commonality for it to occur at all. Various factors contribute to bringing about the commonality the shared symbolic environment and a social relationship among those who participate in communication are the pre-requisites for communication."

According to Rogers and Shoemaker (1971), communication is the process by which messages are transferred from a source to a receiver. Ban and Hawkins (1988) defined communication as the process of sending and receiving messages through channels which establish common meaning between a source and a receiver (In Roy, 1:39). Dhama and Bhatnagar (1987) define communication as a process of social interaction, *i.e.* in a communication situation two or more individuals interact.

In today's world, there is so much to know so quickly that the role of communicator has become very important. The world is experiencing communication revolution and communication explosion. Communication is essential to all human associations. One's ability to influence others is closely linked with his ability to communicate his ideas. For two people to communicate effectively, common goals and a body of common knowledge and ideas are must.

Good communication does not mean only giving orders but creating understanding. It aims at imparting knowledge as well as helping people gain a clear view of the meaning of knowledge. Thus, communication is a social process. It is vital for human survival. It has become a field of study and scientific investigation in modern times. The study of communication has revealed that the process is not only a vital but complicated also. Good communication has the potential to contribute to overcoming the problems like ignorance; poverty, malnutrition, illiteracy and to the attainment of the goals of economic and social well being.

In modern times communication has become very necessary for the existence of human beings. It is a basic need for human beings as the need for food and shelter. It has brought about a human civilization. There are numerous ways through which we communicate such as spoken words, written words, gestures, pictures, paintings, dance and so on.

Communication and Development

Communication plays an important role in the development of a nation. It is an integral part of development. Societies can not change and develop without communication, as it is a process of social interaction through which people are influenced by ideas, attitudes, knowledge and behaviour of each other.

Communication has attained a great importance in the developmental programmes. It is through the process of communication that people are made aware of the nature and objectives of the programmes. The useful developmental messages are conveyed to the target groups through various communication approaches. This helps masses in acquiring new knowledge required for coping with fast changing society. It helps people in adoption of innovations for the improvement of their practices, methods and quality of life.

Development as an objective is planned transformation of society from one stage of life and living to well-defined and known goal. It is a process in which man is the objective as well as the tool of development. All objectives of transformation are to make man live as a human being, with better clothing, food, shelter, health and education. This cannot be achieved without man's involvement. He can not be involved unless the whole process of development is communicated to him as a desirable and acceptable objective. Communication, thus, becomes a key factor in the process of development. Thus, communication is very important in fostering the development process in a country. It can be a powerful instrument in integrating diversified society. It can create an ethos of change and progress. Communicatio by itself does not produce development. Communication should be designed or tailored to fit the various development projects. This can be done by experimenting on communication strategies for development.

Communication is very important for development planners and practitioners as they mediate between specialists and layman. They are required to develop and use effective communication strategies in order to play their role effectively. Communication is the foundation upon which development planner builds various programmes of attaining the goals of economic and social advancement of society by communicating the knowledge of useful technology. It means that the advancement of the country lies in the effectiveness of its communication system at every level. Thus, communication occupies a pivotal position in the process of development.

In the field of extension education, communication serves as the most vital means in convincing people for the acceptance and adoption of innovations. Extension education involves communication of technical know-how to the people. Thus, it is very difficult to draw a distinct line between extension education and communication. In reality, extension education would be dependent to a large extent on the art and technique of effective communication. It is a main vehicle of transmission of the useful messages for their application through implied behavioural change. In other words, communication is a means to achieve the objectives of extension education. Profession of extension education can not exist in the absence of effective communication.

Key Elements of Communication Process

A series of actions take place in the process of communication. These involve various types of expressions, interpretations and responses. Thus, the task of communication is a crucial one. Success at this task requires thorough understanding of the principles and elements of communication and high level skill in their use on the part of all communicators especially working for the development programmes.

According to Paul Leagans. "Successful communication requires a skillful communicator sending useful message, through proper channels, effectively treated, to an appropriate audience, that responds. as desired." These six elements have to be handled skillfully for successful communication. They are related to each other as discussed in the following discussion.

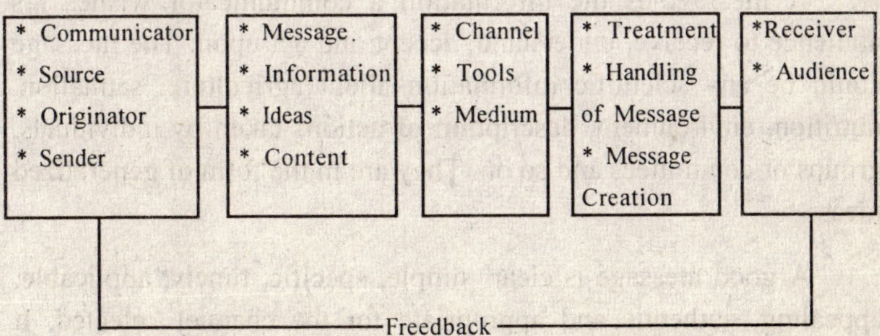

Figure 1: Key elements of communication process.

The Communicator

Communicator is a person who starts the process. He is the source, the originator or the sender of messages. He gives the message intended to reach a specific group of audience. He gives the message in such a manner that it results in correct interpretation and desirable response. He is a key factor in the effectiveness of the communication process. He can be a teacher, extension worker, administrator, leader, writer, or any other person in the role of communicator. A good communicator,

(a) knows his objectives, audience, message, appropriate channels for his message, his abilities and limitations.

(b) is interested in his audience and it's welfare and improving his own communication skills.

(c) has skill in selecting, treating and expressing messages and in understanding his audience and collecting the evidence of results.

The communicator recognizes that his message 'must get through'. He communicates for clear understanding and desirable action by his audience, as this is an indicator of successful communication.

Message or Content

A message is the information a communicator wishes his audience to receive, understand, accept and act upon. The message could be any scientific information about agriculture, sanitation, nutrition, environment, description of actions taken by individuals, groups or committees and so on. They are in the form of generalized ideas.

A good message is clear, simple, specific, timely, applicable, appealing, authentic and appropriate for the channel elected. It should be of significant value to the audience. In extension education and community development programmes, the messages are the content aspects of educational change, such as, on health, income generation, importance of voting, etc.

Channels of Communication

Channels of communication are necessary as they are the link between the sender and receiver. These are the essential tools of the communicator. He gets in contact with his audience through the channel. Channels of communication can be meetings, radio, television, books, newspaper, letters, tours, personal contacts, street plays, drama and so on. To make communication effective, channels should be used in the right way, at the right time and for the right audience and purpose, without channel, no message can reach effectively to the intended audience.

For good selection of channels, objective and nature of the message and the nature of the intended audience, should be considered first. If required, combination of channels also can be considered such as, group meetings and radio talks or television and newspapers. The time available for the use of channel and relative cost of channel in relation to the anticipated effectiveness should be considered too in the selection of the channel. As the channels are the connecting links between communicators and receivers, they must effectively join together these two essential elements of the communication process.

Treatment of Message

Messages need to be treated so that they can be sent over channels to reach the audience effectively. Treatment is a way of handling message in such a manner that it reaches to the audience. This means designing the networks or techniques of presenting messages. Treatment makes the message clear, understandable and realistic to the audience. Treating the message effectively requires skill in creating and using refined techniques of message presentation. The communicator has to make many decisions, such as, whether he will make logical or emotional appeal in presentation of message or he will draw conclusions or leave conclusions to the audience and so on. For example, he may treat the message in a talk form or drama form or a story form.

Treatment is a creative task that has to be 'tailor-made' for each instance of communication. The skill in treatment of message develops with experience and creative thinking. Planning also helps. An understanding of teaching and learning process, knowledge of the subject matter, and skill in the use of channels are also helpful in giving effective treatments to the messages. Any treatment should make the idea of the message specific and concrete.

The Audience

An audience is an individual or a group of persons intended to receive the message, such as, men, women, youth, urban or rural people, students, farmers and so on. In good communication the audience aimed at is already identified by the communicator. Success of the communication process depends on how audience responds to the message received. Audience can be identified according to occupation, profession, educational qualification, age, interest, need, economic status, social status and so on. The homogeneity of the audience increases the chances of successful communication. The communicator must know the characteristics of the audience. This helps in making impact of the message. Without the knowledge of audience and its view points, communicator cannot be sure of the success.

Before making a plan of communication, the communicator must know the people's needs as they see them and why they are in need of changed ways of thinking, feeling and doing.

It is expected from the audience that it will show an immediate action. It can be a mental or physical action. Sometimes audience receives and accepts the message but does not act in response to the message. In the language of communication, until desired action results, programmes of change do not achieve their most essential objectives. Usually the response of the audience is in the form of gaining knowledge as understanding, change in practice or habit, accepting or rejecting the idea and so son.

Thus, response or action resulting from a communication is a complicated phenomenon and should be considered with care and preciseness.

Feedback

Feedback refers to the response or reaction of the receiver to the sender. Feedback can be in various forms, *i.e.* through the same channel or medium or through a different one. Developmental communication is incomplete without feedback. Communication is not an end in itself. Feedback influences communication. How it uinfluences depends on whether the communicator received positive feedback or negative feedback. If one receives laughter or clapping from the audience while delivering a lecture, he feels encouraged. Feedback is immediate in one to one communication. It is more restricted in formal situations. The communication cycle is incomplete without feedback. It is source oriented, and exerts control over future message. It contributes to the stability and equilibrium of a communication process. For any developmental programme to succeed, adequate and correct feedback is necessary when a development practitioner receives feedback, he comes to know the positive and negative sides of his work and he is able to plan his subsequent activities on the basis of this knowledge. Thus, it enhances the confidence of the communicator and receiver in what they have accomplished by communicating with each other. Absence of feedback may give rise to doubts in the minds of both sender and receiver.

Discouragement from the communicator to give feedback, language and cultural barriers, untimely messages, socio-economic barriers or nature of the channel could be some of the reasons for getting no or poor feedback.

Functions of Communication

Communication serves four vital functions in society. Roy summarized these functions as follows:

(i) **Information Function.** The basic requirement of adapting and adjusting oneself to the environment is information. There must be some information about what is going on in the environment which concerns the people. The receiving or giving of information underlines all communication functions, either directly or indirectly.

(ii) **Command or Instructive Function:** Those who are hierarchically superior in the family, society or organisation, often initiate communication either for the purpose of informing their subordinates or for the purpose of telling them, what to do, how to do when to do etc. The command and instructive functions of communication are more observable in formal organisations than in informal organisations.

(iii) Influence or persuasive function: According to Berlo (1960), the sole purpose of communication is to influence people. Persuasive function of communication *i.e.* to induce people is extremely important for extension in changing their behaviour in the desirable direction.

(iv) **Integrative Function:** A major function of communication is integration or of continuously offsetting any disintegration at the interpersonal or at the organisational level. This helps in maintaining individual, societal or organisational stability and identity.

Types of Communication

The word communication means different things in different situations. This can be clarified by understanding types of communication. Communication scholars usually work within one of these types to study how people communicate within that particular setting.

Interpersonal Communication. This type of communication is characterised by face to face communication between two individuals. It is conversation or dialogue between two persons wihtout the use of any machine, such as, telephone. Thus, words and gestures are used for communication. It is more personal, direct and intimate compared to the other types of communication in its most basic sense. It is also called one-to-one communication. This type of communication is the most dynamic, flexible and most interactional in nature. There can be maximum exchange of ideas, feelings, needs and goals. This can be a very casual communication at a coffee shop or serious or formal discussion between two individuals in an office or outside. Intra personal communication refers to dialogue taking place within one's own self or an internal communication. It is an individuals ability to think, feel and use language for understanding and expressing ideas.

Group Communication. This type of communication is characterized by gorup to group or a speaker to group communication. Therefore, it becomes less direct, personal and intimate in nature. However, it provides better scope for quick and easy feedback compared to mass communication. The degree of directness and intimacy depends upon the size of the gorups, the place where it meets, the relationship among group members and the group leader. The group ranges in size from three to twelve or upto twenty. For example, communication in committees, workgroups, family, extension programmes and so on require communicating with the group.

Mass Communication. Mass communication is characterized by communication between a single or a panel of communicators and large sized, heterogeneous and anonymous audience except in rare cases where audience comes in contact with communicator such as author, film maker, development practitioner and so on. It is most indirect and impersonal of all types of communication It requires some kind of mechanical device to transmit duplications of the messages, such as television, radio, films, recordings or magazines and newspapers.

Meaning of Mass Communication

Mass communication is mostly misunderstood as a synonym of communication media such as radio, television or films. Modern technology is essential to the process of mass communication but its presence does not always signify mass communication. For example, the nationwide telecast of independence day celebrations is mass communication whereas closed circuit telecast in a classroom or assembly hall on a topic such as eco-friendly environment is not. Mass communication is directed towards a relatively large, heterogeneous and anonymous audience. It is public, rapid and transient. The concept of mass communication in India has undergone transformation after independence. It has become development supportive, flexible and need-based especially in the areas like health, nutrition, family welfare, agriculture, dairy development, literacy etc.

The development support concept of mass communications is dynamic, purposive, practical and promotional in nature.

In many societies, mass communication has emerged as a result of political needs. People in power encourage the spread of mass media so that they can have a channel at their disposal for publicizing their views, policies and agenda for action. Apart from fulfilling the general functions of communication, they play a very important role in advertising of the various consumer products and thereby bringing the producer and the consumer closer to each other.

Functions of Mass Communication

Communication needs of the society must be met for the existence of the society. Primitive society had sentinels that scanned the environment and repeated dangers. Council of elders interpreted facts and made decisions. Tribal meetings were used to transmit these decisions to the rest of the group. As society became larger and more complex, these jobs also became big and complex to be handled by single individuals. With the advent of technology, these jobs were taken over by the mass media. The major functions of mass communication are:

1. Surveillance
2. Interpretation
3. Transmission of values

4. Lineage

5. Entertainment.

The functions served by mass communication are very similar to those fulfilled by others types of communications. The way mass communication performs these function is discussed here.

Surveillance. Surveillance relates to the constant flow of public information or news about events occurring within the country and in the world. It is the most obvious of all functions of mass communication. It refers to the news and information role of media. They work as the sentinels or guards. Correspondents for wire services, TV networks and newspapers are located across the globe. These individuals gather information for us that we can not get for ourselves. The surveillance function can be divided further into two types.

1. Warning or beware surveillance occurs when the media informs us about threats from weather changes, heavy rains, cyclone, war, etc.

2. Instrumental surveillance occurs when the information useful in everyday life is transmitted, such as, stock market prices, new products, recipes and so on. A TV serial may perform a function of instrumental surveillance by portraying new hair or dress styles or women in changing roles.

Apart from these functions it confers high public status upon certain people by reporting news about individuals and strengthen social control over the individual members of the society by bringing deviant behaviour into public view.

Surveillance thorough mass communication can prove dysfunctional also for the society. If news or information goes uncensored, sometimes it may prove harmful for the society. For example, news of commercial conflicts in some area may result in to communal riots in many areas. Sometimes people are warned frequently about possibility of floods, heavy rains or cyclone. This may lead to panic by the people and increase their anxieties.

Interpretation. Interpretation function is closely related with the surveillance function. It prevents undesirable consequences of communication. Now-a-days, mass communicators have realized their responsibility to evaluate and interpret events for the reader. They select the important news and issues for the attention of the people and not only provide information of the events but they also provide information on the ultimate meaning and significance of these events. This prevents the over stimulation and over modification of the population. For example, the editorial pages of newspapers and magazines interpret the event, comment or opine on it so that the reader gains an added perspective on the event. Many analytical articles, radio and TV documentaries, panel discussions on an event or issue also perform this function. Sometimes cartoons also provide an added perspective on the fact or event.

This function of the mass communication helps the individual to know the viewpoints of various people, which help him to evaluate an issue. A wide range of expertise is available to the individual to which he or she might not have an access through interpersonal communication.

The dysfunction of the interpretation and prescription by mass media can be that people may not get the depth and true picture of the event or issue and may not contribute to the development of an individual's critical faculties.

Transmission of Values. The transmission of values is a subtle but an important function of the mass media. It is also called socialization function. Our society is portrayed in the mass media and by seeing, watching or reading this people learn which are the important values. The media present role models which people try to imitate. Thus, they teach us about people, show us how they act and what is expected of them.

According to Dominick. "At one level, value transmission via the mass media will aid the stability of society. Common values and experiences are passed down to all members, thereby creating common bonds between them. On the other hand, the kinds of values and cultural information that are included in the mass media content are selected by media organisations that may select values and behaviours that encourage the status quo.

Lineage. The mass media are able to link together different elements of society that are not directly connected by interpersonal channel. For example, newspapers generate opinion, develop feeling for whatever happenings are reported. Advertising through mass media links together the needs of buyers with the products of sellers.

It is also possible that media can create new social or professional gorups by linking together the people of same interest. This function is also called 'public making' ability of the mass media. For example, people interested in geography, science, environment form a group and this phenomenon may account for the growth of some movement. Thus, the social gorups can be mobilized quickly and this may lead to some main action. For example, messages regarding literacy motivated NGOs to take up literacy programmes, health programmes motivated people to become health conscious or beauty contests telecasts generated beauty consciousness.

Entertainment. Entertainmentis the most obvious function of all media functions. In the past entertainment functions were fulfilled by interpersonal communication. The importance of the entertainment function has grown as the people have got more leisure time. The work week has decreased for many government offices from six to five day leaving more free time for people. The consequences of this function have been that media entertainment is available to a large number of people at relatively little cost. This helps people to make their recreational and leisure time more enjoyable. Media content is designed to appeal to the lowest common denominator of taste.

Pointing out the consequences of entertainment function of mass media Dominick says, "It is now quite easy to sit back and let others entertain you. Flicking on the TV set, picking up a magazine, and going to a movie require little effort on our part, and some fear that media do such good jobs of entertaining society that they encourage passivity. Instead of playing baseball, people might simply watch it on TV. Instead of learning to play guitar, an adolescent might decide to listen to a record of someone else playing the guitar. On more than one occasion critics have charged that the mass media will turn Americans Into a nation of watchers and listeners instead of doers".

Development of Mass Media-EPS Cycle

John Merrill and Ralph Lowenstein, the mass communication scholars developed progression cycle concept called the Elitist Popular—Specialized (EPS) Cycle. They pointed out that all media develop in three stages.

A mass communication medium usually starts out in the elite stage. Here the media appeal to, and are consumed by, the affluent leaders in the culture. After a nation breaks through the barriers of poverty and illiteracy, its media enter the popular stage and are enjoyed by the mass culture. Eventually, as the elements of higher education, affiuence, leisure time and population growth come together and form one whole, the mass media begin to enter a third stage of the EPS Cycle - specialization. In this stage the—media are consumed by highly fragmented segments of the population, each with its own interests and cultural activities.

Elite Stage. Elite culture is the culture of the educated, aristocratic and wealthy people. It is also called high culture. Until few decades ago there were distinct two types of cultures in India. One was high culture and second, that of the common peasant class, which was known as folk culture. The elite culture revolved around fine arts, literature and classical music. The peasants had their folk culture, which consisted of street carnivals, public drinking, and singing and the telling of folk tales. Although people who participated in the elite culture could also enjoy folk culture, the reverse was not true.

Popular Stage. The popular mass culture was ushered in with the industrial revolution, public education of the masses, and development of political democracy. Popular culture reflects the cultural world around us—our attitudes, habits and actions, our clothing, food practices, our housing, means of travel, entertainment, religion, our beliefs and activities—in short all that surrounds us in our everyday lives. It is our main stream culture, it encompasses all the objects, customs, fads and activities that we take for granted.

Popular culture can be defined as the culture of everyone in a society. Every country has its own popular culture at various stages of development. Most of today's popular culture is mass-produced and is disseminated in large quantities through the mass media. Popular music, cheap paperback novels, soap operas, video cassette movies and advertised products reflect and create popular culture. Mass culture has developed due to mass mediation of our popular culture.

Specialized Stage. With the information explosion, and advanced communication technologies, there is a movement by Indian mass media towards specialization. There is de-massification of the mass media, which means the control of mass communication systems is relocated from the message producer to the media consumer, which reflects the participatory nature of the new media. The mass media are de-massified to an extent that a special message can be exchanged with each individual in a large audience. For example, during election broadcastes, individuals from audience of various places in India could ask questions to the election analysts on TV.

India is entering the age of specialization.

Importance of Mass Communication

With the opening of satellite communication, mass communication has become inseperable part of the human life. The history of mass communication is comparatively recent, but it has become indispensable in today's society, which has become dependent on mass communication. At personal level, mass communication is woven into our day-to-day existence. Individuals'use mass media to satisfy their need for entertainment or enlightenment. They become more aware of the country's problems and issues as well as help people develop understanding of the social problems. They also contribute to increased understanding of culture, politics, economy and so on.

In developed nations, where literacy and industrialization is high, is likely to depend more on mass communication channels for people's knowledge, entertainment and decision making. As people of the country modernize and become more literate, individualistic and cosmopolitan, the use of mass communication channels becomes more and more important as there are many areas of common concern and interest to people about which people want to know.

Today's society has become far more complex to function only through interpersonal or group communication. There are many important messages of common concern which have to reach effectively to masses at a time.

In a country like India, it is not possible to train a mass of Indian population in basic life skills simultaneously and uniformly throug formal education. It is not possible with our meager existing resources and facilities. This requires resorting to effective system of mass communication.

In India a large majority of the population is illiterate and hence beyond the reach of the printed media. Moreover, more than 65 per cent of Indian population is living in villages, bound by traditions, deep rooted attitudes and superstition. This is a challenge for any educator. It is only through persuasive influence of mass communication, the illiterate and backward population in India can be directed towards any social change required for development. Thus, mass communication has important role to play in enlightening the masses to raise the standards of their living and improve quality life.

Communication with rural people is difficult and challenging, as many of them live in inaccessible and isolated villages. In this situation mass communication is the only alternative for reaching them breaking all the barriers of physical distances and illiteracy.

Mass communication becomes very important while communicating ideas intended to change behaviour of people right from developing awareness to adoption of an innovation. When people are exposed to an increasing flow of information, they find themselves in a position which necessitates a change in their aspiration, attitude and effort. Frequent exposure to mass media can create the urge for a higher standard of living. There is adequate research evidence throwing light upon the potentialities of individual medium of mass communication as well as a total effect of mass media exposure in changing cognitive and affective behaviour of rural people.

Radio and Television have invaded almost every corner of the country. People sit glued to watch television. Research have also proved the effectiveness of these media in educating people. Hence mass communication is one of the important inputs for the development of the nation.

Radio, television, newspaper, movies are used widely as means of mass communication for information and entertainment.

Today, mass communication brings people closer by developing common understanding of the event or issue. We are dependent on mass communication not only for information, entertainment and politics but also education, science, religion, charities, agriculture and transportation. In one way or another, almost every major social activity in modern life depends on the use of mass communication media to greater or lesser extent.

Mass communication is important for socialization of people because changes in subtle areas such as the socialization of the individual in regard to knowledge, attitudes, and beliefs, can be brought about through mass communication by using media like television and cinema. Thus, mass communication plays an important role in the transmission of attitudes, perceptions and beliefs. Mass media like television and radio are influential force when the same ideas, people, or behaviours, occur consistently from programme to programme and presented in a stereotype manner.

Mass communication has developed. into industry and has provided jobs to millions of people enabling them to earn their living.

Barriers in Mass Communication

In India if mass communication has to have its maximum impact, the barriers in the system need to be removed.

At present the mass communication channels like television, radio, films operate mainly for urban and elite masses and rural population is neglected as far as the content and accessibility of mass media are concerned. Urban and rural population have different needs and problems which require different content and treatment of the messages.

There is not effective two way system established in our mass communication system because of which no feedback is received on the messages and programmes leaving no scope for developing relevant, need-based messages. This restricts interactive and participatory mass communication system. Thus, there is a need to establish a proper feedback system.

So far, there has been government control over Doordarshan and Akashwani which affected the credibility of the news and information passed on to the masses by these media. Now with the implementation of Prasar Bharati, it is hoped that these two media will increase in the credibility of their messages. When mass media have to function as the instrument of the government it can not contribute to shaping influencing and carrying conviction with the public opinion.

The resistance to change on part of people also becomes a barrier in having the maximum impact of mass communication. People and society have tendency to maintain status quo and resist new messages or ideas. New messages are ignored by the people resulting into lack of development and minimizing the impact of mass communication.

Heterogeneity of the population also becomes an obstacle in maximizing the impact of mass media. People differ in their perceptions depending upon their needs, social environment, level of education, and other personal and cultural characteristics. As a result, people perceive the content or message differently, and interpret and evaluate the information from their own point of view leading to lack of uniformity in understanding and action. This especially affects the action on the development messages by the target group.

Competition in the business or industry of mass media has also become barrier in achieving the objectives of mass communication in our country. This is more applicable to television and print media. It has affected the quality and type of content of these media. They have become more entertainment oriented rather than education or development oriented.

There is a need to overcome these barriers in order to improve the impact of mass communication in our country. It is possible to remove physical barriers, such as, those related to organization, machine etc. by conscious efforts but it is difficult to remove psychological barriers arising out of individual differences.

Impact of Mass Media

In the past, mostly people interacted in groups having face-to-face relationships. Today, they are continuously exposed to messages generated from the centre.

The history of mass media is comparatively recent. The oldest form is the press which was set up first by William Crown at Westminster in 1476. The first wireless communication was made between the Isle of Wight and the English mainland in 1882, the phonograph was patented in 1877. The first cinema film was made in Paris in 1895.

In India, after the independence, new horizons were seen by the country in all the aspects of five year plans stressing the need to solve some of the national problems, such as, lack of cultural identity, absence of economic policy and so on, the development of mass media was boosted. The need for communicating with the masses and influencing them was felt in order to have the impact of the independence. This led to tremendous progress in the fields of print and the broadcast media. Freedom of speech and expression along with freedom of press was provided by the constitution as a fundamental right. Over and above, constitution also granted freedom of movement, right to profession and property, right to hold meetings and cultural gatherings. All these led to the unabated progress of mass media in the country. The developments of each mass media are discussed separately in the following chapters.

With the extending impact of media of mass communication on individuals and groups, the Indian society overall is reacting swiftly. The pervasive effects of the various media on the various spheres of the Indian life economic, social, cultural, intellectual, religious and even moral values are transforming rapidly.

Mass media are capable of creating various kinds of impact on mankind. They play a crucial role in the function and change of any society. A study of social change can not be done without studying mass media. Therefore, in the present times when technology has brought about changes in the society, mass media studies have become important.

Mcluham, the Canadian writer perceives mass media in a very broad perspective. It is his thesis that, the medium is the message, he says that the content of a mass medium can not be divorced from its context and from its technology. A statement made on television will be very different from a statement made through the press, the form and nature of the message's dissemination actually modifies the material. The visual image of television news involves us directly as compared to the news reported in the newspaper. Whether or not we discuss the wheel in the context of mass communication is a moot point, but it is obviously true that the wheel has changed many human societies in a way which is quite as radical as television or the press.

He says that we have been too much pre occupied with the messages, or content, of mass media, and too little concerned with the media themselves, as they function within human society. It was his argument, for example, that the electric light can be taken as a medium, it transmits lights to a large number of people. This notion may not be digestible to many because we are used to ascribing overwhelming importance to content.

The mass media constitute a powerful and pervading force in our lives. We are exposed daily to a bombardment of media messages. Most of the information we receive about our community, our state, the nation and the world comes to us through newspapers, magazines, television and radio. The information and views communicated through these media have great impact on our attitudes toward people, events and problems. Mass media expose people to a flood of informiation almost narcoticising reader, listener or viewer. Due to mass media the range and amount of information available to the people has vastly increased. For example, a villager in India today can have the idea of what the city life is by watching television and cinema.Media use by the people is going through quick shifts. Although urban areas have more access to mass media than the rural areas, it is observed that people in rural areas are becoming increasingly conscious of the power of knowledge. They subscribe to the newspapers and this has led to the growth of regional press. The commercialization of radio and television in India has brought the whole world of advertising to the door steps of the people and made the society consumeristic in nature. Mass media have exposed people to technical subjects which are of their day to day use. For example, use of automatic machines, electronic appliances, pesticides, fertilizers etc.

Media confer a certain social status or peoples position in society is enhanced when they appear upon television or are mentioned in the press. Mass media like films, television and press have particular glamour, which is enjoyed by those who are in them.

Thus, mass media tend to enforce and corroborate social norms and bring personal attitudes and public morality closer.

Mass media are common denominators. They serve the interest of the larger groups. For example, today people use mass media for entertainment or for product information through advertisements. According to Hancock: "This view of mass media as the 'common denominator' of their audiences leads us to the most consistent criticism which is leveled against them; that they spoil public taste and attack art and culture, by becoming lowest common denominators." For example, when literacy was low, print media were required to appeal to a limited audience and writer could write according to his wishes. Even popular writing could be quality writing. With the spread of education and literacy the audience for print media also became larger. This resulted into popular writing.

Media consumers are selective in their consumption of media output. They accept the massages which are easy for them to understand and they do not have to exert themselves in watching a programme or reading a newspaper. They also accept messages which reinforce their beliefs and reject or ignore those which have contrary views. Another criticism about the impact of mass media is that they do not keep pace with the changes that are taking place in society and usually maintain stereotyped roles and values. For example, widow woman in today's society wear dresses of all types and colours but films and television serials show them in their stereotyped white dress with no jewellery. Thus, mass communication process is more likely to sustain rather than challenge the existing political and social power structure in society. As a result, mass media look for supportive :communication and avoid that communication which projects alternative opinions. Mass media play a significant role in the socialization of the young. An extensive exposure necessarily influences young, who are always believed to be passive respondents.

Watz and Hoffman note that: "the social potential of mass communication has hardly been tapped". Effective use of the mass media has the potential for increasing the public's understanding of the goals of development programmes and activities of development workers. It can increase public support for development programmes and it can have a significant impact on the decisions of development planners, policy makers, and legislators that affect these programmes. It can help people function better in the community, by providing information that can support the coping capacities of persons under stress and consequently, it can significantly expand the impact of the development programmes in any community. A much wider range of target groups can be reached, not only those who might benefit form the programmes but also persons and groups that may be willing to provide tangible and intangible support for these development efforts, as a result of being better informed about them.

Mass media in India are actively involved in the tasks related to different aspects of national development and they are assisting government and the masses in social, economic and political development. Thus,. mass media have contributed to the mobilization of human resources for national development. The mobilizing of human resources requires a great deal of attention of what the population knows and thinks of national development, and especially to the encouragement of the attitudes and social customs and the provision of knowledge, which will be favourable to the development, the mass media have undertaken the job quite competently. It is evident from the tremendous changes that have taken place in the entire range of human activity in the country. Research studies by communication scholars also have proved that mass media have immensely aided and assisted the rate and score of development.

The studies conducted by Shramm, Rao and others have shown that the interaction between the media and the society from development point of view is 'constant and cumulative.' This helps people to set common goals of development and arrive at sound consensus. Media have communicated to the people about country's five year plans, development programmes, education system etc. and this has motivated people to become partners in the progress of the country. The farm technology was communicated to the rural masses through mass communication media such as radio and films which became link between university laboratories and farmers. This contributed to tremendous agricultural progress and ushered in green revolution in the country. There have been problems and constraints in the process of development but, on the whole, mass media in India have immensely contributed to bringing about change and development in India. It has been realised that no significant development can take place without using mass media.

In other words, the mass media can have impact on a variety of important development programmes, relations, public education and prevention functions of the development programmes.

It has also been observed that as the time devoted to media increases, people's participation in an organized action decreases. As a result, they remain away from the decision making and action for any personal or national development activities.

Mass media do not involve the individual directly. They bring changes largely in the psychological domain. They capture the audience by changing their opinions, attitudes, beliefs, knowledge and value systems. Psychological changes are considered to be more effective as compared to the change which are introduced directly into the social structure by means of law and government policies to which individuals are forced to adjust.

The new media have brought about changes in the old media for example, due to the impact of television, newspapers and magazines have become more illustrative, radio has been trying to become more innovative in attracting the listeners, advertising has become part of every mass medium and so on. Moreover, due to the review of the programmes offered by every medium, competition to offer more and more interesting programmes of common taste "as increased among the mass media.

What about education? Mass media in India such as television, radio, newspaper, try to offer educational and enrichment messages for farmers, school children, youth, woman, and other groups. This again may be due to the competition among and within the media.

Folk media have been very effective in promoting the message of literacy, mobilising women and bringing them together to discuss issues related to their everyday lives. Street plays have proved very effective in integrating and mobilising women for anti-arrack movement in Andhra Pradesh.

Sometimes too much of exposure to information leads people to saturation. For example, if we are exposed to the events of terrorism in Kashmir or Punjab for a very long period, we become less sensitive to the sufferings of people due to terrorism. Here the immediacy of visual image is lost and media ceases to be an informant.

Mass medium like television has made great impact on the families by changing the way of life. In the last ten years Indian family has under gone drastic changes as far as family relations standard of living, style of living and buying habits are concerned.

To sum up, mass media create impact by playing their role as change agent, reflector and reinforcer of dominant values and attitudes in society which can have a significant impact on the decisions of development planners, policy makers and legislators that affect development programmes.

❐

3

Function of Communication

FUNCTIONS OF ORGANISATIONAL COMMUNICATION

In some important ways communication functions as a tool for members of organisations. It allows them to issue, receive, interpret, and act on commands; it allows them to create and maintain productive business and personal relationships with other members of the organisations; and it allows them to manage ambiguity and uncertainty.

Processes of Communication in Organisations

Communication Process

Monitoring actions of self and others

Processing information about organisational action

Choosing appropriate actions

Organisational Constraints on Actions

Precedents and norms

Individual purposes

Potential effects of different actions

Need for coordination with others

The Command Function

Two types of communication make up the "command" function: direction and feedback. People perform necessary task effectively only when they choose both to initiate action and to limit their actions in clearly prescribed ways. Some members of organisations, usually those given the formal titles of supervisor 'or manager, issue messages which tell other members to take action and to limit that action to a particular series to be taken at a specified time and at a specified place. If the person to whom the message is directed does not act, or if the person acts inappropriately, the command function will not be wholly successful. It is inevitable that people will resist commands to some degree. In order to function, organisations must influence people to act in ways in which they otherwise would not act. For instance, few humans would choose on their own to perform seemingly minor, repetitive tasks hour after hour, day after day. But a large proportion of production-oriented organisations could not exist if it was not possible for some people to persuade other people to perform these tasks at a predetermined rate for a predetermined period of time with a minimal amount of creativity. Assembly lines operate successfully only because a complex array of very specific commands are communicated to a large number of people in a way that somehow persuade them to follow those commands exactly. If any worker a does a job in a new, varied, unanticipated or creative way, the productivity of the assembly line is reduced. When automobile workers respond to the boredom of their jobs by choosing to install parts backward, upside down, or not at all, the quality of the final product usually us reduced. When they respond by celebrating the end of monotonous week with a Thursday afternoon or Thursday through Sunday visit to a local bar, their ability to follow commands exactly on subsequent days usually is reduced. Although these deviations from expected behaviour often do little damage, they create enough problems that most Americans learn at an early age "not to buy a car which was built on Friday." Other types of organisations involve even larger numbers of people whose actions must be initiated and controlled if the organisation is to function.

The command function also involves the production of adequate feedback about the actions that actually are taken by people who have been issued commands. Supervisors often assume that their subordinates will carry out their commands. This assumptions is especially strong when the supervisor has issued a set of routine instructions. Comfortable in the knowledge that their commands will be carried out, supervisors instruct other people to take actions which, when completed, will allow the task that the unit has taken on to be accomplished. If any of the people who are involved in the command process fail to carry out the commands they were given properly or promptly, the supervisors will need to modify the commands that were given to the other people and accurate feedback about the extent to which each of their commands has been carried out.

Almost all people who have worked in organisations which produce tangible products can remember instances in which they found themselves surrounded by piles and piles of partially finished products because some person or group of people failed to receive, understand, or carry out commands. These situations usually strike the workers who are gazing at the piles as being terribly funny, both because they know that the error is someone else's headache and because they have been allowed to take a lengthy break while waiting for the bottleneck to be eliminated and the unfinished products to reach their stations. Rarely does the supervisor who issued the commands find thee situation quite as humorous. The piles of unfinished products do, however, give this supervisor feedback about the effects of the commands. Organisations do seem to function more efficiently when supervisors have access to more timely and less tangible command-related feedback.

Command-related communication typically comes in one of two forms: publications and instructions. The differences between the two forms are important because employees' reactions to a command are related-in part to the form in which it is issued. Organisations produce a variety of formal written policies and procedures. The published communications have three important characteristics. First, they create the impression that the commands is directed to a general audience. No one has been picked out as the recipient; the message seems to be addressed to anyone. Second, they create the impression that the command is official; that is, it is written by the organisation or by someone who represents the organisation rather than by any one individual.

In contrast, instructions are oral commands, .generally given in a face-to-face encounter and addressed to a single person or clearly defined group of persons. Instructions are highly flexible commands which seem to be tranisent rather than permanent. They are viewed as being linked to a specific problem which is relatively new, rare, or unprecedented and are from an individual rather than from the "organisation." Because publications and instructions are different forms of commands, they are appropriate to different kinds of situations. The success of any command depends on part being issued in the proper form.

One function of communication in formal organisations is the command function. Because organisations are composed of large numbers of people who play interdependent roles, their actions must be coordinated effectively. Successful coordination is achieved when members initiate the actions they have been directed to undertake. It occurs when some members of the organisation communicate in ways that create the kind of situations in which other members of the organisation will choose to take the precise actions that are envisioned in the commands. Both the process of creating a appropriate situation and the creation of clear and influential command messages depend on the strategic competence and communication skills of the participants. The command function of organisational communication relies totally on complex processes of constructing, interpreting, and choosing actions in response to a particular type of communication.

The Relational Function

Organisational communication also fulfils a relational function, businesses are composed of human beings who are involved in interpersonal relationships with other human beings. Unlike non-work relationships, in which people have a relatively wide degree of freedom in deciding who to form relationships with the structure of formal organisations dictates that each employee must form relationships with a clearly defined group of people. Sometimes, perhaps most of the time, members of organisations are required to form effective "working relationships" with people with whom they never would choose to form personal relationships. For a number of reasons, imposed relationships are less stable and more prone to friction than are "natural" ones.

Like natural relationships, working relationships can succeed only if the parties involved can achieve at least a minimal degree of understanding and cooperation. To do so they must be able to comprehend the meaning of the messages they exchanges with each other, assess each others' motivations with some degree of accuracy, and negotiate some agreements about how they will act toward one another. Unless these minimal requirements are met, the development of effective working relationships is impossible. Like all relationships, working relationships inevitably will involve some friction, misunderstanding, and conflict about the proper nature of the relationship. However, in non-working relationships the parties usually develop a degree of commitment to each other and to the continuation of the relationship. Typically they will have voluntary started relationship and will made a number of decisions to continue it in spite of conflicts and frictions because they continue to receive benefits from it. To some degree at least, their commitment is mutual and intrinsic to the relationship. In working relationships, the parties may have very little commitment to the relationship itself. Someone or something else a supervisor of the organisation initiated the relationship, the parties stay in it because their roles in the organisation seem to demand that they continue to work together, and the benefits they receive from it are derived from their place in the organisation rather than from the relationship itself.

When people lack an intrinsic commitment to a relationship, it is more difficult to resolve their differences and the degree of communication skills necessary to maintain it is greater. Minor irritations are not overlooked, minor conflicts are not easily resolved and major disagreements erupt into open confrontation because neither party is as concerned that an open conflict might threaten the continuation of the relationship. Fortunately, and almost inevitably, people do form close personal relationships with some of those with whom they have effective working relationships. Although this means that their work situations will be more pleasant than otherwise would be the case, it also adds a number of complicating factors to the relationship. They must negotiate boundaries the two dimensions of their relationship, arriving at some mutual agreement that they will communicate differently with each other while at work than they will while in other contexts. In addition, they must cope with the fact that their personal relationship is being observed by a large number of people with whom they have working relationships and that the existence of the personal relationship may further complicate some of their working relationships. “Don’t have an affair with your boss, or at least don’t let anyone know you are” really is very good advice.

Through processes of communication, working relationships are formed, maintained, and in some cases, transformed into personal relationships. As these relationships begin and develop, the participants in them begin to perceive their jobs, their organisation, and their roles in that organisation differently. These perceptions combine to define the situations that each individual believes one faces at work. Perceptions provide the parameters and guidelines within which each individual makes decisions about how to act. These choices influence the character of the relationships with other members of the organisation, and these changed relationships influence other members’ perceptions of their organisation and thus influence their actions. Other members’ actions in turn alter the character of their relationship and consequently influence the parameters and guidelines within which other members make their choices.

In addition, the relationships that people form at work influence their performance in complicated and important ways. Employees’ perceptions of and satisfaction with the tasks they are asked to perform are affected by the quality of the relationships they form with the people around them. Similarly, their satisfaction with their jobs will influence their ability to form valued and ‘stable relationships with their co-workers. The quality of employees’ relationships with their co-workers influences their ability to gain the information and support they need in order to perform their job and influences their willingness to provide the information and support their co-workers need. The nature of supervisors’ relationships with subordinates influences their ability to understand the messages they exchange and the probability that any particular command will be carried out. For all these reasons, the relational and command functions of organisational communication are interdependent and interactive.

Ambiguity-management Function

The third major function of communication in organisations is the management of ambiguity. Humans are essentially choice-making beings, and their activities at work are essentially choice-making activities. Each day they face a series of decision-making situations. In some of these situations they make choices for the organisation; in others their decisions are more personal. Their choice making is complicated by two factors. The first involves the multitude of motivations an individual generally incorporates into decision-making. In each organisational choice-making situation, a person simultaneously must consider the effects selecting one of a number of available options will have on one, one's co-workers, and one's organisation. In some situations the personal concern will be more important than the relational or organisational ones; in others, the decision maker will be concerned primarily with the interests of the organisation and only indirectly concerned with one's own interests. Some different situations will involve different combinations of self, relationship and organisational interest, organisational choice-making is a complex and potentially confusing process. If the individual faces a situation which provides clear and explicit guidelines for determining how these interests should be balanced, it is relatively easy to make effective choices. However, choice making typically takes place in situations in which the guidelines for action are either unclear or contradictory. Communication then becomes the process through which an actor manages an ambiguous situation.

Second, organisational choice making is complicated by the ambiguity of the organisations themselves. The objectives of an organisation at a particular time often are not clear to its members. In addition, the objectives of a particular unit in the organisation or of particular members also may be ambiguous. In organisations which are undergoing rapid change or which exist in rapidly changing environments, these objectives may be particularly confused.

Also, the complex histories of modern organisations complicate the choice making of their individual members. Most situations are not completely unprecedented. The people involved have faced similar situations in the past and can draw on those experiences to help them make effective choices in the new situation. But precedents sometimes hurt choice making more than they help it. Individuals will recall that in similar situations in the past they made a certain choice. They also remember that their choice was followed by a certain good or bad result. They will tend to believe that it was their decision that led to the result. If the outcome was favourable, they will tend to repeat the decision. If the outcome was negative, they will tend to avoid taking any similar course of action. But in most cases, choices made by a single individual are only one part of a complicated series of events and decisions which lead to an observed outcome. Not realising this, individual tend to make subsequent choices based on the mistaken belief that it was their choice that cause a particular outcome to occur in the past. In this way the availability of precedents can reduce the quality of the choices that are made.

Precedents complicate choice making in another way. When faced with a decision people tend to search their memories for similar situations. When they discover a precedent they feel a great sense of relief because the new situation suddenly becomes clearer and easier to manage. However, people often discover precedents which really are not precedents at all. They recall past situations that they were able to manage and then define the new situation in a way which makes it seems similar to the past, comfortable situation. Through this process they often overlook important differences between the two.

Organisational choice-making situations are inherently complex and almost always ambiguous. They are simplified and sometimes distorted by characteristically human thought processes. They also are simplified and sometimes distorted by typical communication process. Members of organisations use communication in two primary ways in their attempts to manage ambiguity. First, they communicate to each other in order to structure, to make sense out of, new situations. They seek out information which will help them gain a perspective on the problem, and they seek out support from others which will confirm their interpretation, of the problem and strengthen their commitment to a particular course. In addition, they use communication in favour of a particular way of looking at the problem and in support of a preferred option. Through communication with other members of the organisation they are able to create a shared mutual understanding of what a problem is and how it should be addressed. If the information they gain through communication has been sufficient, relevant, and accurate, and if the shared perspective that they have created has been appropriate to the problem, communication will have improved their decision-making.

But if the information gained has been inadequate in any significant way, or if the perspective that has been adopted by the people who were involved in the communication is flawed in any important respect, the availability of communication will have reduced the quality of the decision and further complicated choice making in the future. In the latter case, organisational communication has been used to reduce ambiguity artificially; it has not been used to manage ambiguity successfully. Sometimes processes of communication allow members of organisations to make foolish decisions and become comfortable with and strongly committed to them. In other instances communication allows members to make choices which satisfy their needs and the needs of their organisations. In some cases organisational communication even may provide the basis for making the best possible decisions. A variety of processes inevitably influences the potential effectiveness of the ambiguity-management function of organisational communication.

Communication fulfils three major functions in formal organisations a command function, a relational function, and an ambiguity management function. For any organisation to succeed, each of these functions must operate at or above some minimal level of effectiveness. For any individual members of an organisation to perform their roles successfully, they must be capable of using a variety of communication skills to issue effective commands and respond adequately to commands issued by others, to develop and sustain efficient working relationships, and to manage ambiguity strategically. However, some kinds of organisations are designed in ways which lead their members to rely most heavily on one of these three communication functions. Some organisations rely most heavily on the command function, others on the role of communication in the management of relationships, and others on the effective management of ambiguity.

Every organisation must have adequate command, relational and ambiguity managing communication. However, the relative importance of these three functions varies in the three different types of organisations. Traditional organisations, rely most heavily on the command function of communication and less heavily on the other two. Human relations and resources organisations depend on effective relational communication. Some versions of this type also rely heavily on the command function. In most versions the ambiguity managing function has a limited role.

The final type, "systems-contingency" organisations, relies heavily on ambiguity managing communication. In this type, relational and command functions are important in some situations and less important to others. In fact, it is the assumption that command and relational communication must be combined in different proportions in different situations that distinguishes the systems-contingency type from the traditional and human relations and resources type.

Theory of Ideal Types

The ideas of the German sociologist Max Weber have been an important part of the study of organisations for decades. In America, Weber is best known for his analysis of bureaucracy and bureaucratic organisations and for his discussion of the relationships between the characteristics of a culture and the uses of three different types of leadership traditional, rational-legal, and charismatic authority. An equally important but less well known component of Weber's work is the overall perspective that he took in studying organisations the theory of "ideal types." This perspective rests on a particular set of assumptions about the nature of organisations and the appropriate means of studying them. His ideas provide a method through which employees can understand their organisations and make effective decisions about how to act on them. Weber's primary assumption was that organisations are composed of human actors who are enmeshed in independent activities and who continually are making decisions about how to act. Their choices are based on the meanings they attribute to the actions of others and on their interpretations of the organisational situations in which they are involved. When people enter formal organisations they bring with them a long history of monitoring their actions and the actions of others, of processing the information they obtain, and of choosing from among a number of options. People from a particular culture develop ways of monitoring perceiving, and acting which are very much like another. These perceptual "filters" are not identical, of course, because every individual has had unique experiences and has been part of a particular group of relationships with others. To some extent all members of a culture will have developed their own beliefs about what actions are normal and proper and about what meanings can be attached to different messages. However, within all this diversity and individuality lies a common core, a culture-bound framework for making sense out of people's actions and of deciding how to act in response.

When employees from a particular culture come together within a formal organisation they bring with them a common way of interpreting and responding to one another. But once they come together, their interpretive frameworks begin to change in subtle but important ways. Human develop their interpretive frameworks through their experiences with other people. Relationships formed with people at work provide us with additional experience communicating with and making sense out of the communication of others. As a result, people drawn together in a formal organisation begin to form new "mini-cultures" at work. These new ways of interpreting and acting both retain the basic frame-work of the employees' general culture and reflect the more specific frameworks that develop through working relationships. The complicated interrelationship that exists between the broad patterns of action that characterise a society and the patterns that develop within an organisational "culture" was the basis of Weber's theory of ideal types.

Weber argued that researchers can understand organisations if they can understand how actors (employees) in them interpret their surroundings and choose among the wide variety of different courses of action that are available to them. The study of organisations should begin with careful observations of the choices that employees make. Eventually these observations will reveal that different groups of employees use different sense-making schemes. Researchers will begin to recognise that members of some organisations typically interpret and act in ways which are different from those in which people act in other organisations. At some point these observers will begin to construct mental images of organisations whose employees share the same basic interpretive frameworks.

For example, employees may perceive that their organisation is like an army, a formal structure with a clearly defined administrative staff which, for some as yet unexplained reasons, is obedient to commands issues by superiors. This type of organisation would function properly if it exhibited a number of necessary characteristics: each member of the staff occupies a specific position in the organisation which has been clearly defined, written duties and a clear place in the hierarchy of the organisation: each person knows who the supervisor is, who the subordinates are, and how each of them fits into the hierarchy of the organisation, each employee is selected on the basis of qualifications for the job, determined by some "objective" measure like educational background or a score on an examination; works under a contract which can be terminated if performance is inadequate; and can be promoted to a more responsible or higher paying position only on the basis of performance or seniority.

Of course, there may be no real organisation anywhere which has all these characteristics. Because this type of organisation is an abstraction, which represents the perceptions of a number of different groups of employees, it exists only in the mind of the observer; it is an "idealised" example of a particular "type" of organisation: It is an image of how a certain type of organisation should be designed and how it ought to operate, note a summary of the characteristics and operations of a group of real organisations. But these mental conceptions of ideal types can be useful for researchers. If researchers or managers or any other members of a real organisation understand how different types of organisations should be designed and operated, they can use that knowledge to detect and solve problems in their own organisation. To do so, they would examine their organisation, looking for features of its design or operation which do not correspond to the necessary features of the most relevant ideal type. Armed with perceptions of the essential features of a number of different types, the researcher or manager can discover cases in which the members of the organisation do not choose to act in the ways that are necessary for the organisation to function efficiently. Once these discrepancies are discovered the observer can make careful decisions about how to alter the organisation or change the conditions under which the members make decisions about how to act. When these changes are implemented, the real organisation will begin to operate more like the ideal type to which it is most closely related.

Unfortunately, these are very abstract ideas. A summary of them might increase their clarity. Weber's approach to the study of organisations rests on his theory of ideal types. It suggest that an observer can begin to understand how an organisation operates by attempting to understand how its members interpret and respond to the situations they face in the organisation. The observer then can design the organisation to increase the probability that its members will choose to act in precisely those ways that are in its best interests. Employees always will make their own decisions about how to act. They are human, and consequently they will continually be involved in observing, processing, and responding to their surroundings. But they make their choices based on their interpretations of the situations they face. Both their perceptions and many of the key characteristics of the situations they face can be created strategically through communication. However, appropriate situations can be created only if the people who design organisations know the elements that must be included. The search for these necessary features begins with the construction of a group of ideal types of organisations. Observers ask "What kinds of organisations do employees' interpretive frame works suggest are possible?" And construct a list of features necessary for each of these "mythical" organisations to operate most efficiently. The most important features will involve the conditions under which employees will choose to initiate and limit their actions in desired ways. Among these necessary features will be certain characteristics of organisational communication. After observers have delineated the features of each ideal type of organisation, they can begin to examine existing organisations, searching for points at which the real organisations differ from the ideal type. If they can detect important differences and determine the reasons for them, they can begin to isolate problems in the real organisation and develop strategies for reducing them.

Of course, Weber assumed that most of the "observers" would be scholars involved in academic research. But his perspective can just as readily be used by employees. The social psychologist Fritz Heider once argued that human beings think like researchers think, that the same analytical tools that theorists use to understand the world around them can be used by other people to understand their environment and to decide how to act in the situations they face. Heider's notion that people are "naive theorists" suggest that all theoretical perspectives, of which Weber's of ideal types is one, are based on our interpretations of reality and can be used by us to understand the realities that surround us. This assumption underlies the ideas that will be presented throughout the book. If readers can understand how communication functions in different types of organisations, they can examine their own organisations, determine how communication functions there, and choose the best communicative strategies for responding to the situations they face. Equipped with an understanding of how communication functions in different types of organisations and explanations of why communication functions differently in real organisations, readers can intelligently observe their own organisations and ask themselves these questions: how does communication operate in any organisation? How must people, including myself, act in order for this organisation to operate successfully? Why do they sometimes act in those ways and sometimes act differently? How can I act in order to make the organisation work more effectively and to make the greatest contribution to its success and to my advancement?

These are the kinds of questions Weber suggested that researchers must ask the answers provide the kind of information from organisational theory is made. More important, they are the kinds of questions that members of organisations must ask themselves before they can choose .the best communication strategies to use in different organisational situations. Through understanding how different types of organisations operate and why a particular organisation functions differently, the "naive theorists" who make up an organisation can , adopt the best available communication strategies.

Strategic Organisational Communication

For more than two thousand years communication scholars have argued that people communicate most effectively if they adopt the communication strategies that are most appropriate to the situations they face. Plato's intellectual rival, Gorgias, argued that knowing how to adapt to different situations was the only kind of knowledge that was available to human beings and, consequently, should be the focus of education. Some equivalent to Gorgias' concept of adaptation, an idea he labelled Kairos, has been important to the study of human communication since his time. Historically, training students in the art of adapting their communication to different situations has involved two steps: *(1)* teaching them to analyse the situations they Jace and choose the best strategies for those situations, and *(2)* equipping them with the repertoire of communication skills needed to implement those strategies. This book will concentrate on providing readers with the first kind of knowledge. It will examine the myriad of features which make up organisational situations, plan the kinds of communication in which employees must be competent, they and their organisations are to function effectively, describe the strategic through which they can gain the information necessary for them to adapt intelligently to the situation they face at work, and provide guidelines for choosing the optional communication strategies to use in those situation. Although it will discuss a variety of communication skills and suggest when and how those skills might be used by members of organisations, it will make no attempt to provide detailed training in the skills themselves.

Theory of Communication is widely accepted as one of the main seeds out of which Communication Studies has grown. It is a clear example of the process school, seeing communication as the transmission of messages.

Their work developed during the Second World War in the Bell Telephone Laboratories in the US, and their main concern was to work out a way in which the channels of communication could be used most efficiently. For them, the main channels were the telephone cable and radio wave. They produced a theory that enabled them to approach the programme of how to send a maximum amount of information along a given channel, and how to measure the capacity of, any one channel to carry information. This concentration on the channel and its capacity is appropriate of their engineering and mathematical background, but they claim that their theory is widely applicable over, the whole question of human communication.

Shannon and Weaver's basic model of communication presents it as a simple linear process. Its simplicity has attracted many derivatives, and its linear, process-centred nature has attracted many critics. But we must look at the model before we consider its implications and before we attempt to evaluate it. The model is broadly understandable at first glance. Its obvious characteristics of simplicity and linearity stand out clearly. We will return to the name elements in the process later.

Shannon and Weaver identify three levels of problem in the study of communication. These are:

Level A	How accurately can the symbols of communication be transmitted?
Level B	How precisely do the transmitted symbols convey the desired meaning?
Level C	How effectively does the received meaning affect conduct in the desired way?

The technical problems of level A are the simplest to understand and these are the ones that the model was originally developed to explain.

The semantic problems are again easy to identify, but much harder to solve, and range from the meaning of words to the meaning that a US newsreel picture might have for a Russian. Shannon and Weaver consider that the meaning is contained in the message: the improving the encoding will increase the semantic accuracy. But there are also cultural factors at work here which the model does not specify: the meaning is at least as much in the culture as in the message.

The effectiveness problems may at first sight seem to imply that Shannon and Weaver see communication as manipulation or propaganda: that A has communicated effectively with B when B responds in the way A desires him to. They do lay themselves open to this criticism, and hardly deflect it by claiming that the aesthetic or emotional response to a work of art is an effect of communication.

They claim that the three levels are not watertight, but are interrelated, and interdependent, and that their model, despite its origin in level A, works equally well on all three levels. The point of studying communication at each and all of these levels is to understand how we may improve the accuracy and efficiency of the process.

But let us return to our model. The source seems as the decision maker, that is, the source decides which message to send, or rather selects one out of a set of possible messages, this selected message is then changed by the transmitter into a signal which is sent through the channel to the receiver. For a telephone the channel is a wire, the signal an electrical current in it, and the transmitter and receiver are the telephone handsets. In conversation, my mouth is the transmitter, the signal is the sound waves which pass through the channel of the air (I could not talk to you in a vacuum) and your car is the receiver.

Obviously, some parts of the model can operate more than once. In the telephone message for instance, my mouth transmits a signal to the handset which is at this moment a receiver, and which instantly becomes a transmitter to send the signal to your handset, which receives it and then transmits it via the air to your ear.

Gerbner's model, as we will see later, deals more satisfactorily with this doubling of certain stages of the process.

The Noise

The one term in the model whose meaning is not readily apparent is noise. Noise is anything that is added to the signal between its transmission and reception that is not intended by the source. This can be distortion of sound or crackling in a telephone wire, static in a radio signal or 'snow' on a television screen. These are all examples of noise occurring within the channel and this sort of noise, on level A, is Shannon and Weaver's main concern. But the concept of noise has been extended to mean any signal received that was not transmitted by the source, or anything that makes the intended signal harder to decode accurately. Thus an uncomfortable chair during a lecture can be a source of noise we do not receive messages through our eyes and ears only. Thoughts that are more interesting than the lecturer's words are also noise.

Shannon and Weaver admit that the level A concept of noise needs extending to cope with level B problems. They distinguish between semantic noise (level B) and engineering noise (level A) and suggest that a box labelled 'semantic receiver' may need inserting between the engineering receiver and the destination. Semantic noise is defined as any distortion of meaning occurring in the communication process which is not intended by the source but which affects the reception of the message at its destination.

Noise, whether it originates in the channel, the audience, the sender and thus limits the amount of desired information that can be sent in a given situation in a given time. Overcoming the problems caused by noise led Shannon and Weaver into some further fundamental concepts.

❐

4

Impact on Different Sections

'Media effects' mean different things to different people. A psychologist, for example, has 'psychological' effects in mind when talking about media effects; the sociologist, the 'social' effects, the anthropologist, the 'cultural' effects, the political scientist the 'political' effects, the economist the 'economic' effects, the preacher, the 'moral' effects, the advertiser, the 'market' effects... and so on. Parents too are concerned about the amount of time their children spend with television, music, comics, and films, and the effects this might have on their children's behaviour and attitudes. Then there are school teachers who worry about their students' exposure to adult material, and the police who scapegoat the media for social violence and delinquency. So, any attempt to understand 'effects' must necessarily take into account from whose perspective the 'effects' are being investigated.

'Effects' are of various types and various gradations too. They may be short-term, medium-term or long-term; they may be deep or profound, or transient or superficial as in the case of fashions, mannerisms, and life-styles. Then there are influences of a passing nature or a more permanent nature.

Can influences be termed as 'effects?' How are 'influences', 'effects' distinct from impacts', or are they mere synonyms for the same social phenomena? Few media sociologists have subjected the inadequacy of everyday language to fathom the complexity of media effects to any kind of critical scrutiny.

But what precisely are 'the media?' Are they the technologies printing presses, the telegraph, telephones, radio and TV sets, audio and video recorders, video and movie cameras, satellites, computers, etc.) or the 'genres', the 'programmes' (the software) or the contents of individual media? Or, are they the cultural and entertainment industries which are today one of the fastest growing businesses owned by large media conglomerates? Or, are they the many media organisations involved in the production, distribution and exhibition of media materials? The sheer imprecision in all talk about 'the media' and 'effects' seems to be characteristic of the social sciences. But then, it must be conceded, the social sciences are not 'exact' sciences like the physical and natural sciences. For, while the social sciences study human beings and their behaviour in different situations, the natural sciences study minerals, plants, and animals.

Moreover, social scientists and media professionals rarely consider the infinite variety of 'uses' the different media and the different programmes are put to, in different contexts. In most cases, the use of the term 'effects' is misleading because it suggests that the media "do something" to people, as though people are inorganic creatures, who do not bring their own personalities to play in the communication process. It also implies that the media are actors, and that the people are acted upon. So while the media are active, audiences are unresponsive if not passive. These assumptions about media and audiences have their origin in Aristotelian linear models of communication where persuasion is seen as the primary goal of all communication.

The truth is that we have little precise knowledge or proven data about media effects since they invariably take place in combination with a whole lot of social, economic and cultural variables. Do effects relate to change, however slight, in attitude and behaviour (both elusive terms and comprehensive in meaning)? Perhaps. The extent of change (if any) depends on the variations in the desires and inclinations of individual members of an audience, and in the way they as individuals and as members of different social and cultural groups respond to various types of stimuli from the mass media. It has to be noted moreover, that people can be influenced without paying attention and. without changing at all, that there is often no relationship between what a person learned, knew or recalled on the one hand and what he did or how he felt on the other. It follows therefore that one can learn things without believing them, believe things without doing them, and do things without learning or believing them.

The Interaction

The 'interaction' (a much more accurate term than 'effects') between media and human beings is an extremely complex phenomenon. It becomes even more complex when we realize that there are a great variety of media offering numerous programme genres, and also the fact that there are a whole variety of people and groups listening, viewing, reading in a countless number of socio-cultural environments. Perhaps, the only safe conclusion on 'effects' (or 'interactions') of the media is that arrived at by Bernard Berelson several years ago: 'Some kinds of communication on some kinds of issues, brought to the attention of some kinds of people under some kinds of conditions have some kinds of effects."

Various Theories

Several theories related to the effects or changes brought about by the media (largely television) on individuals and society have been propounded by both 'functionalist' and 'critical' schools of communication. The 'functionalist' theorists begin with the assumption that the media have a role and a function in society: to stabilise, reinforce and maintain the consensus in society. They do notsee the question of power and conflict as a major driving force in society; they assume that the competition among the various groups in society allows for free and fair play, and all groups have an equal chance to "dominate and to control. The 'critical' theorists, on the other hand, place the struggle for power among social classes/ groups at the centre of society; the mass media are invariably employed by the dominant class to propagate its ideology. Further, while the 'functionalists' research media effects using empirical quantitative methods, the 'critical' theorists are so not much concerned with effects as the cultural and political context in which media experiences take place, the ownership and economics of the media, and the various ways in which audiences 'read' the media.

These theories range from one extreme position of all-powerful wide-ranging effects of the media, to the opposing extreme position where the media have no effects at all. At the one extreme are writers and researchers like Marie Winn who take the media, especially television, to be a 'plug-in drug'; at the other extreme is Joseph Klapper who concluded from his longitudinal research that media succeed only in 'reinforcing' old attitudes, habits, and beliefs. In between, are the 'negotiation' or interaction theorists who suggest that effects, like meanings of media texts, are ultimately 'negotiated' by audiences. This is sometimes termed the 'mediation perspective'. Most media theories deal directly with the 'effects' of the contents of programmes on opinions, attitudes, perceptions, beliefs and social behaviour. The theories have their basis largely in research on television and film, though some in speculation or personal experience. The largest number of studies have been on the effects of violence in television programmes on the be haviour of children and adolescents; others on the effects of propaganda on personal opinion and on voting behaviour. Since early effects research was based on the 'persuasion' model of communication (the Lasswell model and the Shanon-Weaver model, for instance) and carried out by social psychologists, the results often pointed to strong effects, for that is what they were looking for in the first place. The social contexts in which the media were experienced (say the family, the home, the theatre, the school or the peer group) were rarely taken into account. The stimulus response experiments to measure effects were frequently carried out in laboratories using mechanical pre-test and post-test methods of research. Thus the results they obtained turned out to be along expected lines.

Reinforcement Limited Effects Theory. Joseph Klapper and others, for example, believed that media reinforce existing values and attitudes. Only then, after all, can programmes of the media be popular with a majority of social groups which have an interest in the perpetuation of their own traditions and statuses. Lazarsfeld and Merton held that the mass media 'cannot be relied upon to work for changes, even minor changes, in the social structure.'

Catharsis and Narcosis

Some mass communication theorists (Lazarsfeld, Merton, and Winn for instance) argue that media have a 'narcotizing dysfunction' that distracts audiences from real problems and in fact prevents their doing anything about them. In other words, the mass media, have a drug-like addictive effect, lulling audiences into passivity and a sense of elation. Exposure to a flood of information, say Lazarsfeld and Merton, may serve to narcotize rather than energize the average reader or listener. As an increasing amount of time is devoted to reading and listening, a decreasing share is available for organized action. The interested and informed citizen can congratulate himself on his lofty state of interest and information and fail to see that he has abstained from decision and action. He comes to mistake knowing about problems of the day for doing something about them.

First proposed in 1948, the theory appears dated particularly after the galvanizing impact together with a combination of many other factors the mass media had in bringing the Vietnam war to an end, and in throwing Nixon out as a result of Watergate. In India, the press publicity given to excesses of the emergency, particularly through underground literature, did contribute to bringing about an end to the Emergency.

Closely related to the 'narcosis' theory, is the 'cartharsis' theory of media effects. Seymour Feshbach, the main exponent of the theory, argued that the media may have a 'cathartic' effect on people that somehow purges them of many anti-social and unfulfilled desires, frustrations and feelings of hostility. In one of his laboratory studies, Feshbach subjected college students to savage insults and criticism at the hands of experimenters; the experimental group was then shown an aggressive film of a brutal boxing-match, while the 'control group' was shown a dull film. When they were later questioned about their opinions of the experimenters, those students who had seen the film on boxing felt less hostile to their experimenters than those students who were shown the 'control' film.

However, in an almost identical laboratory experiment by Leonard Berkowitz, the experimenters were introduced to the students as either a boxer or a rhetoric student. The students were then exposed to either a violent boxing film or a neutral non-violent film. Later, they had the chance to give electrical shocks (under the pretext of a separate experiment) to the 'boxer' or the rhetoric student. It was found that those students who had seen the boxing film gave the largest number of shocks to the 'boxer.' Berkowitz concluded that the boxing film was responsible for the aggressive response of the students. Other experiments have revealed that children in particular are likely to imitate violence in films if the violent actions in the film are rewarded.

Laboratory experiments are by their nature artificial for they cannot re-create the different conditions, environments, and states of mind in which violent films are seen. The reactions to violence in films can be very varied as is well demonstrated in Philip Schlesinger's work on 'Women viewing Violence.'

The 'narcosis' and 'catharsis' theories represent extreme views. So does Ernest Van den Hag's view that 'mass communications, taken together are demeaning, debasing and depersonalizing instruments of manipulation at worst; middle-class hedonism at best.' Yet another extreme theory is that of Frederic Wertham which says that the content of the media is 'corruptive in general and specifically teaches materialism, brutality, antisocial behaviour and callousness towards other humans.'

Incidental Effects

In contrast, Aldous Huxley took the stand that media indeed do teach people things, but most of them are of no consequence; they also have effects, but mostly in unimportant and trivial facets of our lives although we may think that they are important. These trivial facets are fashions, mannerisms, natating habits, and food habits. As Schramm, Lyle and Parker found in their study of children and television, 'television could be an especially effective agent of incidental learning while the child is still young. This is because at that time it seems so real.'

Uses and Gratifications

By the 1950s and sixties, communication researchers began to fine tune their methods and their theories. Elihu Katz, Denis McQuail and Michael Gurevitch introduced what they termed the 'uses and gratifications' theory of media effects. They turned their attention to how audiences used the media to live out their fantasy lives and to seek out other gratifications, or even to inform and educate themselves about the world and its people. Thus media 'effects' were related to the needs and activities of audiences. The theory was largely concerned with the selection, reception and nature of response of audiences to the media, the assumption being that individual members in an audience made conscious and motivated selection of channels and programmes. It was also assumed that audiences made supplementary and compensatory uses of the mass media.

Cultural Indicators Theory

George Gerbner's dissatisfaction with effects research led him to evolve a sophisticated theory grounded on his longitudinal research on American television. He and his team undertook a content analysis of television programmes, looking at portrayals of gender, violence, the family, portrayal of minorities, and then matched these with actual situations, behaviours and attitudes in American society. Take the portrayal of crime, for instance. Gerbner concluded that there was a 'cultivation' effect or enculturation effect on audiences highly exposed to television. Audiences 'adopted' the perceptions and values which were consistently portrayed in different programme genres.

Gerbner and his team attempted 'to move beyond the analysis of effects on individual behaviour and to analyse communication systems at a social structural level.' Television was seen as the arm of the industrial and military establishment, an agent of social control.

Reflex Effects

A rather different kind of effect on which no theory has yet been built is the impact of media among and within themselves. Mass communicators are known to review each other's work, and reporters carefully go through rival papers, and switch on to news programmes on the air. It is no surprise, therefore, that 'copycatting' in content and form has become a common phenomenon. Let a topic be introduced in one paper, and the others take it up with a vengeance. So when a 'health' programme proves popular on TV, every newspaper introduces a 'health' column.

Then there are the effects of new media upon the old, and vice versa. The formats of Doordarshan's newscasts and features have in fact been copied from All India Radio and magazines are all profusely illustrated because of the impact of television. Again, short stories first published in the papers or magazines, are turned into radio, TV and cinema scripts. All these inter-media and intramedia effects may be called "reflex effects" or "bandwagon effects."

Technological Effects

"The medium is the message", wrote Marshall McLuhan, setting the controversy over media effects on its head. No matter what the contents of programmes, he argued, people will watch television; it commands their attention as no other medium has. He warned like a doomsday prophet that "the electronic media are transforming every aspect of man's life and re-structuring civilization, not so much by the content of their messages, as by the nature itself of television, movies, computers and other media." Mass communications, therefore, are neither good nor bad, but rather mystical devices that possess powers to change the way mankind lives and thinks. For instance, Indian cities are already witness to some changes in eating, sleeping and socialising habits as a result of the introduction of television.

Effects on Education

Right from pre-Independence days, attempts have been made by both government and private groups to use the media for educational purposes. Dadasaheb Phalke, the pioneer of Indian cinema, made educational documentaries such as 'The growth of a Pea plant' and 'How to Make a Film' besides fictional films. Radio experiments in the use of radio for promoting literacy and education were conducted as early as the 1930s. Television was introduced into India by the Nehru Government with the primary aim of exploiting the medium for distance education. B.G. Verghese's Chattera experiment attempted to use the daily newspaper to educate urban Delhites about rural people and their problems.

The most ambitious attempt to exploit the mass media for education was of course, SITE (Satellite Instructional Television Experiment). It sought to educate rural people in six states of India about the need for family planning, improved agriculture, hygiene, nutrition and health care. Classroom-type instructions were also provided to school children.

Today, Doordarshan devotes at least ten per cent of its telecast time to educational or enrichment programmes for farmers, school children, youth and other groups. It has taken to promoting literacy on a nationwide scale. UGC's 'Countrywide classroom' and IGNOU's early morning transmissions are ambitious post-SITE attempts to use television for higher education.

Do media educate? How effective are the mass media in educating the people of our country? What are the 'effects' of media on 'education?' These are all loaded and difficult questions to which there can be no straight cut-and-dry answers. Literate and educated people benefit much more from educational media than the less literate and educated, unless the education oriented programmes are specifically geared to the needs, interests and levels of specific groups. This is an essential condition of any educational programme on any medium to have some kind of 'effect.' Even before groups and regions can benefit from education through the print or the electronic media, they will need to become 'media literate.' Media literacy precedes or is simultaneous with the skill to learn from the media.

The folk media are perhaps much more effective in promoting the message of literacy than any of the mass media. In Kerala, Maharashtra, Andhra Pradesh and other states, folk forms of the local regions have been utilised both by voluntary social action groups and by government supported literacy campaigns. For example, in Maharashtra, literacy campaigns have used folk musical forms such as lavani, powada, gondhal, jagar and others. During the campaign, cultural teams went out to the different villages on Kalajathas. The main thrust of the messages conveyed through song, dance and discussions was literacy. However, it was reported that other issues such as mother and child care, family planning, watershed management, the problem of alcoholism and dowry, small savings and agricultural development were also conveyed. In some campaigns, the message of literacy was spread by relating the folk forms to local festivals: akshar kandlis and akshar rangoli at the time of Diwali and Akshar Ganpathi at the time of the popular festivals of Maharashtra. In the campaign at Sindhdurg, haldi-kumkum celebrations were widely used to mobilise women and to bring them together to discuss issues related to their everyday lives. However, in all these campaigns, there were few attempts to place literacy in the context of political, social and economic structures in the rural and urban areas. (for further details Cf. D. Saldanha: 'Cultural Çommunication in Literacy.

It appears then that the media by themselves (whether modern or folk) do not promote literacy. Nor is commitment enough. The social structures obtaining at the grassroots need to be taken into account, as well as the infrastructure in the form of schools, teachers, volunteers, post-literacy facilities, and the caste and communal divides. A factor often overlooked is the time available to agricultural and industrial workers to respond in any meaningful way to literacy drives in the media.

Mass Media and Indian Family

The TV, cable and satellite 'invasion' of urban India is of great concern to parents and teachers. With so much time given to watching the small screen, parents are worried that little or no time will remain for conversation in the family, for family get-togethers and for family visits. However, parents must acknowledge that they too spend a lot of time with television, and that frequently they exercise no control on what their children watch and when. Further, parents frequently us television as a baby-sister or as an excuse for staying at home.

Except for Andal Narayanan's pioneering study on the Impact of Television on Viewers, and Neena Behl's close look at what happens to one 'Indian village when television is introduced in it, there are hardly any studies that take a hard critical look at what happens in the family when television enters the home and how it becomes part of the furniture after a few years. Multi-channel television often creates friction among siblings, or between parents and children, or even between parents themselves. But then TV also helps to bring a family closer especially when all members enjoy a popular programme together. It provides topics for conversation, for expressing opinions and for family discussions. A lot depends upon what the members of the family do with television. Since few Indian families can afford more than one TV set, gathering around the TV set is similar to the earlier practice of gathering round a fireplace. The family, like any other social institution, is a power structure. The exercise of power in the home, in earlier times, was through the breadwinner, generally the man of the house. The remote control device now puts power in the hands that hold it. Ethnographic and focus group studies of the place of television in the lives of families clearly point to the remote control in most families being held by male rather than female members. However, in many Indian homes where the female is dominant, the remote control is invariably in the hands of the mother. In some families though, the remote control is in the hands of the children.

Children and Mass Media

Without communication an individual could never become a human being; without mass communication an individual could never become part of modern society. Socialisation is a life-long active process, beginning on the day of one's birth. The child learns to socialise from the parents and the social groups he or she belongs to. As children grow up they come into contact with other social groups, but their basic loyalties are to their own primary and secondary groups which provide them their sets of attitudes, beliefs, and norms of behaviour. Children come under three kinds of social control: *(1)* tradition orientation-social control based on tradition; *(2)* inner orientation-social control achieved through standards, guidelines or values existing in each individual; and *(3)* external or other orientation-social control achieved by conformity to standards existing in other persons and groups.

The child of today comes into contact with groups other than those in school; for instance, through the, mass media, which give him/her access to remote groups and their cultures. Besides, the mass media provide models of behaviour, and norms of living. The child begins to imitate them, particularly in cases where he or she is least integrated into the family or the peer group. Such children rely heavily on media advice and models; while others do not since their activities outside the home provide them greater stimuli and other role models.

But the socialisation effects of mass media cannot match the power of the home, the neighbourhood and the school where interpersonal relationships exist. In contrast, socialisation through the mass media is depersonalised and hence effective mainly in the peripheral areas of life. One would expect a national outlook to follow from a wide exposure to national news and social advertisements in the mass media. But communalism continues to hold out against all attempts at national integration through the media-so deep rooted are our attitudes and beliefs. So also social evils like the dowry system, child marriages, caste conflicts and the like persist. The mass media are not a panacea for social or economic, under-development as some governments are prone to believe.

In any study of media influence on children, or on the influence of children's interests and needs on the media, the age-group is an important variable. Other equally important variables are social class, religious and cultural background, linguistic background and community. It has been found from research in the West that the pre-operational child (aged 5 years and below), responds differently from the child belonging to the concrete operations stage (6 to 11 years) or to the formal operations stage (11 to 12 years). To illustrate, young children aged five and below see a series of separate and fragmentary incidents rather than the story of a film. They do not invariably recognise the identities of the principal character throughout the film, and they tend to believe implicitly what they see on TV to be real. And, interestingly, they sometimes read incidents into the plot from their own imaginations, or add incidents and events that they think should have occurred.

The 6 to 11 year old child, however, understands the story of a film, but still understands only the concrete physical behaviour of film performers. Only at the age of 10 or 11, does he usually understand the feelings and motivations and put himself in the shoes of a character.

The 11 to 12 year old comprehends films as efficiently as adults, and comes to realize the make-believe fantasy world of films. He also gradually begins to understand the emotional relationships in films, and to appreciate some and dislike other aspects of films. Besides, he can imagine hypothetically the sorts of relationships which may exist between film characters even if the relationships are not presented on the screen. Recent ethnographic and semiotic studies of children's interaction with television suggests that children make for a 'lively audience' and are highly discriminating and critical viewers.

Children and Television

Children below the age of 16 comprise almost 40 per cent of the population of India. Yet barely five per cent of total telecast time is directly aimed at children; this is equally true of radio, fiction and documentary cinema, and the press. On television, programmes for children devote a lot of time to animation films and puppet" shows. Several American animation series like 'Spiderman', 'Heman', and 'Mickey and Donald', have featured on Indian television. The advertisements that usually accompany them relate to toys and dolls. Interestingly, terrorist-related toys like 'G I Joe', 'Barbie' dolls, sold by India toy manufacture like Funskool, an MRF-controlled company based in Goa, and Leo Toys of Blowplast company, are advertised regularly on children's programmes. Funskool is a collaborator of a subsidiary of Hasbro, the world's largest toy manufacturer, and the makers of 'G I Joe'; Leo Toys collaborates with Mattels; the second largest toy manufacturer in the United States. Mattei's produced the TV series on 'He man' to promote the sale of their toys. It has set up a Barbie Friends Club, 'an interactive club where children could emulate the role model' The members of the club-over 12,000 of them between the ages of 6 and 12 years at a subscription fee of Rs. 95 each-write letters to Barbie and she writes back to them. It is claimed that Barbie receives over a hundred letters every day.

Should Doordarshan allow itself to become a commerical medium for the peddling of transnational manufactures and their toys? The Joshi Committee warned against this 'cultural invasion', but Doordarshan has not heeded the warning. The Joshi Committee Report also observed that 'reviews of children's reaction to film and television in India have indicated that animation is not always successful with Indian child audiences. Unfamiliarity with the technique sometimes makes it difficult for Indian children to identify the characters and objects.' For Indian to comprehend them it is necessary to keep the drawings in animation films simple and relistic and the message needs to be conveyed in a direct manner. It therefore urged that research-based software be produced so that programes are appropriate terms of the child's level of development as well as his or her life situation.

The comic strips that daily newspaper, Sunday newspapers, and magazines publish regularly for young readers are mostly

'Syndicated' comics from the United States. Columns for children frequently include quizzes, contests and stories. Children's magazines like Chandamama (in different language) Target, Quest, and Heights carry similar fare.

While there is a National Film Foundation for Children and Young People, and Children's film festivals are organized sporadically very little attention is in fact paid to the production of films for children on a regular basis. The Films Division, or the other hand, is the foremost producer of short animation films, either directly educational in nature, or telling popular stores from the Panchatantra or the wealth of Indian folktale tradition.

The Joshi Committee Report (1984) learned from its extensive analysis of elevision software that 'most of our children's programmes seem to have been deisgned for the upper-class child. This is somewhat paradoxical; the ultimate objective is to use television for education purposes, and it is the urban child who least needs additional educational inputs. Instead, television programmes should be directed primarily towards disadvantaged children in rural and urban areas. The irony is that 'disadvantaged children' do not possess or have access to television receivers.

The Joshi Report also noted that children's programmes are among the most substandard of all programmes produced. Indeed, children's programmes are considered child's play; producers who are under utilized at other work are allocated the children's programme section. Further, the time slotted for telecasting children's programmes is generally at the beginning of the evening's transmission, when most children should be playing outdoors.

Since children do not have any purchasing power, market researchers do not study children as television or radio audiences, or as readers. Except for SITE studies of children's response to educational programmes, and a few other studies, we have little significant research on children's use of; or interaction with, the mass media.

Representations of Women

The Joshi Committee Report observed in 1984 that Doordarshan is 'dominated by feature films and film-based programmes that exploit the female form to titillate and/or, through their socially insensitive approach, simply trivialize and debase the image of womanhood.' It therefore urged not only a reduction of the number of future films and filmbased programmes on television but, more positively, "the incorporation of the 'women's dimension' in all programmes and "the need for a separate focus on and for women."

Other recommendations of the Joshi Committee Report included the following:

(1) The improvement of women's condition, status and image be defined as a major objective of Doordarshan.

(2) The formulation of clear guidelines regarding the positive portrayal of women on television, and a system of monitoring the implementation of these guidelines.

(3) The redefinition of the image and the promotion of the male 'ideal' as one who is carrying and willing to share in household, childcare and contraceptive responsibilities.

(4) The need for orientation courses for all Doordarshan policy makers, programming and production staff so that they are sensitised to social issues with particular reference to women's issues and their implications in society.

(5) The need for a weekly programme on viewers' views, in which the audience, critics, commentators, women's organizations are called upon to analyse and evaluate the week's programmes.

(6) The careful scrutiny (by a special committee) of all advertisements shown on television, to ensure that they do not portray women in derogatory and stereotyped ways.

(7) The involvement of Mahila Mandalas in the installation of community television sets, and in community viewing arrangements in rural areas.

Women's organizations across the country (such as AWAG in Ahmedabad, Vimochana in Bangalore, and the Committees on Portrayal of Women in the Media, in New Delhi and Mumbai), periodicals like Manushi and Stree, and Departments of Women's Studies in universities, have been active for a decade now in carrying out research on representations of women in the various mass media. Over a dozen serious studies, involving both quantitative and qualitative methodologies, have been conducted; the majority of them are available, however; only in mimeo.

Women on Doordarshan

Doordarshan's portrayal of women in its various programmes has been subjected to close critical analysis by a number of researchers. Two major studies are: Affirmation and Denial: Construction of Femininity on Indian Television by Prabha Krishnan and Anita Dighe (1990), and Vision Unveiled by Nandini Prasad (1994). The first study was conducted by Krishnan, Dighe and Rao in 1986. Programmes over a period of 15 days a sample of 30 news programmes, 30 special interest group programmes, 55 general enrichment programmes, 33 art and entertainment programmes, 27 fiction-oriented and cinema programmes, 186 commercials and two audience-contact programmes—a total sample of 363 items were scrutinized for women-related references. The largely quantitative analysis indicated certain definite trends:

In the first place, news related to women did not exceed 2.5 minutes out of the total 20 minutes. Women were news makers in less than ten per cent of the 30 news programmes telecast, mostly in the foreign news items that related to Margaret Thatcher and Corazon Aquino. Further, women invariably figured in the political news as wives, mothers, daughters of well-known men. They also appeared frequently as members of audiences and as victims of some calamity or accident. A significant number of women appeared as shoppers: In development-oriented news items, women featured as workers in tea plantations, sericulture poultry farming, etc., and as beneficiaries of welfare schemes. In women's programmes the focus was on the woman at home. The 'experts' in these programmes were men; in farmers' programmes all the experts were men; women, however, compared most children's programmes.

Where commercials were concerned, the lifestyles promoted were largely elitist; the models in the commercials were overwhelmingly light-skinned. In voice-overs, male voices were presented as 'authoritative'; female voices as informative and 'seductive.' Women featured in all categories of commercials, but they were dominant in ads for foods, grooming and household items.

Nandini Prasad's Study

Prasad's content analysis of Doordarshan programmes was carried out in 1992, using a large sample of two and a half months of national news bulletins. The sample extended from October 1 to December 15, 1992, with every second day's bulletin comprising the sample, *i.e.* a total of 38 news bulletins. Prasad found that a mere 20 news items during the entire period related to women. Of the 20 news items, 5 related to social issues, 3 to mobilising public opinion on women's issues, and 11 to other women-related issues. Prasad's examination of the portrayal of women in Doordarshan's advertisements reveals that out of a total sample of 210 ads, 63 showed women in 'traditional' roles, 35 in a 'non-traditional' role, and 117 in a 'neutral manner.'

Descriptive analyses of the portrayal of women in popular television serials include those by Leela Rao, Jyoti Punwani and others.

Women in Radio Programmes

Less than two per cent of broadcasting time on radio is devoted to programmes on or for women, yet over 25 per cent of radio advertising is directed at women, in the form of advertisements on cosmetics, food products, beverages and fabrics. The songs selected for broadcast on All India Radio and Vividh Bharati are 'by and large on religious themes or depicting themes of coy young women waiting to be married.' The plays convey the message of the ideal woman who is a housewife and mother. If she is employed, then surely she must be neglecting her home and children. Stereotypes of women ,are reinforced in songs, plays and commercial jingles.

An exhaustive study of the portrayal of women in Hindi and Gujarati films was conducted in 1976 by Ila Pathak and her colleagues at AWAG. Their analysis of 12 Hindi and six Gujarati films showed that the films. emphasised young, beautiful and sexually attractive women; portrayed women in terms of their relationship to men; depicted women in traditional female occupations; and as overwhelmingly emotional, dependent, superstitious, and irrational beings. Besides, they stressed marriage as a goal for women, and offered a double standard of morality.

Dasgupta and Hedge did a quantitative analysis of 30 Hindi films available on video in a mid-Western city in the United States, with the objective of investigating how they dealt with 'mistreatment' of women. The analysis led them to conclude that mistreatment was not a central concern of any film; that mis-treatments (such as physical battering, assault, rape, homicide) occurred regularly when women step out of their traditional roles; and that mistreatment served the common function of returning straying women to their stereotypical and socially approved behaviour patterns. The recurrence of mistreatments on the Hindi screen was, therefore, an established mechanism to monitor and perpetuate the patriarchal order. Another study by Vijaya Mulay revealed that women continue to be portrayed in traditional ways, and that in a few films, women beatings were popularized as a form of tanung and romancing. Madhu Kishwar, editor of Manushi, found that Films Division documentaries on family planning contained a strong sexist bias: they underscored the importance of sons over daughters, the responsibility of family planning as a woman's duty, and the general passive nature of women.

Women and Print Media

Studies of the print media have focused on the reporting of rape cases in the press ('as merely spicy news stories'), the presentation of women in women's sections of newspapers, general interest magazines and women's magazines. Ammu Joseph and Kalpana Sharma critiqued the news media's presentation of women's issues in their study, Whose News?

Ila Pathak's study of women's sections in the Gujarati dailies of Ahmedabad, for instance, found that there were hardly any articles devoted to a serious discussion of women's problems at home or in society. Dasgupta's look at the Sunday editions of four English dailies found that articles on women were middle-class and urban-biased, and were restricted to a limited range of themes which did not take into account the political and economic realities of Indian women.

An analysis of fiction in three women's magazines and two general interest magazines concluded that they contained 'images and norms which should discourage female employment, particularly in higher-status occupations.'

Women's magazines have come in for a lot of criticism. Often, they are no more than a mixed bag of recipes, tips on beauty aids, romantic stories, features on women's issues, and discussions on gender problems, and of course women-oriented advertisements. Butalia found that, the advertisements, even in women's magazines, were sexist. Aminu Amin's 1982 study of 'Commercial Ads and the Great Health Robbery of Women and, Children' showed how advertisers and manufacturers play on the susceptibility and, vulnerability of women consumers and cheat them into buying food products, cosmetics, sanitary napkins, soaps and detergents that are positively harmful to the health of their families. The study also revealed that 'men in advertisements are fully clothed, appear confident and dignified' while the women are presented as glamorous but in traditional roles. Further, 'wares for men were sold for durability and economy; those for women for beauty and glamour.' Kalia's analysis of the language used in Indian school textbooks also concluded that it was clearly 'sexist.' Another analysis of the textbook series called Let's: Learn English concluded that women were few in number when it corne to central characters, and they were shown as either mothers or teachers.

Women in the Media

Besides the question of 'representations', the focus of research has been the job opportunities for women, especially at decision-making levels, in the production, administration and technical departments of the various media. The most widely discussed is S.R. Joshi's study for UNESCO entitled Invisible Barriers: Women at Senior Levels. It analyses the status of women's employment at senior levels in Doordarshan. It found that women headed three out of 18 stations; that at the Delhi station 40 per cent of producers are women. Another important finding was that 'although overall employment figures were not available, 28 per cent of the producers at two other stations are women, with responsibility for determining the content of programmes'. Besides, one-third of the women at these levels are unmarried, compared to only one-tenth of the men. The women have fewer children, and are better educated though mostly in the arts, compared to the men half of whom had gone for courses in science, engineering and commerce. According to the study, a large proportion of the women thought that there would be a change in programme content with an increase in the proportion of female employees programme quality would improve and a more balanced perspective would emerge.

But there are more women in senior positions in the government-owned radio and television than in the press which continues to be male-dominated. A 1987 study by the Women and Media Group, Bombay, discovered that women journalists are mainly on the staff of women's magazines; the women journalists in the daily newspapers and the news magazines also confine themselves to women-related issues and 'soft' news stories. Gita Aravamudan's study of the status of women journalists in Kerala, the state with the highest literacy in the land, found that most are employed by women's magazines, or hold desk jobs; dailies such as Malayala Manorama and Kerala Koumadi however, did not employ women as a matter of policy.

Need for Audience Studies

A largely neglected area in women-and-the-media studies has been audience research. Most of the audience research available has been conducted by market researchers where women are taken to be 'consumers'. The kind of research questions that need to be looked at are: How do women from different social classes 'read' the stereotypes in the various mass media and their genres? Do they, for instance, swallow the stereotypical representations hook, line and sinker, or reject or even 're-read' them? Again, how are programmes for women on radio and television produced? Who takes the vital decisions on programme content? Does the very fact that women are producers necessarily add a women's dimension to the programme? Women film directors like Aparna Sen and Sai Paranjpe have sensitized us to women's issues, but so have Satyajit Ray, Kumar Shahani, Mani Kaul, Basu Chatterjee, and Shyam Benegal. Further, women-con centred serials on Doordarshan (Rajani; It's A Woman's World, Kashmakesh. Chehre, Poornima, Rathachakra, Rathen Au Bhai Hain, Swayamsiddha, Basanti, Shanti, and several others) have attempted, some with greater success than others, to probe the woman/gender question through interesting narratives.

Further, several women have entered print and electronic journalism, but one wonders whether this alone has made any difference to professional values and news values which have been evolved and moulded by patriarchy, politics and the market. The core of professional journalism is still 'hard news'; 'soft news' which women reporters and featurewriters are generally asked to cover, is considered less important.

Media and Consumerism

To most advertisers, people are not customers or even people but mere 'consumers.' Advertisers seek to entice target consumers to consume as much as possible, as frequently as possible, and with as much relish and envy or vanity as possible. It is not without significance that we are urged to buy and to consume wherever we are and whenever we switch on the radio, TV, cable or satellite TV, or read newspapers and magazines. Day in and day out we are bombarded with print and electronic messages promising us fun, frolic and happiness if we 'consume.' It does not matter whether we have the purchasing power to tryout 'impulse products' like ice-creams, chocolates, candies, or soft drinks, but if we do not consume like the rest of the world we are likely to be left behind in the rat-race.

It is not only advertising that directly promotes consumption beyond one's means, but also 'sponsdred' programmes and columns and supplements. The subtle messages of soap-operas, quiz and game shows (where expensive prizes are gifted by business and industrial houses), elite-oriented news and current affairs programmes, ports programmes, fashion shows, children's magazines and programmes, cartoon shows, 'advertorials' and almost every programme—all tell one persuasive story: consume or be damned. Advertisers like to believe that the consumer enjoys the freedom of choice. He is, after all, not compelled to buy. He must learn to live within his means. What is more, the consumer is not a moron; she is your wife!.

The question that needs to be raised is: Do the mass media which thrive on advertising lead to excessive consumption in society, or is the other way around: Does an affluent and economically developed society or community persuade the mass media to turn consumerist? It is true that both manufacturing and service industries in developed economies spend more on advertising and media relations than those in developing economies. However, it is equally true that the world's biggest markets for consumer product as well as tor consumer durable are in the less developed countries. Further, during the past decade or so, growth in advertising expenditure in Asian countries has been steadily rising, while it has been reduced in the United States and other western countries.

In sum, consumerism is a fall-out of an industrial society, especially a society that swears by the economic laws of the free market and a liberal democracy. The assumption of such a society is that an 'invisible hand' controls the forces that compete freely with one another, and that justice and equity is promoted by such competition. The reality is that in a so-called open and free market the law of the jungle prevails, and only the most aggressive survive. Public welfare and concern fall by the wayside. The Indian experience of 'privatization' and 'liberalization' during the post-Rajiv Gandhi years suggests that some 'regulation' is imperative if the public will is to be maintained..

Violence in Media Society

Over three thousand studies have been conducted during the past forty years in the United States alone that suggest that there is a 'correlation' between social aggression and the viewing of violence on the big and small screens. According to the American Psychological Association, by the time an average American child is ten or eleven years old, he/she would have seen 8,000 murders and 10,000 acts of violence on television.

Few studies on the subject have been conducted in India, and Indian children are not yet exposed to the excessive violence that American children are, at least on television. However, with the arrival of satellite television which is dominated by American films and television programmes, the Indian child is no doubt likely to be exposed to more and more violent fare. Of course, popular Indian films too have a surfeit of violence, much of it stylised, but some of it vivid and realistic, often bordering on the pornographic. There have been cases of children and adults imitating on-screen violence and the modus operandi of gangsters, robbers and murderers. Such cases get prominent coverage in the press and other media. But all this does not lead one to the conclusion that cinema or television violence is the primary or even the secondary cause of violence in our society. At the most, screen violence may be one of the many contributory factors. More influential factors are poverty, frustration, unemployment, revenge, family clashes, urban decay, loss of self-esteem, a sense of failure in other words, a combination of sociological, psychological, economic and cultural factors. In any case, the 'correlations' that the American studies have found between screen violence and individual acts of violence do not mean that screen violence has 'caused' the violent behaviour. Statistical correlations, however significant, may point to an 'association' but hardly ever to a cause-and-effect relationship. What is of greater concern is the effect of 'desensitization' which could result from repeated exposure to scenes of violence in programmes, news and cartoons. Exposure to violence constantly and on a daily basis can desensitize us to violence in real life: violence against women and children, for instance, will shock or move us much less than we ought to as human beings: Further, we might be convinced that violence is a part of society, and that it is normal, even glamorous to be aggressive and 'macho' in one's behaviour. It might lead us to believe that some groups (for instance, tribais, dalits and leftists) are naturally violent, and such stereotypes might endure.

Violence in News

Violence in the news and in comic strips is rarely talked about. While the portrayal of violence in the press and broadcast media is condoned because it is 'factual' and deals with real-life incidents, the caricatures of violent fights and clashes between heroes and villains are condoned because they are presented in a light and humorous manner. There has been hardly any study in India or elsewhere in Asia about the influence of such violent portrayals on society.

A recent study sponsored by AMIC, Singapore, of television violence in six Asian countries concluded that where American origin fare dominated, as in the Philippines and Thailand, the violent scenes were more numerous than in indigenous programmes, though this was not the case in Japanese television. The violence on the Indian television screen was found to be mostly in the popular Hindi and regional language films. The Indian Institute of Mass Communication, New Delhi, undertook a study of television violence in 1996, using the Gerbner model of 'cultivation analysis.'

But violence is not related to crime alone. It must take into account state violence, like that of the police and the armed forces, or the violence of the law which does not bring the guilty to book, or which delays justice, or worse, punishes the innocent. Such violence too is sometimes the subject of cinema and television. The portrayal of such violence could help raise consciousness and thus lead to social reform (*e.g.* the film Ardh Satya, and the television serial, Tamas). Violence in the mass media is frequently associated with sex.

Indeed, rape or forced sex is the most violent crime that is often depicted graphically on the big and small screen. In recent years, a rape sequence has almost become obligatory in the popular film. Rape sequences are sometimes followed by scenes of blood and gore, since scores have to be settled and the rape avenged. Further, villains need to frequent night clubs where titillating cabarets are put on for their entertainment. The censors come 'down heavily on a few films, but the majority of popular films are 'passed' as okay for the entire family. Foreign television soap-operas, sitcoms, detective serials, music videos, and even talk shows and sports relays (especially those from the United States, Australia and Britain) have dollops of sex and violence, often verging on soft-core pornography. Doordarshan and Zee TV, in order to compete with STAR-TV, have begun imitating the fare on the satellite channels uplinked from Hong Kong, and other Asian cities.

THE NATURE AND CHANGING SOCIETY AND MASS MEDIA IN IT

Our society is a changing society. There are various elements in our society which makes it to change frequently. This is called as social change by sociologists. Social change means the changes that are taking place in the entire fabric of our society. Some changes can be seen and some of the changes can't be seen. Some changes take place gradually, yet some other changes take place too fast. We have which is called a social evolution meaning the changes taking place slowly in the society. We have also some thing called revolution which sees changes taking place too violently. The society undergoes changes from time to time due to various reasons. We mayor may not like these changes and some changes are acceptable to us and some other changes are not. Let us look at the role of mass media in changing society.

Mass media act as open force in providing changes in our society. We need change for betterment of the people and for providing modernisation to our people. Let us look at how media helps in a changing society.

1. Media first of all provide various kinds of information relating to the people's development and progress. These provide general information and specific information. General information is provided through the reporting of the general scene. Specific information is provided through advertising which is a paid form of communication and some personal representation of ideas, goods and services by an identified sponsor. People make use of both the general and specific information in our country.

2. Media persuades us through various forms of communication technics. We are persuaded constantly by advertising. Advertising talks to us about product and its various attributes. Depending upon the information and need, people buy various programmes, goods and services. Education is kind of progressive communication aimed at building goodwill and advertising for an organisation. Sales promotion involves presentations and mass communication in a persuasive medium. TV persuades us through its powerful combination of sight and sound, whereas Radio persuades us through its commercial broadcasting. It interacts us through the advts. it carries. Thus, all media are well oriented towards persuasion.

3. We get both general education and specific education from the mass media. General education comes in the form of news and commentaries whereas specific education comes through specific articles/advts. targetted against the people concerned. This is also yet another function of mass media.

4. Entertainment is yet another function which is needed to be stressed here. No doubt, mass media perform it. Here also we get both specific entertainment and general entertainment. General entertainment is drawn from the mass media in a general way. This means that it could be the case of, for example, a person who is drawing entertainment by watching a TV programme or reading a

news article past time etc. Specific entertainment function includes watching a programme like 'Chitrahar' which contains song and dance schemes or 'Superhit Muqabla' etc. One need to distinguish between general entertainment and specific entertainment at this stage.

5. Apart from these all the three media perform a number of yet another function. These include keeping a surveillance over the environment, correlation and or introspection of ongoing events to act people. We need media and media need us. Even in a closed society there is a definite role for mass media to play.

Apart from these functions, news media also play powerful role in a changing society. The feedback of mass media is delayed and often it is difficult to get. The mass media act as opinion leaders in many cases whereby they shape up our opinion. We form opinions on various cases and events only through mass media and without the help of mass media we could not be in a position to shape up our opinion on many crucial issues. Mass media are a force to reckon with in our society and Daniel Lerner, in his classic study, On the passing of Traditional Society says that where there has been media exposure (viewership to films) there has been modernisation found. He tracks out the concepts of urbanisation, literacy and modernisation in his theory on national development and modernisation. Daniel Lerner was a well known theorist in the area of mass communication.

The changing society needs mass media because without it, it can't change. As mass media develop, so do the changing society. We never go back and we only move forward. This is true of mass media and the changing society.

In conclusion, we can say that news media's message is needed in the changing society. The mass media serves several functions and preparing citizens to keep up with the changes in one of them. For example, before that in order to do banking we needed to go to bank and spend sometime. The technology has become so advanced that we can do the banking 24 hours and in various places and not necessarily in the banking premises. The role of mass media here is to inform about the changes to his place in the fabric of the society. This and has been the role of mass media in our society. Preparing citizens to take up various challenges during the upcoming days has been the main job of mass media. These should perform it well and the job of mass media have been to prepare us to take up the challenges of the day. This will be the role of mass media of future in our country and elsewhere. We will be seeing that the mass media play a dynamic role in our society and as well everywhere. With the help of mass media, we would be able to meet the challenges of tomorrow and play our role as citizens in our society.

ROLE OF MASS MEDIA IN SOCIETY

The mass media can play a powerful role in any society and its importance in the 20th century, which is coming to close, can never be disputed. People thought during 1960's that mass media playa very powerful role in any society. This concept of thinking came to be called 'Magic Bullet Theory of Mass Communication'. That is, the messages of mass media are injected as bullets in people's minds but, subsequent research has shown that mass media messages are not that powerful but other societal factors are important. These theories have come to be known as limited effects model and moderate effects model of mass communication.

The mass media, apart from exerting influence on the members of the society can play a definite role as far as citizens are concerned. There have been a number of studies on the impact of mass media among the audience. These studies have tried to find out how effective the media have been on the audience. Scholars like Wilbur Schramm, Daniel Lerner and scores of other have tried to find out the influence that is exerted by the media on society. The agenda setting theory by Maxwell Mcloney and Donald Shaw says that media set the agenda and the media act as the gate keeper in providing information to the people.

People get only selected information and this selected information reaches them after being filtered by the mass media. The social learning theory of Albert Bandura traces how people learn generally in the social setting. All these and more are glaring examples to tell the role played by mass media in society.

Apart from performing the functions of communication, media give what the society require. An average American according to Dr. Gerald Flannery, a Professor in the University of South Western Louisiania, is targeted at least 1500 advertising messages everyday. This figure was 10 years old. He or she must be targeted or receiving now double the amount of arts and commercials by now. Not all the messages he or she utilises or grasps and he leaves most of them out and selects only a few according to his interests and likes. This is called as media selecting metaphor in which he receives the messages depends on the likes and dislikes.

This concept has resulted in what is called as media consumerism where in this cintext media being used as a consuming agent in the society. The role played by mass media in this that it is being consumed by the audience consuming means utilising them for various purposes apart context is from the regular ones. As we talk of consumer oriented society or economy, so we also talk of consumer oriented media. That is, the media, in 20th century, have grown so big and powerful in the society. Apart from being playing the regular role of information other two, education and entertainment, being the two major functions of mass media in our society.

We can talk of the media and society in our society now and the fact remains that those who are living in urban areas get exposed to mass media more frequently than those who are living in rural areas. It also means that those who are rich, are also, information rich than those who lack it. This kind of situation do exist in our society, where the number of mass media are more in number. But their reach and frequency are less. It is true that India produces largest feature films in the world, but it is also true that their quality is equally not good. We have more number of publications in our society but the reach and coverage is less. We also have the largest population of illiterates in our country.

The question that comes to our mind is that what is going to be the situation in the days to come? We will see the following things happening.

1. There will be more number of population getting exposed to media. Thanks to the literacy and efforts made by government, we are going to see more and more people getting exposed to mass media in our society. The current literacy rate is at 36% and it is likely to go up in the upcoming days. Radio produces programmes to 90% of the population and print media circulations are about 55 million copies long ago. This is likely to go up. Television has emerged a popular medium among the masses whereas the cinema is continued to be popular with the rural people. This would remain to be the same.

2. There would be more demand for electronic media than print media in our country although former will continue to exist and have existed in the past in developed societies. The coming days are for electronic media in our country and the growth of satellite and cable TV will continue to be more as well as govt. owned TV. Efforts will be made towards promoting autonomy to radio and television in our country.

The single most important part is that electronic media will continue to mesmerise the audience. By the sheer power of the media, people will be spellbound and continued to be attracted towards the electronic media. The person who categorically cited this influence was Marshall McLuhan than anyone else.

We would also be borrowing more from the west as far as the development of TV and its adaptations. Here we can distinguish between ordinary TV and satellite/cable TV and the Satellite/cable TV are extensions of existing TV broadcasting or telecasting for that matter. TV do not know the barrier of illiteracy since it is an audio-visual medium. It combines both sight and sound where people are generally attracted to it. The satellite and cable TV has provided multitude of choices in viewerships and opened the market for vast amount of advertisers. This is not possible only with television alone. In America, where there were more than 1000 TV stations in 1984 and people have access to programming of about 8-9 channels at a single time with more than 30-40 through the use of cable shows the advancement of TV. The cable TV technology has been borrowed from the west and people use it as it has been used in the West. Thus electronic media will continue to be the popular medium as far as people are concerned.

The print media will continue to have its advantages and disadvantages in spite of the guidance of news of electronic media. People will, continue to patronise this although, day by day, it might see text as with all the electronic media cannot replace the all powerful print media. The electronic media cannot be recorded as effectively or we use print media but no doubt this dimension will continue to changing. We need both the print and electronic media in our country as much.

3. Print media remedy newspapers and magazines will continue to play the traditional role rather than playing newer roles. The news role will be restricted to the electronic media in our country.

4. Print media will continue to attract less number of advertisers and most of them will switch over to electronic media. The reason is that print media is not as glamorous as electronic media in attracting viewers. The traditional advertisers of print media will continue to be with the print media and the new advertisers are prone to switch over to the electronic media.

5. Print media will promote literacy in our country and the electronic media can promote more of visual literacy.

6. People will be dependent more on print media for information and education as well as for advertising and turn to electronic media for mostly entertainment.

7. The film medium will remain unaffected by the advent of electronic media because of illiteracy and such other factors.

8. The electronic media namely radio and TV will play much more dynamic role than it used to play now.

9. We will be borrowing much of the communication technology from the west although there would be a resentment towards this in our society. The use of communication media will suit more of the requirements of the west than us.

10. There would be an increase in number of language news than it is now. In every language some newspapers and magazines will meet premature death as there is too little money available for them in the direct to be provided and support them financially.

11. Newspapers and magazines owned by large conglomerate will have mor circulation and enjoy advertising support because these are better equipped to face the challenges posed to them.

12. There will be competition to the Doordarshan *i.e.*, the television media from cable networks and satellite television in the coming days.

13. Doordarshan will continue to be a govt. owned medium although efforts will be on to make it privately owned.

14. There will be threats to press freedom from time to time in our country although by and large, the press media will continue to be free. Leonard Susman in his book, on Freedom Around the Countries of the World says that India has only a nominally free press media.

15. There won't be much of problem regarding the availability of newsprint quota to newspapers in our society. The demand will be met by the indigenous newsprints and imports.

16. The thrust would be to go in for professionalised training in the entire field of mass media. By professionalism, we mean that those who are trained in journalism and communication would be required to work far as news media managers would opt for those who are professionally trained in the field of mass communication than those who are not.

17. The thrust would be to provide better training facility in the area of journalism then that is available at the present moment. The

use of Ion printers and other electronic equipments will become more in the area of training in productions in journalism.

18. By this, this doesn't mean journalism will become a glamorous profession. It will continue to be as popular or so as it is now.

19. The exact role to be played by the entire mass media will be decided by the media themselves and not by the people who are affected by it. Apart from playing a traditional role, the media will be expected to play a more dynamic role. The mass media have become a part of our lives in many ways. We need it for information, education and entertainment, and this will continue to serve. Apart from these functions, mass media will be expected to serve more functions which are in addition to these. *The Hindustan Times* brings out a supplement title 'Infotainment' which contains information and entertainment is an example in this case. Like these, the Song and Drama Division of the Ministry of Information and Broadcasting reaches people through the performance of song and dramas. We will see the sophistication in the use and operation of various media in our country.

20. There would be more leisure times for the people and mass media will have to keep them occupied. No medium can afford to becme boring to the people. This means that the programme executives of news media have to invent newer methods to keep the people from getting bored.

21. The mass media will continue to be popular subject of study among and for academicians, sociologists and others.

22. It will be used by doctors, scientists and engineers and such others in performing their profession, know in future that the concept of media literacy will emerge in the days to come.

23. The concept of feedback of the mass media will also be talked by people in the days to come. People will want feedback from the mass media for various reasons. Now the feedback is often

delayed and difficult. In the days to come newer methods will be invented to make the feedback easier for the people.

24. There would be close relationship between the mass media and politics in the days to come in our country. Mass media will help politicians and politicians will also provide sufficient material to learn in the mass media.

25. Finally, the urban bias of the mass media will continue to be there but there would be an effort to shift towards rural areas and people.

These are the different aspects and criteria that are mentioned on the role of mass media in society which cannot be ignored. Not only mass media will continue to be a powerful force in our society, but also shape up peoples lives. We come to know about many things happening around ourselves only through and mass media and primarily we need these for providing information, entertainment and for secondarily we need mass media to become part and parcel of our society. The relationship between mass media and society cannot be denied by any single person in our society, and are powerful force in our society as well as in other developing societies, shaking up the peoples lives in many ways. In the days to come, we will see a dominant role for individual citizens as well as for the collective social psyche in our society.

❐

5

Kinds and Theories of Communication

People often speculate about the existence of other forms of life on one of the millions of planets in the rest of the universe. Interesting questions that come up are: Are there intelligent life forms? if so, are they more advanced than our societies on Earth? Are they peaceful or warlike? In fact, our society constantly monitors "noise" from outer space, using electronic sensing equipment. We do this for many reasons, one of those being to detect possible "communications" from alien beings. From the opposite point of view, scholars of life on other planets have questioned what kind of impression our world would make on other possible societies in outer space. Someone out there may even now be monitoring our television and radio broadcast signals as they make their way toward outer space. Would such alien societies assume we all spend our days trying to win consumer items on game shows?

And now that we have begun to travel in space we know that travel may also be possible for alien societies. Probably everyone has at some time imagined a future encounter between our world and some travelling group of space aliens. Many of the popular science fiction movies with such themes commonly assume that such visitors would take the responsibility to learn and then communicate with us English (or some other language spoken on earth). But would communication necessarily even be possible with them? What exactly would we do to attempt to communicate with them? Would we speak? Gesture? Touch? Paint pictures? After all they might not have eyes and ears in the form with which we are familiar. Imagine that you are standing in an open area with some of these visitors from outer space who look very different from you. What will the first minutes be like? How will you respond to a set of "peculiar" sounds coming from the aliens (assuming a friendly encounter)?

Now and then we have put these questions to groups or students in my communication classes. I invite them to engage in problem-solving sessions in order to develop ideas. Frequently, the solutions involve some type of gestural sign language or pointing and pantomime. Grosos usually decide to teach the alien group the meanings of these visual signals so that they can eventually communicate with the hypothetical visitors. In fact, one group devised a system where they proposed to take pictures of various items to be communicated about (*e.g.*, specific people, objects, or actions). They then planned to demonstrate the meaning of teach picture by temporarily placing aliens the meaning of each picture. After the proposed training period, they planned to create different messages by selecting various sequences of pictures. With each set of pictures they would make a type of visual "sentence". Other groups essentially developed similar strategies using hand gestures instead of pictures.

How well such strategies would work, of course, is open to question. However, the basic problem in attempting to communicate with these hypothetical visitors from space would involve overcoming at least five obstacles. One obstacle is that the parties involved must be aware that communication is being attempted. It might not always be obvious that the other is attempting to communicate. A second obstacle is that both parties would have to be able to recognize the physical form of each other's communicative signals. These signals would be auditory, visual, thermal, or even involve puffs of air reaching the skin or some other novel form. A third obstacle is that both parties. Of course, for communication to take place they would both need to understand correctly the references made by each' other's messages. If this four obstacle is not passed, no one understands anyone else. Finally, a fifth obstacle is that the participants must be able to engage jointly in a purposeful communicative act. Comprehension of messages is not enough in itself. For communication to succeed, there must be an outcome. Information must be successfully shared, or activity must be coordinated, or intentions must be signalled. In other words, the participants must understand the overall purpose of the communicative activity they engage in. They must then achieve this purpose.

The problem we have just discussed might be a little easier if we were to consider communication with someone from another culture here on Earth. If you have travelled in a foreign country you have probably experienced trying to communicate with someone who did not speak English, or you may have encountered someone visiting the United States who did not speak English. Commumcation would be easier in this situation because with a foreign visitor it is easy to tell when the other person is attempting to communicate. It would also be easy to recognize the form of the signals (words, gestures, facial expressions). And both parties normally will be able to experience thoughts and feelings in a similar way. Of course, the basic obstacles in this situation are for the participants to identify correctly the references made by each other's messages and, likewise, to be able to participate jointly in a communicative act with a purpose.

Historically speaking, at least two groups have developed strategies for communicating across language barriers: the American Plains, Indians and the European explorers of the fifteenth and sixteenth centuries. Both groups developed sign language systems that used hand and facial gestures. Although simple in design, these systems did enable basic types of communication to take place among parties who did not speak the same language. These groups would rely on their systems of gestures to, among other things, greet each other, trade for desired items, indicate intentions, tell about previous experiences, and coordinate activities. The gestures used would have conventionalized meanings for such ideas as 'me,' 'you/'sunrise/'sunset/and 'water'.

Fortunately, adult members within the same culture find communication easier than individuals in the situations described so far. However, even here obstacles can prevent people from correctly understanding each other or from relating to each other in mutually satisfying ways. One sign of this is when one person complains about another by saying, "We just don't seem able to communicate anymore!" When communication does work it can function for the participants in very complex ways. It can enable them jointly to think out loud, feel emotions, dwell on objects of perception or on each other or on their relationship together. It can be blunt and explicit or it can be subtle and convey fine shades of meaning. For example, you can agree to do something for someone by shouting, "I will do it?" You can also agree by simply lowering your head as little as one quarter of an inch while blinking your eyes once. Children born within a culture must learn to do these things with their communicative behaviour. Although we have already used the word "communication" several times, our discussion of the concept has been informal. However, because the word can be used to mean different things in different situations, we will devote some time in the next sections to clarifying exactly what the term can mean.

The simplest way to begin is by pointing out how communication experts traditionally identify types of communication. There are five different categories of communication. Each category represents a broad area of communication. Communication scholars usually work within one of these broad areas to study how people communicate within that particular setting. The five categories are:

Various Types

Mass Communication: This includes television, radio, newspapers, magazines, films or movies, musical recordings, and mass mailings. This type of communication always concern large number of people and involves some type of machinery to transmit many duplications of the messages. Mass media generally are used by the media-consuming public for entertainment, companionship, or for getting information or education. The media are used by political leaders, governments, and business organizations that advertise in order to influence the behaviour of individuals and to influence the day-today workings of society.

Public Commanication. This is when one person (*e.g.*, public speaker, entertainer, lecturer) assumes the responsibility for doing most of the talking, while several dozen to several thousand others do most of the listening. This form of communication is used to inform, persuade, motivate, or entertain an audience. To inform, a speaker brings the audience up-to-date on some topic through an organized delivery of information and ideas.

To persuade, a speaker uses logical and emotional arguments to change people's minds about some topic or to reinforce existing attitudes. Speakers who entertain usually tell funny stories. The face-to-face nature of public communication allows the audience to participate in the communication through its occasional responses to what the speaker says. This immediate response permits the speaker to make on-the-spot adjustments in the message.

Small-group Communication. Examples of small groups are committees, work groups, the family, and social groups. Small groups frequently range in size from three to about twelve members. This form of communication is used basically to enable people to accomplish things collectively (such as solving problems or making decisions). At other times group members use the group to satisfy personal needs. This might occur in the family or in a therapy group. Small groups rely heavily on leadership in order to reach established goals.

Interpersonal Communication. This concerns communication between just two persons who create a relationship. This setting represents communication in its most basic sense. It involves the two individuals in a mutual disclosure of themselves. It involves them in shared thought and feelings and in the shared construction of a unique interpersonal relationship. Interpersonal communication is what is shared between friends, lovers, parent and child, worker and boss, or teacher and student. The "inter" in the word "interpersonal" means between.

Intrapersonal Communication. This refers to the individual's ability to think, feel, and use language for understanding and expressing ideas. It sometimes refers to an internal dialogue held solely within the self.

The most obvious of behaviours that count as communication are speech behaviours. Beyond there are other types that communicate to others. The way you walk down the street may tell others what mood you are in. Similarly, the fact that you don't show up at a party may signal you feelings about the people who were expecting you. Raising your fist at an explosive school board meeting on book-banning may indicate your reaction to what has just been said by a speaker.

Communication Code

A communication code is a set of signals or symbols hat creates meanings for people. We live by many codes. The words of a language concern a code. When you don't understand a language you don't know the code. Less obvious are the non-verbal codes we use so extensively but pay so little attention to. We use dress codes (try coming to class in formal evening wear or a swimsuit). We even have a sense of a time code. For example, in: North America and Europe if you show up 20 minutes after a set time for an important appointment you are late. However, in many parts of Latin America or the Mediterranean area you might show up an hour or more after the set time and not be considered late. These; are some of the codes we all learn to use for social communication as we grow up within our cultures. As we learn to use these codes we learn social behaviour.

Noise is anything that interferes with the shared understanding of a message by the sender and receiver. Noise can come from external causes, such as a loud sound that interferes with what you are saying. It can come from a visual distraction, for example, someone wearing a purple polka-dot suit while trying to give a serious speech. In addition, noise can sometimes come from internal sources, for instance, when a listener starts to daydream or pay attention to someone's lisp rather than to what the speaker is saying. Similarly, off-color language or highly emotional words sometimes create noise effects. In a sense, noise opposes communication. Communication concerns the successful sharing of ideas and feelings, while noise involves distorted understanding of messages or a failure to receive the message at all.

Feedback refers to the response a sender gets from the receiver, it is an important concept because in any communicative situation (except media situations) feedback is continuously affecting the ongoing behaviour of the participants. For example, on a job interview you get feedback from the interviewer. The way in interviewer says "Come in" (nicely, or not so nicely) when you knock is feedback for you. You also give feedback to the interviewer by how you respond to questions, suggestions, jokes, etc. Feedback responses can come in the form of verbal statements—*e.g.*, "Oh, that sounds interesting" or "Do you really think that is the best way to handle such a situation?" Feedback can also be nonverbal—the interviewer looking directly at you and smiling, or the interviewer failing to look at you at all as you speak. Similarly, you might receive enthusiastic nods or receive very unenthusiastic nods or expressions. Feedback is important because it can dramatically influence you during communication. For instance, imagine that you are standing in front of 500 people, telling a long joke, and as you get to the punch line, everyone stares in silence—how would you feel? Or instead, imagine that as you reach the punch line they roar with laughter, almost rolling in the aisles-now how would you feel? This possibility for feedback to be either positive or negative is the source of its power to shape the communicator's future behaviour. That is why teachers sometimes look at and pay more attention to students who give more positive feedback by smiling, looking, and giving verbal responses to the lecture. In fact, one mischievous class conditioned parts of their instructor's classroom behaviour by secretly agreeing among themselves to reinforce certain behaviour. Outside class they conspired to give only positive responses (interested looks, smiles, head nods, etc.) when the teacher stood on the right side of the room. At other times they would act bored (blank stares, yawns, looking out the window, etc.). In a short time the teacher was delivering the entire lecture from the right side of the room.

The last of the ingredients we will discuss is the context in which communication occurs. That is, all communication must, by definition, take place in some physical location and in some social situation. These contexts influence the meanings of communicative behaviours. For instance, if you lived next door to a judge; you might on occasion lean across the back fence and say, "Hi, John." Such a greeting would probably be interpreted by your neighbour as a sign of friendliness. If, however, you were passing by this same person's court during an important trial and leaned in from the back door and yelled, "Hi, John!" your message would probably be interpreted very differently. The thumb-jerk gesture is still another example of how context influences meaning. Do it or the side of a road and it means one thing. Do it while standing behind first base during a baseball game and it means another. To some extent the meaning of every word we use and every gesture we make is affected by the social, physical, and linguistic contexts in which we are' communicating hence, the familiar complaint sometimes heard during conflicts, "You took my words out of context."

Important Aspects of Communication

The concepts do help to clarify several important aspects of communication. In addition, communication experts have traditionally relied on visual diagrams or models to help explain how communication works. The simplest view of the communication process would show a sender (S) who used a channel (CH) to create a message (M) that a receiver (R) actively attends to (Resp) and, it is hoped, understands:

The above model would be good for illustrating such communicative acts as a public announcement in a department store or an individual writing a letter to a friend. However, being so simple the model does not represent any of the complexities of communicative behaviour.

For example, many acts of communication involve two-way transmission,as when two people engage in a conversation. And so, we could modify above model in the following away in order to show this two-way dimension of most kinds of face-to-face communication:

This revised model could now be used to show what happens, for example when one person asks another, "Do you know the time?" and the second person responds with, "Yes, it's past ten".

The model could also be used to illustrate a telephone conversation or an interview or two people who are pen pals. Notice also the ever-present potential of noise to disrupt communication at various points in the above diagram.

Still, we have not yet diagrammed any of the complexities of human communication. For example, you might want to get the other person to tell you the time, buy something you from you, or experience a positive feeling you have for him/her. Or you may want the person to listen to a story, accept something as true, commit to something, or accept a greeting from you. Something the two participants will have the same goals in a situation (*e.g.*, to greet each other). More often, however the two will have different goals. For example, if you asked a stranger for the time your goal would be to get the time (as well as some kindly attention); the stranger's goal would be to convey the time, to feel useful, and to have your gratitude temporarily (this is why two strangers standing together will sometimes compete to give you directions when you ask).

To perform a given communication role in the participant engages in the particular types of behaviours that belong to the role. These behaviours are shown to be either verbal or non-verbal in the diagram. The participant's ability to perform these behaviours that belong to the role. These behaviours are shown to be either verbal or non-verbal in the diagram. The participant's ability to perform these behaviours is represented by the large S, while the large R represents the ability to comprehend the meanings of these behaviours. In order to pursue communication goals, play communication. This last point represents what must go on inside the person during communication. Successful communication occurs when the participants experience similar meanings for each other's behaviours. The word "dysfunction" means to not function effectively. Communication dysfunctions can be total or partial. Imagine for a moment what would happen if all communication among all people ceased for one day. Media would be turned of. You could not talk to anyone you could not write. You could not even off. You could not talk to anyone; you could not write. You could not even gesture or whose expression on your face. The result would be anarchy, disarray, and randomness. In addition, without communication the individual, and the group individuals from, would not grow and develop and probably would not survive very long. Fortunately, however, communication failure is more often partial in nature than total.

For example, it is common to hear people say "We don't seem to be able to communicate anymore" or "We have a communication breakdown." What people mean by such statement frequently differs from person to person. It is important to distinguish; then among the many ways that communication can be dysfunctional. At all simplest' level, communication fails whenever mutual attentions or contract is not achieved as, for example when on person feels a need to greet another across a crowded room and the second person does not hear or respond to the first person. In a different way, if a speaker were to misarticulate what he or she was saying, communication would fail because of poor 'performance'. Similarly, if two people were a conversion, one of the two might mishear what the other has said, wrongfully challenging the other with, "How can you say that" Communication would fail here because the two are no experiencing meanings in a similar way.

At a different level, if one person were to say to another during an intimate conversation, "Why don't ideas to yourself" communication will have partly failed at this point. It will have failed because while one person was trying to play the role of "counsellor" or "suggestion giver" the "suggestion taker." And if the participants do not have any clear communication goals whatsoever, communication will falter. Anyone. who has experienced the discomfort of a prolonged silence at a party among people who don't know one another can testify to this. Similarly seeking inappropriate communication goals may also cause communication failure *e.g.* at tempting to organize party games among adults who want to sit and converse.

People sometimes speak of communication failure across generation. This'type of failure usually concerns parents and their children who don't seem to express similar values and attitudes. In addition, parents and children sometimes "disagree" about how and when certain communication roles ought to be played by each other. This last problem can be seen whereever the son or daughter wants the parent to play the role of friend or peer and the parent insists on playing the role of mother or father. This conflict especially surfaces when the son or daughter reaches the late tens or early twenties. The following dialogue is a good example of the problem:

At the farthest extreme are those of us whose emotional problem are tied to communication failure. Such people are sometimes called "crazy" or "emotionally disturbed." For example I recently noticed a woman having a terrible argument with someone while taking on a public telephone. Passing by about 10 minutes later I could still hear screaming the same arguments into the phone and I noticed she was using exactly the same words I had heard earlier. Lingering a little, I then noticed that she would repeat the same dialogue every 20 or 30 seconds (sort of a recorded message). The woman was playing the communication role in inappropriate circumstances because no one was on the other end of the line.

On another occasion I saw a man sitting in a park making very elaborate but strange, slow gestures in the air. After watching him for a while I came to realize that although neither I nor other passers by could understand what he was doing or why he was doing it, he probably did. His weird gestures probably had some significance for him as he performed them. The problem was, however, that the gestures did not communicate recognizable meanings to other people. The gestures were part of a private code, not a socially understood code. For such people, communication failure is a fundamental part of life.

From the discussion of communication dysfunctions, we can see that people have a need for effective communication in many aspects of their lives. In one sense, effective communication involves an art that is very difficult to master and just as difficult to study scientifically. In another sense communication can be used as a tool to accomplish specific things. That is just as we use the more physical tools such as an ax a shove'l, or a soup ladle to get particular thing done, we also use communicative behaviours to get specific things done. For instance, we use communication as a tool to get other to help us when we are in trouble. We also do it to persuade other to accept our beliefs. We use it to give social recognition to other we meet, to help establish opposite sex relationships, to resolve conflicts, and to promote our abilities to do certain things (*e.g.*, during a job interview).

In a different sense, our societies survive because we can use communication as a tool to collect, pool, and disseminate information and because we can teach others to do and understand things. As a tool, communication helps societies discover knowledge, carry out business or legal transactions, and stimulate economies. Clearly, without linguistic communication we might not even be able to think the way we do. At a social level, communication is the basic currency of our dealings with others.

MASS COMMUNICATION IN INDIA

Mass Communication can be defined as communicating to the audience through a mass media like radio, TV, films and newspapers etc. According to Friedrich Williams 'Mass Communication' seems communication through the use of radio, TV and films etc. The functions of mass communication include information, education; entertainment and persuasion. Mass media inform, educate, and entertain the persuasion. Mass media inform, educate, and entertain and persuade people. According to Charles Wright the following are the functions performed by the Mass media: *(a)* correlation *(b)* socialisation *(c)* entertainment and *(d)* education.

All these functions are important for the study of communication and society decline in an age in which these media are threatened to be replaced by advanced communication technologies like Internet and Teleconferencing and other newer innovations.

News communication provides more entertainment than anything else. People turn to news media for entertainment with a said circulation exceeding 55 million. We are covered up to 90% both area and population wise as well as TV reaching 55% of the population and area.

Mass Communication offers consumer of the opportunities to those who are qualified starting with the print media to public selection. It is highly glamorous and exciting to enter the field of mass communication. Journalism is being complained as a profession which doesn't pay well. But it is not the case with advertising. Big opportunities are opening up and more number of people are needed. It is not that early people with poor including enter the field of advertising and PR. Even people who have high IQ and who have achieved distinction in studies like people who have completed B.Tech. From IIT's do enter or make up career in journalism and mass communication. This shows the amount of potential that are there in the fields of mass communication and journalism.

To qualify for a job in mass communication, one needs to register in a college or university or private institute which offers such courses. The intelligent and academically bright students visitor take to going up to USA or abroad to have higher education in mass communication. They return back to India after studying there.

To succeed in journalism and or mass communication, these days are needed not only good English, but also knowledge or background in social. sciences. This is especially useful to people who would like to take up advanced studies in journalism and communication in India as well as abroad. A strong requirement is wish to work hard for the chosen field of study which is of course is mass communication.

There are more than 50 universities and colleges in the country which provide training in mass communication. The type of people who do these studies don't replace the students who are studying in private colleges and universities which offer similar courses. The graduates of private institutes ideally fit in the jobs available in the industry. The jobs available in government/public and some private sectors go to those who are qualified from universities and government sponsored institutes and colleges.

Any way, that is common is to find people who have done this course in and employed here and there. Almost all of them get jobs or create jobs to do their work of their choice. The metropolitan cities would be the hunting ground for people without work and jobs are opening up in places like Bangalore, Hyderabad and other cities. With certain amount of sincerity and hard work one would be able to get a job quite easily.

There are opportunities for furthering studies and research for those who are employed in the field. A number of colleges and universities offer postgraduate as well as beyond normal degree courses. One can learn further through cities the formal which is university/college/or institute oriented as well as through informal research. It all depends on one's convenience and willingness to do study and research.

We have had heard about internet and newer means of communication changing the work place and offering a number of opportunities and challenges for people. The opportunities provide people with further scope and opportunity to purpose their career with deeper interest. No doubt, we will see more and more people entering into mass communication in the future. This will further advance the field of mass communication and accommodate people who we will qualified and talented. Sooner mass communication would be recognised as a profession on par with engineering, medicine, law and or sciences. Those who are already in the field would be benefitted out of this and they would be blessed with more opportunities for advancement.

As days become complex and which needs the services of specialists and not generalists in various fields, mass conununication is bound to grow more and provide ample scope for specialisation. Gone are the days in which a person can do many things. We need specialists and the scope for opting for specialisation in mass conununication is boundless. We will see of that in our coming days in our country and abroad.

VARIOUS THEORIES AND BARRIERS

Indian Theories

In recent years communication scholars in India and Sri Lanka have made attempts to develop theories of communication based.

According to Tewari, the Indian theory of communication forms a part of Indian poetics; and can be traced to a period between second century B.C. and first century AD. in the works of Bharata. It hinges on the concept of 'sadharanikaran' which is quite close in meaning to the Latin term communis, commonness, from which the word 'communication' is derived.

The most important assumption in the process of sadharanikaran is that it can be achieved only among sahridayas, *i.e.*, only those who have a capacity to accept a message. This is an innate ability acquired through culture, adaptation and learning. Thus communication is an activity among sahridayas. It is to be noted, says Tewari, that the concept of 'sahridaya' is not co-terminus with predisposition or in favour or against. It only denotes the quality of mind or receptivity on the part of the audience. It does not speak of the quality positive or negative of attitude on the part of the audience. It may, however, qualify the depth or level of sensory experience that shapes the human personality.

The human psyche in terms of this theory is composed of permanent moods, called *sthaibhava*. These moods are capable of arousing a corresponding state of feeling, *rasa*. There are nine permanent moods and they give rise to nine rasas or forms of aesthetic pleasure. For instance, the permanent mood bhayanaka arouses the *bhayanak* (furious) rasa, the *hrsha* Joy) triggers the *hasya* (laughter) rasa, the dina the *karuna* (compassion) rasa and so on. The entire range of human emotions is encompassed in this categorisation. The state of arousal of the nine permanent moods is termed *rasa utpathi*.

The sthai bhavas are accompanied also by many fleeting or secondary moods that are common to several dominant moods and serve the purpose of completely manifesting the permanent mood, such as *nirveda* (despondency) or *glani* (fatigue), and may help to manifest' the permanent moods, like the erotic helps the pathetic. These are called sancharis or vyabhichari bhavas. In addition, there are vibhavas and anubhavas, the emotions that unite a man and woman in love. It is at the climax of this relationship that sadharanikaran is attained.

The concept of sadharanikaran, one of the fundamental concepts in Indian aesthetics, also has religious implications. As in the Vedanta, objects of experience are held to be not the ultimate reality but only manifestations of that reality; so words and the expressed meaning are regarded as the mere external experience of art, and the emotional mood which a work communicates is thus the essence of reality the highest communication endeavour indeed.

There is a certain elitism present in the concept, however. Rasa is the art of the ordinary, but it can be understood only by the sahridaya and the only proof of its existence is the aswada, the taste, which only a saridaya has. He or she alone is capable of sadharanikaran.

Yadava points out that the term was first used in the tenth century by Bhattanayaka in a commentary on the Natya Shastrato explain the sutras related to rasa. Bhattanayaka stressed that the essence of communication lay in achieving commonness and oneness.

Yadava draws out two implications or resonances of the term, sahridaya, literally of one heart. He believes that the term is synonymous with 'identification' and 'simplification'the identification of communicator with the receiver through the process of simplification. Mahatma Gandhi, for instance, achieved this identification with the masses through 'simplification' of his message, the common religious symbols he employed, and above all, the utter simplicity of his life.

At the community level, Yadava notes, the saints, sufis and brahmins of old propagated religious and cultural values through simplification and illustration. He sees this practice as continuing today in the conversation and traditional media of rural folk throughout the Indian sub-continent. This dimension of sadharanikaran seems to have become the common heritage of the Indian people.

Yet, the process of sadharanikaran is fundamentally 'asymmetrical', and the sharing or oneness it connotes is among sahridayas alone, unequal perhaps but one in heart. The goal of sadharnikaran, therefore, is not persuasion so much as the very enjoyment of the process of sharing. At the same time, the source is perceived as having a higher status, and the receiver of the message, a lower status. As Yadava puts it, the relationship is hierarchical, of 'domination' and 'subordination.' The source is held in high esteem by the receiver of information, a relationship idealized and romanticised in the guru-chela tradition.

Yadava hypothesises that the asymmetrical aspects of sadharanikaran helped in the blossoming of Indian civilization in earlier, times through efficient communication and division of labour, but in centuries resulted in highly rigid and hierarchical closed social structures.

Wimal Dissanayake draws on the Vedas, the Upanishads and non-philosophical traditions (such as Bhartrhari's Vakyapadiya, a fifth century text on grammar) to build an Indian model of communication. The primary focus of interest in his model is how the receiver makes sense of the stimuli he receives so as to deepen his self-awareness. In Indian tradition, he argues, 'communication is an inward search for meaning-a process leading to self awareness, then to freedom, and finally to truth'. Thus it transcends language and meaning and is interpretation or reception-oriented, not expression-oriented like the Western models. The intrapersonal dimension is of greater importance than the interpersonal in the Indian approach, for individualism and manipulation have no place in it.

Neville Jayaweera, also a Sri Lankan with a deep interest in Indian philosophy, observes that the Vedantic philosophy of 'advaita' (absolute monism) has profound implications for contemporary understanding of communication.

Dissanayake also propounds a Buddhist theory of communication derived from the concept of dependent co-origination, pattica-samupadda/pratitya-samutpada. This concept lies at the heart of the Buddha's teaching. It is related to the three principles that sum up worldly existence: anitya or impermanence, dukkha or suffering and anatma or no-self. It is a highly connotative concept which implies that every phenomenon, including communication, is in a state of impermanence and flux.

A Philosophical View

T.B. Saral looks at communication theory from a Hindu philosophical perspective. The Hindu's concept of the universe is based on the 'Virat Purush' (cosmic man) view. A natural extension of this concept is that it espouses the systems approach, the authority of Universal law, the law of Dharma. Dharma is the basic principle of the whole Universe and is existing eternally. This natural law of Dharma regulates human existence and governs relations of individual beings; communication too is governed by the same law.

Saral believes that most western studies of communication are confined to the study of what may be termed 'surface structure' features, such as verbal language, body language, non-verbal gestures, facial expressions, etc. But it is often the 'deep structure' features that make a critical difference to our understanding of communication. This 'deep structure' is shaped by the cultural and metaphysical assumptions about the definition of truth and reality, the place of an individual in the universe, and one's relationship with other living and non-living elements of the environment, the concepts of time and space, and so on.

Western models and theories of communication are thus reflective of the biases of western thought and culture. The distinctive marks of this philosophy are categorisation, classification, linear sequencing and rational logic. Indian philosophy on the other hand, is characterised by complexity and pluralism; it is holistic and intuitive, and believes that reality is one. In Indian rhetoric, opposites are coordinates, contradictions are illusory, and the world is a dramatic portrayal of God playing hide-and-seek with himself, trying to reassemble all the divergent parts back into their original unity.

An Islamic 'Communitarian' View

Hamid Mowlana and Majid Teharanian, two Iranian-American media scholars have developed an Islamic or 'Communitarian' model of communication. The 'umma' or the community is at the centre of communication in Islam, as against the individual who is the primary focus of attention in Western models. The primary purpose and experience of communication, according to this view, is to build relationships in a community rather than persuasion or propaganda.

Barriers to Communication

'Barriers' are any obstacles or difficulties that corne in the way of communication. They may be physical, mechanical, psychological, cultural or linguistic in nature. In business communication, for instance, the major obstacles arise because of the set-up of an organisation the organisational barriers. The size of an organisation, the physical distance between employees of an organisation, the specialisation of jobs and activities, and the power and status relationships, are the main organisational barriers. Besides, there are the barriers, raised by interpersonal relationships between individual and groups, the prejudices of both individuals and groups, and the channels they use to communicate.

In the 'jargon' of communication, all barriers whatever their nature are clubbed under a common label-noise'. A term from modern physics, it denotes not only atmospheric or channel disturbance, but all barriers that distort communications in any manner.

Is there such a thing then as 'perfect' communication free of all barriers? This is hardly ever true, except perhaps at higher spiritual or mystic levels where communication is transformed into a 'communion.' For us, mere mortals, the wrestling with imperfect communications must continue.

Physical Barriers

Four main kinds of distractions act as 'physical barriers' to the communication process. These are:

(1) The Competing stimulus in the form of another conversation going on within hearing distance, or loud music or traffic noise in the background. The cawing of crows or a plane passing overhead can, for example, drown out messages altogether.

(2) Environmental Stress. A high temperature and humidity, poor ventilation, vibrations felt, a strong glare-all can contribute to distortions in the sending and receiving of messages.

(3) Subjective Stress. Sleeplessness, ill health, the effects of drugs and mood variations give rise to forms of subjective stress that often lead to great difficulties in listening and interpretation.

(4) Ignorance of the Medium. The various media for communication are: oral, written, audio, visual and audio-visual. The use of a medium with which the communicators are not familiar would turn the medium itself into a barrier. For instance, the use of visual media like maps and charts to instruct workers who have not been taught to read maps and charts would alienate the workers immediately; they would switch off for lack of knowledge of the medium.

Psychological Barriers

Each of us has a certain 'frame of reference,' a kind of window through which we look out at the world, at people, and events and situations. A frame of reference is a system of standards and values, usually implicit, underlying and to some extent controlling an action, or the expression of any belief, attitude or idea. No two individuals possess exactly similar frames of reference, even if they should be identical twins. To a large extent our frames of reference are influenced by our experiences, particulary our childhood experiences, and the cultural environment we have grown up in. Heredity too has a great influence.

However, learning and deeper experiences modify these 'mental sets' as we grow and mature, and develop diverse frames of reference to meet different needs our own and that of the group we identify ourselves with. This is the 'reference group', whose attitudes towards religion, politics, education and so on we adopt as our own, without being fully aware that we are doing so.

Self Image

Tied up with the term 'frame of reference' is the term 'self-image' or 'self-concept'—*i.e.*, the way an individual looks at himself, or the picture he has of himself. It is this 'self-image' that makes us always defend our point of view, to interpret messages in the way we wish to interpret them, and to see 'reality' according to our own pre-conceived notions. That is why few people see things alike: Freud, Jung and Adler interpreted the same dream in three different ways; Indian historians differ on who was responsible for 'the partition', and people understand 'love', 'beauty', 'honour' and 'freedom' according to what suits their 'self-image.' The American poet Wallac Stevens wrote that there were 13 ways of looking at a blackbird. He was mistaken, for there were as many ways as there were cultural contexts. Thus, we tend to listen attentively to, and interpret favourably those messages which give a boost to our self-image, and reject or misinterpret messages which threaten that same image. The consequence is: Communication selectivity. It is not only with regard to the sending and receiving of messages that we are selective, but also in the extent we remember them. For instance, we retain only that information that is pleasant to us or reinforces our ego, and very conveniently forget details that are unpleasant or humiliating.

Resistance to Change

"The risk of being changed is one of the most frightening prospects many of us can face" (Carl Rogers). No wonder, we resist change in any form except where we are convinced it is to out benefit. So new ideas that do not support our own views are resisted outright. In fact, most of the time we do not actually hear views which conflict with our own. But we hear with rapt attention any communication that reinforces our beliefs, and our self image.

The effective communicator, therefore, does not wait till resistance builds up against an intended change or innovation, but takes the people into confidence even at the planning stage. Instead of springing a surprise on them, he listens to their point of view with respect, involves them in the change; talks to them about the benefits the change will bring; assures them their security will not be affected; and explains the reasons why the change is necessary.

Defensiveness and Fear

Closely related to the barrier raised by our 'resistance to change' is the barrier of defensiveness. One of man's most compelling needs is to justify himself. Even when we are convinced we are wrong, few of us admit it, as it means a loss of face. More often than not, therefore, we tend to 'rationalize' (explain away) the mistakes we make, the attitudes and opinions we hold so dear.

'Fear is an affect of great potency in determining what the individual will perceive, think and do' (Izard and Tomkins). Indeed, together with the allied emotions of nervousness, anxiety and tension, fear is the most constricting of all the affects, resulting often in 'tunnel vision' (near-blindness to a great part of the communication). It also gives rise to slow and narrow thinking which selects and distorts communication.

During an interview, a candidate's fear, tension and anxiety tells on his performance: he fumbles 'for words, misinterprets questions and in general gives a poor show of himself. During a written examination, nervous candidates misread the instructions, misunderstand the questions asked. Some psychologists, however, are of the view that a little anxiety is good, for it brings into use brain-cells otherwise inactive, and heightens attention, improves performance, releases certain hormones, and facilitates learning by a greater spread of nerve messages in the brain.

Linguistic and Cultural Barriers

A language is the expression of the thoughts and experiences of a people in terms of their cultural environment. When the same language is made use of in a different culture, it takes on another colour, another meaning. When, for instance, English is employed in India, it comes under the influence not only of the accent of the local language, but also of the meanings and connotations of words, phrases, and idioms of that language, and of the culture that has given rise to it.

Each language shapes the reasoning of its speakers. Thus English enforces 'either/or' thinking and reasoning, which Chinese does not. Indeed, no human is free to describe nature with strict objectivity; he is a prisoner of his language and even the same language has to cross not only cultural and generation gaps, but political and social-gaps as well.

What is more, in our own familiar environment we switch our type of language fairly frequently, probably quite unconsciously; we modify it according to whom we are talking to, where we are, and according to what we talk about; there is a different language for discussing profit margins and for talking about the merits of the domestic help we are aware of the situational differences. This is equally true of non-verbal language: a nod of the head does not mean assent in all cultures; the 'thumbs up' gesture has different associations for urban and rural groups in India; the touching of an elder's feet is a mark of respect in North India, but a mark of humiliation in other cultures.

Language and Meaning

Language facilitates understanding, but there are times when it can be a barrier to communication. In the first place, a language (whether verbal or non-verbal) is ambiguous by nature. The words of language, for instance, are mere symbols, and by themselves rarely represent only one meaning. Further, these symbols are understood differently by participants in communication. And words (or symbols) possess objective and subjective meanings. While objective (or denotative or dictionary) meanings point to objects, people and events, subjective (or connotative) meanings point to emotional and evaluational responses. The favourable and unfavourable associations of a word depend upon the cultural context in which it is used. Take the words 'fascist', 'capitalist' or 'communist', for example, they carry different associations in communist and non-communist states.

Meanings, therefore, exist not in words themselves but in the minds of people who use them. Even simple words like 'love', 'freedom', 'happiness' and 'tragedy' carry numerous associations depending upon the political and cultural situations people find themselves a part of.

Mechanical Barriers

Mechanical barriers are those raised by the channels employed for interpersonal, group or mass communication. Channels become barriers when the message is interfered with by some disturbance, which *(1)* increased the difficulty in reception or *(2)* prevented some elements of the message reaching its destination or both. The absence of communication facilities too would be a mechanical barrier. Technically, such barriers are clubbed together under one general term 'channel noise'.

This type of barrier includes any disturbance which interferes with the fidelity of the physical transmission of the message. A telephone that is in poor working. order, making demands on the yelling ability of Sender and Receiver, is a mechanical barrier in interpersonal communication. So also is 'cross-talk' often heard over an 'intercom' link in an office, or during long-distance calls. Thus, hearing is the physical act of receiving sound waves, a natural process. Listening, however, is a skill that has to be learned and developed, requiring hard work and practice. In Group Communication, a rundown or 'whistling microphone, and the wrong placement of loudspeakers are disturbances which are mechanical in nature. (The communicator who stands too close or too far from the mike is another matter). In mass communication, mechanical barriers would include such disturbances as static on the radio, smeared ink in a newspaper, a rolling screen on television, a barely readable point-size, or a film projector or video that does not function perfectly.

Information Technology and Society

The beginnings of modern mass communication where the use of technology defines the nature of communication, are perhaps traceable to the invention of printing in China and other parts of Asia, more than two centuries before Guttenberg or Caxton's invention in

Europe. It was around 1450 in Mainz, Germany, that Johannes Guttenberg's introduced his machine for printing from movable type. Instead of having to make copies laboriously by hand, numerous copies could be turned out of a machine that was worked by hand. Books like the Bible became easily available to all those who were literate. Indeed, the invention of printing made possible the spread of education in schools and universities. No more was learning the monopoly of a few monks with access to handcopied manuscripts in remote monasteries.

With the growing sophistication in the techniques of printing, communication with the literate masses by writers and leaders became a simple matter. Political revolutions like the French and the American and freedom struggles like those in Asia and Africa could involve the masses in the uprisings because of speedy and efficient communication.

The First Wave

The invention of printing (which Marshall McLuhan, the Canadian media sociologist, considered an 'extension of the eye') led to the tendency to see reality in discrete units, to find causal relations and linear serial order, and to find orderly structure in nature.' It allowed individuals to withdraw, to contemplate and meditate outside of communal activities. Printing, therefore, encouraged privatization, the lonely scholar, and the development of private points of view. Indeed, the very linear and rectilinear layout of words on the printed page transformed the nature of spelling, grammar and prose style. An oral face-to-face 'tribal' culture gave way with the help of the new technology of printing to a 'detribalized' visual, linear and symmetrical culture. The logical, the orderly, and the linear now come to prominence in man's ways of seeing and communicating. So did McLuhan speculate on the deterministic nature of technology. To McLuhan, all the media (not just the communication media) were 'the extensions of man.'

By the early 19th century, power press printing helped introduce the daily newspaper the greatest challenge to the printed book. The arrangement of news and later of pictures as well on the pages of a newspaper was not linear, but in the form of a mosaic and montage. There was no specific order in which the news and pictures were arranged, and no specific order in which they had to be read or looked at. Thus, the linear and the symmetrical communication culture gave way under the onslaught of the mosaic and montage modes of communication. Technology had once again revolutionised our way of seeing and of sending and receiving communication.

The Second Wave

The 19th century also saw the inventions of the telegraph, the telephone and photography. Then along came Thomas Edison with his phonograph and his movie camera and projector which made it possible to store sound and moving pictures. DeForest's invention of the triode vacuum tube in 1907, opened up the new worlds of radio and television. All these technological innovations led to another revolution in communication. This dramatic development has been called 'the second wave' of modern communication, 'the first wave' being ushered in by print technology.

Just as print extended the eye, radio proved to be an extension of the ear. McLuhan argued that 'printing upset the balance between oral and written speech; photography upset the balance of ear and eye.' With radio, oral speech and the sense of hearing regained their importance. Together with the phonograph (or gramophone), a new aural culture was beginning to take shape, when the movies and later television launched an audio-visual revolution in communication. In McLuhan's words, "If the movie was the mechanization of movement and gesture, TV was the electronification of the same."

Satellite communication via television and cable has now transformed the world into a 'global village'. Man has been 'retribalized', returned to the state of the tribe, to his 'sensorial wholeness' (the balanced use of all his senses). "The speed of information in the global viilage", wrote McLuhan, "means that every human action or event involves everybody in the village in the consequences of every event" Wishful thinking! While this might have been true of the small close-knit primitive tribe, it does not apply to the scattered millions of the universe who are caught up in the little worlds of their own castes, religions, communities and nationalities.

The Third Wave

The third wave of modern communication between man and machine was set in motion almost at the same time as the first, but climaxed only in the 20th century. Computers, and the concept of information storage and retrieval have brought about mind-boggling changes in the processing of information and communication. It is now possible for computer programmers to instruct machines to develop and work other machines ('artificial intelligence'). This has resulted in automation and the dawn of the fourth wave.

The Fourth Wave

First it was 'Teletext', then 'Videotex' bringing us the latest headlines on the TV screen; but from the early nineties, the rapid diffusion of multi-media, paging and cellular telephony, and above all, the Internet, especially in developed societies, has given rise to the 'Age of Information', an age in which information has been turned into the primary commodity of commerce and trade.

Further, Cable TV technology combined with satellite and digital technologies, has led to a profusion of broadcasting channels worldwide. (Direct-to-Home or DTH broadcasting promises to bring more than a hundred channels to the small screen). The choice in communication has become virtually unlimited for the urban affluent. The 'information explosion' is however largely restricted to the young, university-educated upper classes in developed societies, and the business and academic elite in developing societies.

In India, multinational companies and several public and private sector organisations have already gone in for the use of computers, though on a limited scale for fear of generating unemployment. But the armed forces, the police departments, the airlines, railways, meteorological departments and the telecommunications division, find the computer indispensable for efficiency. The INSAT series of domestic satellites, and our membership in INTELSAT, INMARSAT and other consortia, are helping us considerably in improving communications on a nationwide and international scale. McLuhan is a media-centric account of the development of Western civilization, largely influenced by his compatriot, Harold Innis. Other futurists Alvin Toffler (author of Future Shock, The Third Wave, and, Powershift), Daniel Bell (author of The Post-industrial Society), John Naisbitt (author of Megatrends), have advocated a similar view. Like Jacob Bronowski, such writers see the 'ascent of man' only in terms of the history and experience of Western civilization. The domination of the social sciences by such one-sided linear accounts has made other more ancient traditions 'invisible'. The colonisation of history, knowledge and information continues unchallenged.

Mass Communication and Culture

Modes of communication and culture are not as far apart, nor as distinct from each other, as is often argued. Both communication and culture develop together, one supporting the other. Indeed, communication is an expression of a community's culture, and culture in its turn embodies a community's communication and information needs and practices. Communication and Culture are thus inextricably tied to each other; we cannot understand one without understanding the other; nor can we speak of one without referring to the other. Most Indian languages do not have separate words for each; 'Sanskriti' for instance takes both within its compass; so does 'sadharanikaran.' Communication, language, culture, society and civilization, and their Indian equivalents, may have meanings of their own, but they are intimately linked to each other, and have evolved together, though the pace of evolution might differ from community to community. Moreover, changes and developments in one influence the others.

Has mass communication led to changes in the people's various cultures? Has the Hindi cinema which is in every sense the most popular and the most widespread form of mass entertainment in our country made any dent in our centuries old cultural values and behaviour? Or, has television (which in the Indian context is nothing more than an extension of cinema) in any way affected the culture of our city folk in any significant manner?

The reach of mass communication through the electronic media is mostly limited to the urban areas. It would, therefore, be ridiculous to suggest that the modern mass media have in any tangible way influenced Indian culture which itself is an extremely composite phenomenon, and impossible to define precisely. Indeed, the word 'culture' too is so comprehensive that it encompasses every facet of our lives from the most superficial to the most profound and intimate.

Mass Communication does influence (and even reflect) social values and practices, but this influence is always in combination with a whole lot of other socio-cultural and economic and political factors. By themselves, the media have little power to influence, change or develop.

For instance, Hindi films may start new fashions for men and women in the areas "'Of clothes, hairstyles, manner of speech (the use of 'yaar' for example, or the sprinkling of conversation with English expressions), manner of greeting, or ways of socializing. We may even go to the extreme of acting out what we see or hear in the mass media, say a violent gesture or a protest, but it takes much more than film or TV to change our social and cultural. values.

The Phenomenon of 'Mass Culture'

The understanding of 'mass culture' depends on our point of view and on what 'culture' means to us. Thus the term 'mass culture' can be used prejoratively or positively. The 'mass' is the rabble, the uncouth, illiterate and uncultured lot; the 'mass' is also vast, homogenous, scattered, anonymous. But from a positive perspective, the mass is volatile, dynamic, revolutionary; what Carl Sandburg, the American poet, termed the 'teeming, seething mass.' The concept of mass culture refers to a whole range of popular activities and artefacts to entertainments, spectacles, music books, films but it has become identified with the typical content of the mass media, and especially with the fictional, dramatic and entertainment material which they provide.

So, 'mass culture' according to this definition, has little reference to the culture of the masses, that is the vast general population of a nation. It primarily refers to the 'content' of radio, TV, cinema and the press. What there is the relationship between this 'mass culture' of the media and the people's own cultures?

The reach of the mass media is so limited in India that one wonders what relevance Denis McQuail's description of mass culture has to our society. 'Mass' culture in our country is still by and large the one that prevails in our villages where over 77% of our people live, and where Indian culture is barely touched by the mass media, except perhaps in South India. Folk media continue to provide the main source of entertainment, and also of instruction and education in religious, social, economic and political matters. While there are a great variety of folk forms in every region, and numerous languages and dialects in which they are presented, the themes have their source in the two epics, the Ramayana and the Mahabharata. The Muslims who make up the second largest religious community in the country have preserved their own traditional folk forms like the Ghazal, the Quwali and the Mushaira. The tribals too continue to entertain themselves with age-old folk songs and folk dances. The mass media have, however, entered into the lives of the upper and middle classes in cities and towns. The cinema is the most popular entertainment, as is evident from the production of nearly 800 films a year, and the screening of them in over 12,500 theaters. This popularity is also seen in the number of film-oriented programmes on Vividh Bharati and Doordarshan, as well as on the many cable and satellite television channels.

The Indian cinema has the qualities of a mass culture product, but it is doubtful if it has given rise to a 'mass culture' among the general population.

As understood by Western sociology, Mass Culture has three main features:

(1) Immense popularity among all classes, but particularly among the working class in industrial societies.

(2) Mass production and mass distribution.

(3) Unlike elite or 'high' culture, its aesthetic and literary standards are low, and commercialised, as its mass produced programmes aim at the mass market.

Examples of such mass culture products are the films for the big and the small screens (what is sometimes decisively termed 'the commercial cinema'), soap operas like HumLog, Buniyaad, Shanti, and Chandrakanta; the 'mythologicals' such as the Mahabharat, Ramayana, Shri Krishna, situation Comedies ('sitcoms'), film-based programmes, game shows and the like.

The culture propagated by the mass media is not necessarily the popular culture of the masses. More often than not, as in the Hindi cinema, it is a 'synthetic' North-Indian or Mumbai culture, paying lip service occasionally to the values of popular culture. This is not to suggest that there are no links whatsoever to the popular cultures; these links, however tenuous, make for 'connections' with the myths of the community and the nation. But 'mass culture' is itself a non-entity; like mass communication it largely exists in the minds of the elite fearful of the 'vulgar mob', the common people.

The mainstream Hindi. and regional language cinema, the glossy film magazines; and the garish type of calendar art, greeting cards, and cinema and advertising posters, offer examples of mass culture in our cities. But are they mere 'kitsch'? 'Kitsch' is an expressive German word often used to describe the art forms of the new culture of the mass media. It may well be defined 'as artistic rubbish'. The German verb from which 'kitsch' is derived means 'to make cheap', to 'vulgarise.' A well-known commentator on the Indian cultural scene, Ka Naa Subramaniam, dismisses the division between elite and 'pop' ('high' and 'mass') culture as meaningless in the Indian context, since the mass media have not yet advanced much, and the spirit of the community still prevails. He argues that 'to talk of pop and elitist art in India is to confuse the issues in an already confused milieu. Neither 'pop' nor elitist art exists in India as of today. We have not yet lost the old purpose of art nor discovered new ones.'

'Mass culture' is a complex cultural phenomenon which is a creation of the mass media. It is, therefore, more precise to term it 'mass media culture', to distinguish it from the majority culture or folk culture. Mass media culture is an entirely urban phenomenon, resulting from rapid industrialization, and alienation from the majority culture.

Dwight MacDonald sums up the characteristics of this culture which is manufactured collectively by production line specialists to tested formulas, packaging and marketing, in these words:

"The lords of Kitsch (or mass culture) sell culture to the masses. It is a debased, trivial culture that voids both the deep realities (sex, death, failure, tragedy) and also the simple, spontaneous pleasures... The masses, debauched by several generations of this sort of things, in turn come to demand trivial and comfortable cultural products which came first... the mass demand or its satisfaction (and further stimulation) is a question as academic as it is unanswerable."

This is evidently an elitist and patronizing view of what culture is and what the masses are susceptible to. A more balanced approach to the popular forms of various cultures, would make for a more realistic evaluation of the relationship between the mass media and the mass culture. Do television audiences, for instance, watch a soap opera as a 'mass' or rather as members of a cultural community, in terms of what James Lull calls 'interpretative communities'?

❐

6

Mass Media Development

India, as is well known, is a nation of diverse and divergent cultures and sub-cultures, languages and dialects that run into several hundreds, varied religions and faiths. An ancient country with civilisation some 4,000-year-old, India, now a land of teeming millions, is abounding with challenging themes and problems of development. The 640 million people are waiting for a revolution in all aspects of human endeavour, a rich field for mass media to exert the influence and cast their impact. It is unfortunate that prior to 1947, when India formed a part of the British rulers acted only in those directions which either aided in extending their influence or perpetuating their power.

With the consequences that no consistent attitudes or patterns of behaviour could be formed or inculcated among the masses. Newspapers were not permitted freedom of writing, radio was under the control of the government, television had not even been conceived, although Britain had a well-established television and radio networks at home, black and white cinema was unaware of developments in colour techniques in the west and other media of mass communication did not progress in any systematic, planned direction to assist the country in any way. The advent of independence in August 1947 removed the shackles of the colonial era and a new horizon breathed in all aspects of the country's life. The media of mass communication also rose to the occasion. There was a tremendous progress in the fields of print and the broadcast media, the rate of literacy rose, more cinemas came into being, more and more people came in contact with one another in the countryside and the urban areas. The impact of the wide world was beginning to be felt at large.

Most of the laws restriction or controlling the activities of the journalists and writers were either withdrawn or suspended. Freedom of speech and expression (including thereby the freedom of the press) was guaranteed by the Constitution as a fundamental right (ArtIcle 19 A). The Constitution also granted freedom of movement, right to profession and property and also to hold meetings and cultural gatherings. All this added to the momentum of growth of mass media immensely. Since the Indian Constitution racognises 16 provincial and regional languages, equal opportunities were available to all of them for instituting newspapers and periodicals in their respective regions for their proliferation and development. Radio though remained under the control of the Central Government, but several new stations were planned to give coverage to all national and regional languages including several dialects.

In 1976, twenty-nine years after independence, India had 13,320 newspapers in 65 languages. Of which, 10,947 or 78 per cent were started after independence. The largest number of newspapers was in Hindi-a language spoken by about 40 percent of the country's population, followed by English. The number in Hindi was 3,289 and in English 2,765 next probably only to the USSR. The total circulation of all the newspapers, though not very large as compared to the Western standards, amounted to over 34 million copies. Weekly and other journals in the Indian and regional languages numbered 12,445. The progress has continued unabated, despite several hurdles of low advertising and shortage of newsprint, specially in the field of regional and provincial languages.

Started with only six broadcasting stations in 1947, All India Radio (AIR) has also greatly extended its services and progressively created its impact on the masses. In 1977, 155 radio stations including relay station, were functioning and these stations were broadcasting in several foreign, national and regional languages. A regular feedback was in existence in most languages wherein listeners could have a say in programming and broadcasting scheduled in these languages. AIR went commercial in 1967.

Television arrived in India in 1959, though pretty late and on a rather too restricted scale. The United Nations Educational, Scientific and Cultural Organisation (UNESCO), the USA, West Germany, Yugoslavia and Japan helped india in establishing, extending and programming of the television network in India.

In 1975, the US- loaned satellite enabled India to initiate the SITE (Satellite Instructional Television Experiment) programme. It was the first experiment of its kind ever made in the world. Some 3,000 villages in the six Indian states were. brought under the focus of the television programs for four hours every day. This was the greatest achievement for the country's mass media. Although the NASA (National Aeronautics Space Administration of the USA) has now withdrawn the satellite, the Indian Government is determined to establish the television link to the 70 per cent of the 3,000 villages to the television stations to be started in the near by' states to these villages. This is being done expeditiously with a view to keeping these villages further exposed to the new medium the "magic box." Besides the seventeen television stations set up in various towns of the country are now covering 15 per cent of the population, as per the UNESCCD figures published in the publication entitled "World Communication."

The Indian cinema has also taken rapid strides: some 619 films in 15 Indian regional languages were produced in 1978 and there were over 8,000 cinemas in the country's various states. Right now, the Indian mass media are actively involved in the different aspects of national development. After the national emergency declared in India in June 1975, the mass media, especially the press, came under stress. But it should be stated to the credit of the media that in spite ot severe restraints, they gave increasingly contributed to improvement of the situation and assisted the government and the masses in social, economic and political endeavour. People are being systematically educated in the new and modern means of production. Much more needs to be done however.

The coming of huge industry and large-scale construction works in India after independence have brought problem: complex working groups human resources mobilisation for national development, which have in turn changed the skill, training and attitudes which usually go side by side. As the "mobilising of human resources requires a great deal of attention of what the population knows and thinks of national development, and especially to the encouragement of the attitudes and social customs and the provision of knowledge, which will be favourable to the development", the mass media have undertaken the job quite competently.

This task of creating and encouraging attitudes and providing adequate information is being increasingly entrusted to the mass media. For, unless, according to Wilbur Schramm, there is enough information designed to encourage productive attitudes, social patterns and customs, the development process is bound to suffer and be blocked. The individual differences perspective, the social categories perspective and the social relations perspective theories as enunciated by Melvin De Fleur and Sandra Ball-Rokeach find a fair amount of application in the present Indian situation, if we assess the economic, social and political perspectives in the country in the last three decades or so since the dawn of independence.

Schramm notices change in social, cultural, religious and personal attitudes which subsequently have helped change and shape a society completely differently. The Indian society has by and large reacted almost in an identical manner. This has been amply established by some well known studies conducted by Indian mass communication scholars such as Rao, Damle and several others. These researches have proved that mass media have immensely aided and assisted the rate and score of development and the pace of people in absorbing the new media which has completely revolutionised the style of people.

In bringing about these changes in which the various media are fully participating and getting involved include political consciousness, urbanisation, professional mobility, adult literacy, media consumption, and a broad general participation in the nation's reconstruction and similar activities. This has given a new dimension to the media's role in a developing situation and this is media in action in a country well on a road to progress which India presents today in the last quarter of the twentieth century. Considering its size, swelling population and a fairly developing economy and a comparatively stable political system, India is the largest country in Asia today, second only to China. A great task of building up the country and developing its various latent human and natural resources *lies am head* of the people in numerous fields. For its economic recovery and raising a complex infrastructure, India has already executed its four five-year development plans; the fifth commenced from April 1976 and will cost the country about $1,000 billion (Rs. 70,000 crores) on its completion and full execution in 1981. It is a colossal task requiring close cooperation and thorough coordination of the various factors including the mass media.

The Indian people "raised in different social environments" are therefore passing through a series of changes in "attitudes, values and beliefs that constitute their personal-psychological make-up." No system of mass media are "poorly developed." They have not been put to work "for economic development nor have they been used to bring about common anxieties, common concerns, and common emotions for India as a whole."

But it must be recognised that "it is through communication that people can learn about new ideas, can be stimulated by change which is conveyed to them or be cognizant of change and what it means, and can understand what is going around them." Mass media are essentially agents of social change, and the "specific kind of social change they are expected to help accomplish in the transition to new customs and practices, and in some cases, to different social relationships. Behind such changes in behaviour must necessarily present substantial alterations in attitudes, beliefs, skills and social norms."

Thus the carious people would take the perspective that media present to them not in the same uniform way but in varying manners suiting their personal and psychological viewpoints which the media would possibly focus on resulting in individual differences in perspective on the mass communication process.

In fact, the initial stages, as Rokeach and DeFleur point out in their Dependency Model, the cognitive effects of mass media may be creation and resolution of ambiguity which "can occur because people lack enough information to understand the meaning of an event, or because they lack adequate information to determine which of several possible interpretations of an event is correct one." Besides, in such a situation "attitude formation", "agenda-setting," "the expansion of people's beliefs" and "the values" of a society are also affected in a changing situation. Since the most media messages at present are closely linked to the Indian audience dependence, perceptible influence on their activities, attitudes, values, aspirations and endeavours have been keenly noticed. The active media message reception of the people has been effectively instrumental in changing "individual needs, psychological and social characteristics. And in some cases they flow back to alter the nature of social system itself." These factors play an overriding role in shaping the developmental attitudes of a people and which changes the developmental strategy of a nation.

Communication Use

As India is passing through an era of economic transition, people's attitudes and values are changing fast; media use by the people is also going through quick shifts. Although communication facilities prevalent in the urban areas are much more than in the rural areas, villagers are becoming increasingly conscious of the power of knowledge. There has been quite a spurt in the rural press in the recent times in almost all regional dialects and national languages.

This has led in rural families now have one or two members who either subscribe to the newspapers, borrow from others or read in the village reading rooms. More villagers now visit cities, there is more interpersonal communication. The rural people now get more opportunities to see films as cinema houses have been brought to the villages. Actually, the shows are always full to the capacity now than ever. With transistor revolution, more radios are used by the rural people; there were some 150 million licences issued until December

1973 by the various radio stations in the country. A farmer with a radio transistor tucked on his shoulder working in the fields is a common sight now. As the portable television set has already been manufactured in India itself, the radio transistor would, it is hoped be replaced by the portable television.

The commercialisation of radio and television in India has brought the whole world of advertising to his door steps. As the messages about the new goods and products reach the rural homes and "if they (the messages) relate to their (people's) interests, consistent with their attitudes, congruent with their beliefs, and supportive to their values", as De Fleur and Rokeach point out, these ate quickly acted upon and "hotly" pursued.

The proof of this, if one were required, lies in the improved living standards of the farmers, their better dressed and well-fed families, their awakening to health and family planning methods, their awareness of modern agricultural techniques and latest innovations. In fact, they are deriving the maximum use of media messages concern directly individually and jointly.

But it is true that majority of people are not gaining or are not able to benefit so much from the media messages. "Since there are individual differences in personality characteristics among such members, it is natural to assume that there will be variations in effect which correspond to these individual differences."

Another aspect of the Indian life, an altogether different and novel, is in the urban areas. The journals and periodicals published in most regional and national languages have fairly good circulations; majority of the people have seen television at some place or the other and a good number have them in their drawing rooms. They watch all that this "mafic box" has to offer day in and day out.

The programme presented by the SITE offered a year-long contact with the modern information science and technology in kaleidoscopic forms and fashion. People have learnt from media and acquired ability to cope with new ideas and innovative techniques.

Most people are acquainted with the human machines called the computers; they are familiar with A-bomb; they try to keep themselves abreast with what is happening in the most important parts of the world through radio, newspapers, journals and television. When they learnt about the murder of John Kennedy, many people stopped work and mourned; news about the forthcoming change in the American administration and Carter's victory were widely acclaimed all over.

Awareness of the media message even among the old people, who were markedly passive to political, social, economic and cultural developments, is also rising. Even a 70-year-old illiterate woman in a middleclass Delhi home knows how to switch on/off radio and television, aircooler and fan, often enjoys the radio and television programmes that concern her and interest her. More and more people are being exposed to technical subjects which one can use in everyday life. Some of these include things such as the DDT powder, chemical fertilizers, pesticides automatic machines and the intricate electronic gadgets. This is also raising their general level of understanding and information. The level of knowledge on abstract subjects like the local and national politics, diplomacy, air-carriers, pollution, ecology, elections, dictatorship, democracy, etc. expanding steadily.

The elites are still better off: It is, however, interesting and significant that the sense of change separates the elite from the masses most dramatically. Some 30 percent of the Indian people belong to the elite class and these people are as Westernised as could be conceived. They have completely shrugged off old traditional ways, attitudes and customs. And the Western media, newspapers, magazines films and television show have drastically transformed them into entirely new personalities. Living in the urban areas also means frequent mixing with the people from other advanced nations who come there as tourists or on business or in international gatherings and conferences (which are now a common feature). These intercourses have brought them nearer to the people in the United States, the U.K., West Germany, Canada, Australia and the USSR. And this has taken them away from superstitions, obselete habits and beliefs of the yore. There is a great desire for change in life styles, values, economic status, social position and overall thinking.

Media have immensely contributed to this change and this development taking place in the Indian society. Like a wild magic media have placed the Indian society "up to hill higher than we can see on the horizon and let him look beyond." Media are like magic because "they can lit a man see and hear where he has never been and know people has never met." This indeed is a tremendous achievement for the Indian media and their yeoman's service in concrete terms to the national development and the common man.

MEDIA SOCIETY AND DEVELOPMENT

It has been prominently borne out by several research studies conducted in the carious developing countries that modern communication media have immeasurable potency for improving and changing the face of a traditional society like that of India.

The studies conducted by Lerner, Schramm, Rao, and Doop, etc., have amply demonstrated that the interaction between the media and the society from development point of view is "constant and cumulative." The prominent reason, according to De Fleur and Rokeach, is that "people located at similar positions in a similar social structure would be similar in personality because of similarity of their immediate social environment." And they would naturally react and are most likely to grasp identically the gains in the form of knowledge of new techniques and new ideas have to offer.

Thus with constant communication flow, people will have a great deal in common in setting before them their developmental goals, deciding whin and how they should change and what they want their society to be changing when such a communication is available and established in a society, the job of arriving at social consensus, designing a policy and directing action is entrusted to the government, but social and political organisations and the mass media become the most powerful instruments of change and development. The communication is fundamental to all social and development processes.

Development in India has been more or less on these very lines. Media, print and electronic, have played their role in framing economic and development attitudes for the five-year plans, directing and helping action by the government with people's participation, as far as practicable under the existing limitations of literacy and access. Of course, success has been slow and tardy. Huge economic and development five-year plans for overall economic emancipation, giant industrial establishments and mammoth power works, enormous network of state undertakings, elaborately spread health and family welfare programmes and well-developed telecommunications, air and rail transportation networks arm primary and higher education systems would not have been possible without a responsible and responsive mass media asserting their influence. These projects may only have come about slowly in the ordinary course of history by continuing contact with other economic systems through mass media.

It seems to be a simple and straight procedure, but actually it is a long drawn-out programme. To work this out would not have been easy and the process not so smooth. But the media helped expedite it and manoeuvre it through engineering human cooperation, consent and skill.

It is indeed a great task, which media could assist in bringing about in most amiable way. In its drain, change is also introduced in cultural and group relationship by participation, decision making and action. India has organised and successfully held six general elections for the 520 seat Parliament and several for the 22 state legislatures, wherein thousands of candidates and millions of electorates had complete liberty of "formulating voting decisions and actually going to the polls" where mass communication media barring radio and television had a full free-play of their potentialities, where people had not only "direction of exposure to mass communicated campaign material, but also the kind of effects that such material would have upon them". The mass media effects on the Indian situation have been indeed invaluable, of late specially.

In fact, India's swift agricultural progress, commonly termed as the "green revolution" in the late sixties and the early seventies. It is a living tribute to the power of mass communication which has carried the results of the university laboratories to the farmer in the field and has made India almost self-sufficient in feeding its 630 million people. As social relations perspectives of the Indian people are being progressively altered by the all-pervasive force of the mass media, family system, relations between parents and children, old and young, clothing habits and fashions, dressing and eating, and cultural and moral values are being assessed and reassessed. Large families, arranged marriages, women confining to kitchen drudgery and bearing children, etc. are becoming things of the past. Diehards are losing ground and masscommunicated youngsters with modern ideals are rapidly taking over even in the tradition-ridden homes and changing the society tremendously.

Although the government in India is very powerful in the field of mass communication and has complete monopoly of radio and television, and its films division produces a heavy proportion of the films made in the country, the government also publishes a large number of journals and periodicals—states and the central governments together are certainly the largest publishers in the country nevertheless other mass communication media too have a heavy impact in the total situation of the nation.

That the mass media are trying to involve themselves and participate in the overall national development process is apparent from glancing through any issue of a newspaper or magazine. There has been an active realisation to the fact that :there cannot be and significant economic development without the use of mass media. You cannot increase agricultural yields, convince people about family welfare, persuade them to hold off from buying or to bring their crops to the market, or teach them the value of sending their daughters to schools, without reaching them through radio, television, films or newspapers. Nor can one hope, without better mass communications, to weld together a vast country with many languages; bring about a concern for the same thing, see to it...that the citizens talk about the same national problems and, further take positions about them which are not primarily dictated by regional or other narrow considerations. For this we need, of course, the expansion of media....

Mass media in India are therefore striving to perform three developmental tasks (as outlined by Schramm): the populace must have information about national development: their attention must be focussed on the need to change, the opportunities inviting change, the methods and means of change; and if possible their aspiration for themselves and their country must be raised and highlighted.

In the second place, there must be opportunity to participate intelligently in the decision process, and thirdly, the needed skills must be taught: adults must be taught to read, children must be educated, farmers must learn the methods of modern farming, teachers, doctors, engineers must be trained, workers must master technical skills, people in general must learn more about how to keep themselves healthy and strong. The end result of this process in the situation as it develops would ultimately play a very vital role and would lead to the emergence of informal social relationships which would be helpful in "modifying the manner in which given individuals will act upon a message that comes to their attention via the mass media."

Media in India by and large in the near future would be able to assist in decision-making process which must accompany the country's overall developments and allround progress. The result indeed would be much better if the media get more and more opportunities and their activities have a free, unfettered flow.

There are, however, serious hurdles indeed: financial, technological, political, and social. But these would certainly be overcome as the nation moves further in the realms of development and progresses with the impact of its media of mass communication.

MASS MEDIA AND FUTURE

Of late, the concept of development itself is undergoing vast changes, and mass media's role in this process is being redefined and reassessed. Everette Rogers of Stanford University has recently tried to improve upon Schramm's concept of development. He states, "...equality of distribution of information, socio economic benefits;. popular participation in self development planning and execution usually accompanied by the decentralisation of certain of these activities to the village level; self-reliance and independence in development, within an emphasis upon the potential of local resources; integration of traditional with modern system, so that modernisation is a syncretisation of old and new ideas, with the exact mixture somewhat different in each locale" form the essential elements in the new concept of development.

There has already been immense realisation in India of the type of development envisaged by Rogers. With mass communication media constantly "bombarding" these concepts, the rural and urban poor are receiving keen attention, and getting priority audience in development programmes so that the gap between the rich and the poor is being bridged as ably and quickly as possible.

Media have already started giving ample space and time to the villages, which they were earlier either doing casually or not doing at all. And with stimulus and incentives being promised, villagers and people of the lowest rung of the society are themselves being induced to develop themselves. Radio, television and cinema are persistently focussing on the plight of the downtrodden, the underprivileged and the unprivileged. Some old habits and customs are being yoked to reinforce new ideals on development so that every village, township or city may develop in their own way. Newspapers are adopting villages and with their influence, colleges and universities are following suit. As the news media report about the changes taking place in these villages at regular intervals and the spotlight works as a catalyst agent for the development of the entire community, a pattern suited to a particular enviromnent is being worked out. This would also be determined by local and personal behaviour, style of living or community patterns. Thus Indian mass media are striking to focus development as a widely participatory process of social change in a society, intended to bring about both social and material advancement (including greater equality, freedom, and other valued qualities) for the majority of the people through their gaining greater control over their environment.

But there are still huge problems awaiting solutions. Agriculture, health and family welfare, education, and adult literacy, obscure habits and outdated customs yet untouched and unearthed. These need media's urgent attention. There is lot to be done to accomplish these problems. This will immensely stimulate the people in their self-development patterns and would provoke them to outline their own achievements and successes in the various fields. At political plane, masses still need to be educated about the necessity of stable political environments, they require to be enlightened about the importance of a pliable democratic process, and the role of a common citizen in the over-all administration of the country.

As Y.V.L. Rao points out in his study on the role of communication in the growth and development of the various aspects of the village life, the mass media should help the Indian people to raise their economic status, bring about greater respect for human dignity and greater equality among the masses, make cultural, social, political and economic chances a perpetuating process. It is, therefore, clear that mass media have an eminently significant role in the total development and is "tied inseparably" in the entire process in India. However, as De Fleur and Rokeach underline that there is need to recognise and establish that "the effects of a given mass-communicated message sent out on a given channel will depend upon a large number of psychological characteristics and social categories similarities which audience members bring to their encounters with the quickly gaining momentum of the mass communication function. The method is to involve in the innumerable fields of activity. Communication specialists and researchers over the world are looking at the outcome of media's this involvement in India development with interest, and perhaps with an amount of concern.

Communication, as it is known today, has originated and evolved in the West, particularly in the United States of America.

With the development of technologies, the communication methods also developed. The methods became complex and sophisticated. But the concept of 'communication' has been with us since the creation of man. The methods and the process is differ from region to region, country to country. Even now, with the idea of 'global village' becoming a reality, we differ as far as methods and process of communication are concerned.

You must be aware of various seminars and workshops being conducted to formulate a policy regarding satellite communication. Some experts say as a result of exposures to foreign television programmes, our values and culture may be damaged beyond repair. The negative influence of such telecasts may prove detrimental to the development of the nation.

Some scholars say that the Indian tradition has hardly. any thoughts on communications. Those who grant such thoughts have negative views on the issue. 'Communication' is a word coined in the recent past to explain a particular area of study. Therefore, in our ancient literature this view was not dealt with separately. But, a lot has been said on the process and methods of communication is an integral part of our socio-political and cultural life. It was as important then as it is now. It worked according to the social and cultural norms. At present, we must ensure that it works as per the socio-cultural ethos of our nation. Otherwise the fabric of the nation may be disturbed.

Our way of life is influenced by religion and various philosophical teachings. As a God fearing people, we have found various ways to worship. Mysticism is one such way. Mysticism has given birth to a new method of communicating one's deep realisation and understanding of God and the Universe. Mysticism is centered on oneself. It is a process by which one plunges into the deepest core of one's heart of self. A profound communication takes place in one's innermost care. This communication process can be termed as interpersonal communication—communication with oneself. Mira Bai and Kabir communicated so much in a very easy way because their realisation was clear. We have not explored this mystical process. This mystical approach possibly can help us to communicate with our people more effectively. Interpersonal Communication enriched interpersonal communication. This area of communication has not been sufficiently explored. Some enthusiastic communication professionals take a parochial view and try desperately to invent a communication theory or a model which existed in the ancient times. Having discussed the importance of interpersonal and interpersonal communication, we shall discuss the importance of Indian philosophy in Communication. We come to know about the process of communication in ancient India through treatises on arts, religion, and mysticism.

Accounts of Vedanta, Bhakti, Vaishnavism and Sufism speak volumes on communication. To be effective in our communication we should be able to establish their relevance to the people of modern India. This Indian orientation will help us to recast and reframe the whole outlook towards communication concepts norms, and beliefs. We ought to turn to the Indian philosophical tradition which has tremendous intellectual and spiritual resources and can easily supply us with basic framework for a creative and relevant communication process. The impact of this heritage has been felt through the ages and its richness and university has been acknowledged by the world. Since the present communication concept and discipline has developed in the west, we do get carried away by its Western perception and hence become ineffective in the Indian situation. It is necessary, therefore that we ground ourselves firmly in our culture, beliefs and ethos. We need not copy the western models blindly. And thus consequently suffer the loss of inspiration.

INDIAN HERITAGE AND COMMUNICATION VALUES

In India, communication is inextricably linked with philosophy and religion. Sarvapalli Radhakrishnan says, "the pursuit of philosophy is deemed a religious vocation. Therefore, in order to come to terms with the cultural ideal that animates Indian society, we need to examine, brief though they may be, the outlines of Indian philosophy".

The Upanishads call attention to the value of the knowledge of ultimate truth as a means of liberation. The Upanishads, greatly emphasise the need to look inward for a clearer understanding of reality. The basic tenet of the Upanishads is the need to acquire self-knowledge and thereby liberate oneself from worldly bondages.

With the passage to time, a number of non-Vedic philosophical traditions sprang up. The Charvakas placed heavy emphasis on the material world on the material world and discarded all notions of transcendentality. Jainism was another tradition of philosophy which was non-vedic in character. In maintained that both the animate and the inanimate world were eternal and independent. Therefore one has to be tolerant to all that exists on earth. Buddhism, another non-vedic philosophy constituted a powerful reaction against the ritualism that characterized the Vedas and the transcendentalism that was associated with the Upanishads. The individual, according to Buddhism, should diligently work out his salvation, from pain and suffering.

Later, Indian Philosophy began to move further and further away from the original ways of thinking and, indeed, split into different and competing systems. Although these systems do not by any means constitute mutually exclusive categories, they display sufficient variation for each to warrant on autonomous conceptual status. Of these, there are six that deserve close attention. They are the Nyaya; Vaisesika; Sankhya; Yoga; Mimamsa; Vedanta and Advaita. These schools, too, contributed to the formation of the Indian tradition.

The Indian schools philosophy originated from the Vedas; two schools are Vedic—the Mimamsa and the Vedanta; the four-Samkhya, Yoga, Vaisesika, and Nyaya have their base in the Vedas. Therefore, these six schools are classed as Vedic or Astika. The two schools of Buddhism and Jainism are called Nastika as they do not accept Vedic authority. These eight schools are products of the great thought that characterised the post-Vedic age. Each school of philosophy is called a Darsana, meaning a view or a vision of the truth. The aims and aspirations of life are not only the pursuit of material gains and pleasure but also, virtue and morality which chasten life and spiritual enlightment and freedom. Each school is associated with a sage as its first promulgator-Samkhya with Kapila, Yoga with Paanjali, Vaịsesika with Kanada, Nayaya with Gautama, Mimamsa with Jaiminị and Vedanta with Badarayana-Vyasa. Because of their mutual relationship, these six schools fall into three groups of allied systems, Samkhya is accepted by Yoga, with the addition of God as the omniscient first Teacher. The speciality of Yoga is the practical aspect of the methods of mental control by which the philosophical ideal of the Samkhya, namely, the isolation of the Spirit from Matter is achieved. But Yoga as a Sadhana or preparatory discipline and means came to be accepted by all schools.

Today, it has, with, the help of science, grown in strength and gained a world-wide vogue. The vaisesika doctrines form the basis of Nyaya, both being schools of realism and pluralism. The Mimamsa and Vedanta go together because of their common Vedic basis but otherwise they differ fundamentally. The former is concerned with Karma and Dharma, the performance of ordained duty, but the latter to the opposite of Karma, namely, renunication from activity; according to Vedanta, knowledge is the means of salvation. Mimamsa is thus related to the Karma-kanda, and Vedanta to the Upanishads. The Mimamsa also made a valuable contribution to the science of interpreting texts; it came to be known therefore as Vakya Sastra.

But what do all these mean to us today. Our tradition, philosophy, culture, and religion are not dead. We still practice our ancient religion. We do study our ancient philosophy and theology. Our beliefs are largely based on Karma and Dharmạ.

Therefore, these things have meaning in our day to day life. The words coined in various philosophical and theological books are still being used by us to convey the same meaning. Thus, to communicate meaningfully, we must be well grounded in this rich heritage. But a little caution we must not be so heavily grounded in these, so as not to be able to fly and explore the richness of clear blue sky. What implication does this survey of Indian philosophy have for communication theory? On the basis of these philosophical tenets, we can construct a workable model of communication for the Indian situation. This may differ substantially from models found in the Western countries. Each culture may have models of communication of its own. What is essential is that any communication model must be based on a cultural context. Otherwise the meaning conveyed may differ from the intended meaning to be conveying in a communication. Many times, we may fail to communicate if we do not take this cultural context into consideration. In India generally the primary focus of interest in communication is how does the receiver make sense of the stimuli that he receives so as to deepen his self-awareness. In the Western model, the basic question that present themselves are how does the Communicator affect/influence/ manipulate the receiver and how does the communicator and receiver share information and enter into a two-way relationship. According to traditional Indian views, meaning should necessarily lead to self-awareness. Hence the Indian definition of communication would be that it is an inward search for meaning a process of intra-personal communication.

In the West, communication is seen as the transference of meaning with the intention of influencing the receiver. But in Indian meaning brings enlightenment. Meaning, according to traditional Indian thought, was seen as process which leads to selfawareness, then to freedom, and finally to truth. Here, by freedom we mean the liberation of persons from ignorance, from illusion of the world, and the web of the artificial categories constructed all around us.

Another significant point of divergence between the Indian and the Western ways is that the Indian way focuses attention on the intra-personal dimension as opposed to the inter-personal dimension. The Western way is expression-oriented but the Indian way is interpretation oriented. The Indian way seems to suggest that what is important in human communication is to find out how a receiver makes sense of the verbal stimuli that are received by him and engages in a search for meaning. This search is an inward one. The traditional authorities maintain that the reality is indeed within man. To know it is to be. In other words, distinction between the knower and the known narrows down considerably. The realization of truth is facilitated neither by language nor by logic and rationality. To know is to be; to know is to become aware of the artificial categorization imposed on the world by language and logic. It is only through an intuitive process that man will be able to lift himself out of the illusory world, which according to the Indian viewpoint, is indeed the aim of communication. People may differ with this view. But we all must agree that in India realisation dawns when we internalise the communication. It needs to be pointed out that one may not understand the current development in communication solely in the light of this model. We are living in a world where the border lines between countries are disappearing very fast. We do know and feel at one with the happenings in other parts of the globe. We are passing though a phase of civilisation which could be termed, at best, the transition, and 'chaotic' at worst.

Indian communication centres on the word Sadharanikaran. It is derived from the Sanskrit world Sadharan meaning simple, common or ordinary. Sadharanikaran would thus imply simplification. The word has a familiar ring and is equivalent to the Latin word "communs" that is communication, meaning commonness of experience.

Sadharanikaran has been vividly described in Bharata's natya Shastra, which though discovered in the 10th century A.D. by Bhattanayak, has now been established to have its authorship in a period as early as 500 B.C. It is also known as the fifth Veda, as in it Bharata Muni had condensed the essence of the four Vedas for the benefit of the common man.

How does Sadharanikaran take place? Bharata describes Sadharanikaran as that point in the climax of a drama when the audience becomes one with the actor who lives an experience through his acting on stage and starts simultaneously reliving the same experience. The process has been described as rasa swadan. When Sadharanikaran happens, universalisation or commonness of experience takes place in full form. According Bhattanayak, the essence of communication is to achieve commonness or oneness among the people. Later, this word was extensively used in literacy circles for explaining poetics, aesthetics and drama.

But today, Sadharanikaran is often employed to convey the idea of commonness and simplification. The entire superstructure of Indian aesthetic centres on the act of Sadharanikaran through rasa swadan.

Rasa has been explained thus: man in his essential characteristics is a bundle of bhawa that constitute his being and form part of his total consciousness. These have been categorised as 50 in number. Of these nine are described as *Sthai bhawa* 33 as *Vyabhicari bhawa* and the remaining as *Satwik bhawa*. Bharata, after an intensive study of these moods, has grouped them under one all encompassing expression *bhawa* for purposes of establishing Sadharanikaran.

Coomaraswamy describes 'bhawa' as springing from aesthetic emotion of person who derives its existence ,from sensory experience. Each mood is capable of arousing a relevant state of feeling/quality of response.

Bharat Muni also postulated that for Sadharanikaran to take place, Sthai Bhava, that is, permanent moods in the audience, have to be aroused which will result in the unleashing of the attendant Rasas, feeling or aesthetic pleasures, thereby completing the process of communication.

A Bhava is the first reaction or sensation caused in the sympathetic mind by a stimulus called *Vibhavas* sone, a bird, a picture. A sustained *Bhnva* that leads to Rasa is the Sthayee *Bhava.*

An Anubhava is the physical manifestation that takes place immediately as *Bhava* registers itself in the mind.

The Sthayee *Bhava* is stimulated by the *Vibhava* in the mind and is heightened by Anubhavas and *Sanchari Bhavas*. In this state, the mind will be highly receptive to the Rasa experience.

When a person experiences the intensity of the *Bhavas* of the *Vaibhavas* he overcomes his own personality and completely identifies himself with actual state of the *Vibhava*. This is state of universalisation. The universalisation leads to identification and involvement. Whatever is communicated leaves deep impact. Rasa can be understood only by the Sahridaya the person who alone is capable of rasaswadan. Who is Sahridaya? He/she is person in state of emotional intensity *i.e.* a quality of emotional dimension coequal to that of the sender of the message of communicator. Both must be *sahridayas*.

In India, communication lays great stress on the communicator and the one who receives communication belonging to the same cultural group. The same cultural context will help the communicator and the receiver to communicate effectively. The sender and receiver of a communication belonging to same culture, would be able to communicate more effectively. In other world, it is emphasised that communication may be ineffective between an individuals or groups, not belonging to the same culture as total grasp of symbols, signs and meanings are essential for effective communication. The relevance of the message, the code and the experience that the code stands for, to the group with which communication is sought to be established, is an important factor in communication. In Western societies sources and receivers, at least in principle, communicate as equals, but in Indian society, it is not the case. The source is viewed as higher and the receiver as lower in status. The relationship is a hierarchical one of dominance and subordination. The source is held in high esteem by the receiver of communication, a relationship idealized in the gurushishya relationship. Even though the source and receiver are unequal, they are Sahridayas, having a common cultural orientation. This makes the communication is their unequal relationship satisfying.

The hierarchical aspect of Sadharanikaran contributed to the blossoming of Indian civilization through efficient communication. This was, however, later taken to the level of absurdity, resulting in highly rigid and hierarchical society. To some extent, it made Indian society into a more or less closed system and thereby contributed towards its stagnancy and decay. It is true Natyashastra was written by Bharat Muni to simplify the complex Vedas for the benefit of the common man and thereby bridge the gap between the elites, the priests, the nobles and Sudras. However, with the passage of time, Sadharanikaran resulted in divisions within society. Later, with institutionalization of difference the society became stagnant.

Sadharanikaran, through communication, between unequals over a period of time, contributed toward the development of more or less permanent and rigid hierarchical social relationships, as reflected in the caste system. Not only that, it seems that the values supporting the hierarchical nature of social arousal of permanent mood and particular aesthetic pleasure made them natural and acceptable as well as satisfying. Acceptance of this type of communication pattern by the people belonging to different castes, made the system stronger and permanent. Today, to a great extent, the caste system influences communication patterns, particularly in Indian villages. Within a village community, far more communication takes place among the members of a caste than between castes because of the highly stratified and hierarchical nature of the caste system. People of high and low castes accept their position as natural. The asymmetrical relationship between high and low caste members is hereditary and is accepted by those who are in a disadvantageous position.

It may be pointed out here that in Indian many sages and saints, in different times, launched reform movements against social inequalities. They attempted to further simplify and reinterpret Indian philosophy for the benefit of the common people and thereby bridge the gap between elites and commoners.

However, the question arises: apart from the academic exercise, is there any use of studying of the Indian view on communication? In think, it is necessary and the need is urgent. Some the reasons are as follow:

(a) The Indian view of communication takes into consideration the man and his environment as healthy unit as against the mechanical and quantitative view of man.

(b) The use of technology has added a new dimension to use of world as a tool of communication. The printing press, radio TV and satellite have multiplied words and their use to an immeasurable extent. The knowledge of Indian view of communication may help in minimising the use of words to create a greater effect with aid of visuals.

(c) The emergence and use of large number of words has resulted in the distortion of the meaning or words. Words, however, would continue to occupy primacy in human communication in future despite the expansion of electronic media. "Better than a collection of thousand meaningless words is one word full of meaning on hearing which one becomes peaceful", says the Dhammapada.

(d) The Sadharanikaran theory underlines the role of communication. It is total communication and communication at its best. It is more integrated approach to communication because it seeks to affect the behaviour of human beings by arousing emotional and physical response simultaneously.

INDIAN SOCIETY AND COMMUNICATION

Indian society is often characterised as one of "unity in diversity" and its villages as "independent republics". These characterizations have important implications for the patterns of human communication in India.

In ancient India, cultures blossomed in different parts of the sub-continent. These were unique and independent of each other. These cultures derived strength and inspirations from each other. The merits of cultures were communicated through the long established oral tradition.

The roving saints and sufies performed the task of communicating messages. They propagated the gospels of truth enshrined in the Vedas, Puranas, epic stories like Ramayana and Mahabharata and other scriptures. They reinterpreted these messages. as per the realities prevailing in the society. In the process, they succeeded in communicating the norms values proper for decent social living.

At the communicating level, known as a class of knowledgeable people, Brahmins enjoyed the highest social status. They played an effective role as "link persons" between the common man of their own community and persons from outside the community.

Village communities were mostly self-sufficient. Each community had strong and extensive cultural links with other communities beyond the neighbouring villages and towns. Administrative contract were minimal, largely confined to revenue collection. Even this task was performed through intermediaries such as the Nawabs Zamindars and Lambardars. Thus, in ancient or traditional India, there existed effective systems of communication which were both local and pan-Indian in character. Such communication provided meaning and justification for the social order. It inculcated the spirit of devotion, love and faith.

Indian society was highly stratified and hierarchical. Communication tended to flow from persons of higher status to persons of lower status. In any communication situation, the relationship between the source and the receiver was that of dominance and subordination. In spite of this there as some dialogue between the two. Both shared a common frame of reference which made communication smooth and effective.

Emergence of Modem Mass Media

With the advent of British rule in India, there was an increase in administrative links, and physical mobility was encouraged through rails and roads. A new philosophy and culture spread by Macaulay's education system started making inroads into traditional Indian society and culture. The two were incompatible in many ways. However, the communication of foreign concepts, ideas and philosophies was successful as a lot of Indians accepted them. At the same time the conflict between the Indian and British ways of life became evident. As a consequence, there were upheavals, and turmoils, which ultimately led to the birth of independent India.

Free India has adopted democracy based on universal adult franchise as form of government. As welfare state it has opted for planned development. The technological growth and developments, huge development in communication and increases in the scale of economic activities have enlarged the range of choices. The philosophy of equality, irrespective of caste, creed and religion and the compulsions of democratic elections at all levels-village panchayats to the Parliament help to minimise the disadvantages of the traditional social and political relationships.

Communication is not confined only through to religion and practice of social norms. Its task is much more than maintaining the order and stability in society. Though the speaker is till viewed as an authority figure, particularly in rural areas and the listener as subordinate, such a relationship does not go unchallenged in many parts of our country to day. Tensions centred on such relationship do exit and report of social tensions from different parts of the country are frequently published. At the same time, there are situations where communication patterns are more on a basis of equality. Communication is no longer viewed only as a means to stability and harmony but for change as well. Thus communication in India has become a complex subject.

We are well aware of societal conditions that have given rise to various mass media. It is normally assumed that technology has been necessary for the reproduction of communications for mass audiences. Industrialisation, with the division of labour and urbanization, has created mass and heterogenous audiences. The proponents of this idea also hold that in the pre-industrial period, the communication system was restricted to direct face-to-face communication between individuals.

These assumptions, as far as India is concerned, are not wholly true. First, despite passing from the First Information and Communication Revolution the Indian society has largely retained the traditions of oral and interpersonal communication. Therefore, when we consider the distinguishing features of modern society, it is not the 'mass' of people that constitutes 'a mass society', but the relationships between the members. The western concept of mass society explains its heterogenous nature due to its being alienated by technology, socially differentiated due to occupation and physically separated through expansion of urbanisation. Thus the need to reach out to this highly "impersonalized" mass society, requires various "mass media" not only to bring together its members into mainstream, but also to seek their consent for social action.

However, in recent years, even among communication scholars, there has been tendency to transplant communication models from the West to developing countries. They have transplanted the idea that rational independent messages beamed at "individuals" will lead to motivation and attitude change. This basically the advertising and marketing model of a society believing in perfect competition.

We are now beginning to realise that there is another model of society in which the individual derives his legitimacy from the system. In such a society the role of "communication" is quite different. Therefore, attempts to inform, educate and motivate the individual in many a times do not succeed. However, messages with symbols appealing to the "collective" consciousness' many times do succeed. The Indian society, with its unique concept of the "collective" nature of interpersonal networks, affirms that while we keep our windows open to the world, our feet are rooted in the innate wisdom that has come down to us over the last 5000 years. It is within these parameters, that India's transition from the oral to the modern mass media-based society, has to perceive.

In India, the print media took roots first in the major provincial capitals of British Indian-Calcutta and Madras and later Bombay. These cities with their surrounding areas accounted for the bulk of their newspaper circulations. Advertising also developed in these metropolitan centres. As the freedom struggle gained momentum, newspapers were published from main centres of the agitation like Delhi, Lahore, Lucknow and Kanpur. Other newspaper centres were concentrated in the princely states of Mysore, Hyderabad, Bhopal and Baroda. These cities also had their own radio stations.

Newspaper readership continued to remain in urban areas. After independence the print medium emerged from its pre-colonial past and spread into the semi urban and rural areas. Advanced technology, better roads and transport helped the press to move into semi urban centres, but they were still rotted in the cities. A new class emerged the information rich who were already modernised, literate and economically well off. With development and growth of newspaper technology and sharp competition the costs of publishing a newspaper also rose. The advertising world the backbone of newspaper-hitched its wagon to the highly-circulated newspaper and magazines, fuelling the growing difference between big and small newspapers and magazines. The power of the print media attracted bit industrialists to invest in the newspaper industry. Monopolies and chain newspapers became the order of the day. Suddenly, the missionary zeal of preindependence days gave away to a competitive frenzy in commerce, Today we have chain-newspapers controlled by business tycoons who run them purely on commercial lines.

What has been the impact of newspapers on Indian society? A difficult question to answer. But a few pointers would give us somewhat clear picture. Newspapers have become a class medium, catering only to the rich and the powerful. However, the language newspapers do cater to the lower levels of society. But their reach and access are linked to literacy and capacity to purchase. According to present estimates, newspapers are purchased and read by less than 20 per cent of India's 900 million population. A wide gulf has been created between the "information-rich" and "information-poor". Instead of a democratising and bringing equity the newspapers have helped to perpetuate a class structure in society.

The broadcasting media though government conlrol, have the capacity to reach out to the people in every nook and corner of the country. While both are highly capital-intensive, it is their capacity to reach out to millions that makes them a people's medium. The development of Akashwani and Doordarshan in India has had its ups and downs, but today we have about 545 TV stations covering about 90 per cent of area and catering to about 60 per cent of the population. Radio has much wider reach and access. But in case of the two media, it is not the development of infrastructure that we need to look into, but their programme content and how it is being received by the people. It is in this area that both AIR and Doordarshan have not been found wanting. While "news" has been accepted as the important segment in their programme content, other aspects lime development and education have been given adequate attention. However, entertainment has become synonymous with these two corporations.

AIR has opened various channels for entertainment; but has failed to evoke the same kind of audience response to other development-oriented programmes as to entertainment. Even its educational programmes have restricted listenership. Researchers have pointed out to the lack of quality programmes over AIR.

Doordarshan has fared no better. The criticism levelled against AIR also applies to Doordarshan. The criticism levelled against Doordarshan is sometimes more severe as the policy formulated for it says that it should serve the developmental aspirations of the majority. The Doordarshan has ended up with more entertainment than any other type of programmes. Except for news and few current affairs programmes. DD largely depends on films and film-based programmes to fill in its telecast time criticism about lack of professionalism, creativity and production skills, have been levelled against DD. What has bean its impact on society? People do say that TV is an "idiot box" and has harmful effects on children. But TV is a tool of learning also and so far, has been well-received. Further, information on health, family planning and eradication of social evils like drugs, smoking, alcoholism and dowry, have all been successfully projected over Doordarshan.

Let us take another important mass medium-films. Films can be produced on almost all subjects of human interest and include, broadly speaking, feature films, documentaries and newsreels. The themes may encompass such diverse subjects as industry, agriculture -development, education, environment and vital national issues like family welfare, national integration and untouchability. In fact, a large number of films are not commercial in the usual sense. Contemporary film making more than ever before, is a big financial venture. It is usually controlled by commercial consideration rather than the demands of the art. The star system, lavish promotion and publicity and huge budgets for formula pictures are all frantic attempts to minimise the financial risk involve in film making. No wonder such films aim to please the audience by creating a synthetic worl·˙ of unreal emotions. They make no demands on the power of thinking and ignores are for the sake of commerce. Films seeks to attract the audience by providing rather glib and naive entertainment in order to covert people's childishness into cash. For the majority of the viewers, a film is day-dreaming device in which they forget their worries and get lost in world of fantasy-full of melodramatic sentiments, songs and dance, violence and sex. In fact, with only a few honourable exceptions cinema in India has been overwhelmingly entertainment-oriented almost since its beginning. The Indian film stars have exerted such a hypnotic hold on the masses that they have made a place for themselves in public life, politics and even influenced the living style of the people. Exceptional Indian Films, with their intens realism and abiding concern for the common map, have found their way to international acclaim. The emergence of the new cinema as a movement, presenting a modern humanistic approach, offered a refreshing contrast to the commercial cinema.

Video has grown to be a very popular mass medium within a remarkably short times. It has endless possibilities for entertainment and education. Video in India in India is largely perceived as an alternative source of entertainment. However, video news magazine has caught the popular fancy and many leading newspapers have come forward to launch news magazines in audio-visual form. Public sector companies have utilised the video medium for bringing out house journals. But video has also come to occupy an important place in political and poll campaigns in India.

Satellite Communication

A communication satellite is a man-made platform launched into space; it remains relatively stationary over the earth. It serves as a platform for radio relay stations which receive radio signals beamed to it from the earth and relays those signals back to other locations on earth. Satellite communication greatly benefitted the newspaper industry. It made possible fascimiles of newspaper pages to be sent electronically via satellite to receiving station anywhere in the world where printing facilities may be located.

The satellite distribution systems give the newspapers a flexibility hitherto not possible. Satellites now link news bureaus all over the country and can instantly transmit news reports to any station. Computers can automatically set the stories in type and start the process rolling. The cable TV system can receive programmes through satellite and deliver them by cable to subscribers' sets. In another form of transmission, called Direct Broadcast Satellite, television programmes are directly received by the dish antenna at home, totally bypassing the cable system.

But the strongest impact of TV comes through the Hong Kong-based STAR-TV, CNN, the BBC and Pakistan TV, using satellites to beam programmes right into our homes. There has been a furore over the role of these foreign satellite broadcasts, referred to as post-colonial cultural imperialism. They have made serious inroads into DD viewership. Innumerable dish antennae dot the horizon of Delhi, Bombay, Calcutta, Madras, Bangalore and Ahmedabad and a large number of smaller cities in the country. DD replied to this "invasion from the sky" by opening the 5 Metro channels to Indian viewers from August 15, 1993. It also hopes to use the terrestial links to further upgrade the coverage geographically. Multiplicity of channels has increased the choice for the viewers. The question always is as to which channel will win the audience-ratings race. It has been observed that a large majority of TV viewers seem to be convinced that the foreign-based TV channels, thought better produced, are not culturally conducive to a large number of viewers.

FUTURE OF COMMUNICATION IN INDIA

It should be obvious by now that for an Indian approach to communication a sound knowledge of its philosophical, cultural and linguistic traditions is necessary. It is also necessary to go to Sanskrit, as it may provide us with a lot of materials on communication which could be of use to communicate to our people properly and effectively. It is only by undertaking such kind of studies and by relating these to the demands of modern life that we will be able to re-cast and reframe our whole outlook toward communication concepts, norms and beliefs.

In this connection, we have to look at the trends in characteristic of the highly industrialised west and particularly of the USA. There, the are the science of communication have been mastered, but because of a highly materialistic focus, who are losing the true purpose of communication is lost sight of in their eagerness to consume more and provide themselves with more free time and leisure, the listener has unleashed a Frankensteinian unstoppable momentum to the growth of sophisticated technology. The wisdom of the East, from India and China, may help them to reframe their communication priorities.

It is a matter of concern, that the lure of technology is creating a wide gap among various communities and classes in Indian society. We require to prioritize our use of technology, particularly those needs related to the socio-cultural and linguistic demands. According to many scholars, catering to this large number of people with diverse needs has become a problem. Faced with spectre of proliferating communication technology, India is on the threshold of a giant leap forward. Just acquisition of communication technology may not help the Indian society. India has used a lot of communication technology in almost five decades since Independence. But the increase in the use of modern technology for development did not make our communication better. Analysis reveals that during this process of modernisation, very powerful political and economic forces have gained control over the communication system. This in turn had led to either distortion, discrimination of even total obstruction of the communication flow from and to the grassroot level. This has not only resulted in cultural erosion, but at the same time has pushed large masses of people below the poverty line of information. This needs to be guarded against. India with its teeming millions cannot afford to sustain an imbalanced system of communication.

This theme—popular entertainment is harmful to the minds of the young—has been a consistent one from the beginnings of mass communication. It has been claimed from time to time that such charges can be validated by scientific evidence, but repeatedly this evidence has turned out to be difficult to interpret and therefore controversial. Social sciences insist that any important conclusions about the effects of the media be supported by solid evidence. Because of such insistence upon data rather than emotion, they sometimes find themselves in the awkward position of seeming to defend the media when actually they are simply refusing to accept the inadequately supported claims of critics.

Nevertheless, the insistence that conclusions be based on adequate evidence has never deterred the literacy critic from charging the media with a deep responsibility for society's problems. Most nineteenth century American writers at some point in their careers took time to criticize and condemn the newspaper for superficiality and distortion.

THE BASICS OF FUNCTIONAL ANALYSIS

The *tenacity* and *stability* of the mass media generally in the face of such a long history of criticism by powerful voices needs explanation. The problem at first seems deceptively simple: the media appeal to the masses and the masses want the kind of content they get and so the media continue to give it to them.

Many social scientists, such as Skornia, have exposed the inadequacy of this explanation by nothing the old chicken-and-egg problem. It is difficult at best to know if the public taste determines the media fare or if the media fare determines public taste. The answer probably lies somewhere in between with public taste being. both a cause and effect of media fare. The relationship between public taste and media fare thus becomes a circular one which, in terms of the chicken-egg analogy, is an ongoing process of chickens producing eggs and eggs producing chickens.

The structural functional analysis of social systems (or "functional analysis" for short) concerns itself with the patterns of action exhibited by individuals or subgroups who relate themselves to one another within such systems. A social system is, for this reason, an abstraction but one not too far removed from the observable and empirically verifiable behaviours of the persons who are doing the acting. The social system, then, is a complex of stable, repetitive, and patterned action that is in part a manifestation of the culture shared by the actors, and in part a manifestation of the psychological orientations of the actors (which are in turn derived from that culture). The cultural system, the social system, and' the personality systems (of the individual actors), therefore, are different kinds of abstractions made from the same basic data, namely, the overt and symbolic behaviours of individual human beings. They are equally legitimate abstractions, each providing in its own right a basis for various kinds of explanations and predictions. Generally speaking, it may be difficult or nearly impossible to analyse or understand fully one such abstraction without some reference to the others.

But, granted that the term "social system" is a legitimate scientific abstraction, how does this general conceptual strategy help in understanding the mass media of communication? To answer this question, we need to set forth in greater detail exactly what is meant by the term social system, and what type of analysis it provides. To aid in providing such an explanation we turn briefly to several ideas that are important aspects of the study of social systems. One of the most important of these ideas is the concept of the function" of some particular repetitive phenomenon (set of actions) within such a system. The fact that such content has long survived the jibes of influential critics was said to require explanation. One form of explanation will be provided by noting the function of such a repetitive phenomenon within some stable system of action. The term" function" in the present context means little more than "consequence." To illustrate briefly, we might hypothesize that the repetitive practice of wearing wedding rings on the part of a given married couple has the function (consequence) of reminding, them as well as others that the two are bound together by the obligations and ties that matrimony implies. This practice thereby contributes indirectly to maintaining the permanence of the marriage—the stability of that particular social system. The practice is in a sense "explained" by noting its contribution to the context within which it occurs.

In the above example, the social system is a relatively simple one. There are only two "components," and each of these happen to be the behaviour pattern of an individual. Their patterns are derived both from the individual psychological makeup of the partners and from the cultural norms concerning marriage prevailing in their community, social class, and society. It is a miniature system whose stability is dependent upon satisfaction of its "needs." For example, such a system requires that the partners perform roles that meet the expectations each has of the other and the expectations the community has of married couples. This can be thought of as a "need" for adequate role performance, without which the stability of the system would be endangered. Other "needs," related to economic matters and emotional satisfactions, could be cited.

More complex illustrations of social systems can easily be pointed to, where the "components" of the system are not the actions of individual persons but sub-systems. A department store, for example, is a complex social system consisting of the actions of managerial personnel, buyers, salespersons, the clerical staff, customers, transportation workers, a janitorial team,and security employees. Each of these components is a smaller system of action within the broader system of the store itself, and it in turn is a complex system of action carried out within the context of the external social conditions of the community. In spite of the complexity, any given set of repetitive actions might be analysed in terms of their contribution to maintaining or undermining the system's stability. Granting to employees the right to buy merchandise at cost could have the function (consequence) of maintaining their morale and loyalty, and thus would contribute fairly directly to the maintenance of the system. Rigid insistence on the observance of petty rules, such as docking the pay of an employee who on rare occasions was late for work, might be disruptive of morale and loyalty, and by contributing to labour turnover it could be dysfunctional. Instead of contributing to the maintenance of the system, it could cause disruptions and instability. Such inductively derived conclusions would be subject to testing for validity, of course, but the functional analysis would have generated the hypothesis to be tested (an important role of theory).

Structure and Function in Media Systems

A "functional analysis," then, focuses on some specific phenomenon occurring within a social system. It then attempts to show how this phenomenon has consequences that contribute to the stability and permanence of the system as a whole. The phenomenon may, of course, have a negative influence, and if so, it would be said to have "dysfunctions" rather than "functions." The analysis is a strategy for inducing or locating hypotheses that can be tested empirically by comparative studies or other appropriate research methods.

The analysis of social system is extremely difficult, No infallible rules specify precisely how to locate and define the exact boundaries of a given social system, particularly if it is relatively complex. As yet, no completely agreed upon criteria exist for establishing linkages between the components of a system, and no standard formulas can uncover the precise contribution that a given repetitive form of action makes to the stability of a system. A functional analysis of the contribution of some item to the stability of a system, then, is a procedure that is somewhat less than rigorous. But in spite of this source of potential criticism, this strategy has proved useful in our attempts to understand complex social phenomena, such as the mass media.

Low-taste Content as a Repetitive Phenomenon

How can this type of analysis be applied to the mass media? First, we can identify that portion of the content of the mass media that is in "low" cultural taste or provides gratifications to the mass audience in such a manner that it is widely held to be potentially debasing as the "relatively persistent trait or disposition" of the mass media we seek to explain. It would be difficult in practice to construct a set of categories under which to analyse the content of the media so that material of "low" cultural taste can be identified readily. It would be difficult, but actually it would not be impossible. Excessive violence, the portrayal of criminal techniques, horror and monster themes, open pornography, suggestive music, and dreary formula melodramas are typical categories of content that arouse the ire of critics. Considerable disagreement would probably occur as to the exact content that should be included in any given category. There would also be debates over the number of categories used. There would also be debates over the number of categories used. Nevertheless, it is theoretically possible to identify the content of any given medium that is most objected to by the largest number of critics. We will assume that given sufficient time and resources, and using survey techniques, preference scales, attitude measuring instruments, and other research procedures now available that the content of any given medium could be divided roughly into something like the following three categories:

> **Low-taste Content.** This would be media content widely distributed and attended to by the mass audience, but which has consistently aroused the ire of critics. Examples would be crime dramas on television that emphasize violence, openly pornographic motion pictures, day time, confession magazines, crime comics, suggestive music or other content that has been widely held to contribute to a lowering of taste, disruption of morals, or stimulation toward socially unacceptable conduct. (Whether or not such charges are true.)

> **Nondebated Content.** This would be media content, widely distributed and attended to, about which media critics have said very little. It is not an issue in the debate over the impact of the media on the masses. Examples would be television weather reports, some news content, music that is neither symphonic nor popular, magazines devoted to specialized interests, motion pictures using "wholesome" themes, and many others. Such content is not believed either to elevate or lower taste, and it is not seen as a threat to moral standards.

High-taste Content. This would be media content sometimes widely distributed but not necessarily widely attended to. It is content that media critics feel is in better taste, morally uplifting, educational, or in some way inspiring. Examples would be serious music, sophisticated drama, political discussions, art films, or magazines devoted to political commentary. Such content is championed by critics as the opposite of the low-taste material, which they see as distinctly objectionable.

Of course, the first of the above categories is the one to which we wish to direct most of our attention. It is the repetitive phenomenon whose contribution to the media (as a social system) needs analysis. Nevertheless, it would also be possible to study the other two categories with somewhat parallel perspectives, but this will receive relatively little attention in the present discussion.

Components and Boundaries of the System

We need now to begin to identify the components and boundaries of the social system within which low-taste content occurs so that eventually the contribution it makes to the system can be inductively hypothesized.

Rather than develop a purely descriptively scheme that will apply only to a single medium, it will be more fruitful to attempt to develop a general conceptual scheme into which any or all media could be placed, with suitable minor modifications in details. Such a general scheme will emphasize the similarities between media, particularly in terms of relationships between the components in the system.

Audiences. The first major component of the social system of mass communication is the audience. This is an exceedingly complex component. The audience is stratified, differentiated, and interrelated in the many ways that social scientists have studied for years. Some of the major variables that play a part in determining how this component will operate within the system are the major needs and interests of audience members, the various social categories represented in an audience, and the nature of the social relationships between audience members. These variables point to behavioural mechanisms that determine the patterns of attention, interpretation, and response of an audience with respect to content of a given type.

Research Organisations. The rough typology of content suggested is in some degree related to the characteristics of the audience. Organizations devoted to research, to measuring the performances of media audiences, or to various forms of market research provide information to those responsible for selecting the categories of content that will be distributed to the audience. There is a link, then, between the audience as a component in the system and the market research-rating service organizations as a second component. In purely theoretical terms, both components are role system themselves and are thus actually sub-systems. This is in a sense a one-way link. For very minor (or usually no) personal reward, audience members selected for study provide data about themselves to such an agency, but very little flows back. This linkage between components is by comparison relatively simple.

Distributors. The content itself, of whatever type, flows from some distributor to the audience. The role system of the distributor component varies in detail from one medium to another. In addition, several somewhat distinct sub-systems exist within this general component. First, there are local outlets, which are likely to be in the most immediate contact with the audience. The local newspaper, the local theatre, the local broadcasting station play the most immediate part in placing messages before their respective audiences. But inseparably tied to them are other sub-systems of this general component. Newspaper syndicates, broadcasting networks, or chains of movie theatres pass content on to their local outlets. The link between these two sub-systems is a two-way one. The local outlet provides money, and the larger distributor supplies content. Or the link age may be that the local outlet provides a service, and the distributor (who is paid elsewhere) provides money.

The relationship between audience and distributor seems at first to be mostly a one-way link. The distributor provides entertainment content (and often advertising), but the audience provides little back in a direct sense. However, it does provide its attention. In fact, it is precisely the attention of the audience that distributors are attempting to solicit. They sell this "commodity" directly to their financial backer or sponsor. In addition, the audience supplies information to the research component and this is indirectly supplied to distributors in the form of feedback so that they may gauge the amount of attention they are eliciting. The linkages between components grow more complex as we seek the boundaries of the system.

Producers and Their Sponsors. To the audience, the research, and the distributing component, we may add the role system of the producer of content. This component's primary link is with the financial backer (or sponsor) component and with the distributor, from whom money is obtained and for whom various forms of entertainment content are manufactured. A host of sub-systems are included in this producer component, depending upon the particular medium. Examples are actors, directors, television producers, technicians, foreign correspondents, wire-service editors, film producers, labour union leaders, publishers, copyeditors, clerical staff, and many, many more.

Advertising Agencies. Linking the sponsor, distributor, producer, and research organization are the advertising agencies. Paid primarily by the sponsor, this component provides (in return) certain ideas and services. For the most part, it provides the distributor with advertising messages. It may have links with the research component as well.

Sub-systems of Control. Over this complex set of interrelated components, there are other sub-systems that exert control. The legislative bodies, at both the state and national level, which enact regulative statutes concerning the media, constitute an important part of such a control component. Another important part of this role sub-system is the official regulative agencies, which implement the policies that have been legislated. The link between the legislative body (control component) and the audience is, course, one of votes and public opinion, to which the component is presumably sensitive and dependent. Information lines between audience, legislative bodies, and regulatory agencies are more or less open. To the regulatory components whose role definitions are found in legal statute can be added the private voluntary associations that develop "codes" and to some degree serve as a control over the distributors. Such distributors provide them with money, and they in turn provide surveillance and other services.

The regulatory sub-systems draw definitions of permissible and non-permissible content from the general set of external conditions within which this extremely complicated system operates. Surrounding the entire structure as an external condition are our society's general norms concerning morality, and the expressions that these find in formal law. Similar, although less likely to be incorporated into law, are our general cultural norms and beliefs regarding what will be likely to entertain or otherwise gratify Americans. Thus, we seldom see traditional Chinese opera but frequently see western horse opera. We seldom hear the strains of Hindu temple music but frequently hear the "strains" and other noises of the latest singer whom teen-agers admire. If our interests run to more serious fare, we are likely to hear the music of a relatively small list of European or American composers who created their works within a span of about three centuries.

Each of the several media will fit into this general model of a social system in slightly different ways. A complete description of each of the media separately would be tedious. Indeed, each could well occupy the contents of an entire book. Two decades ago, Opotowsky attempted just such a detailed analysis of the television industry, although he did not use the social system concept.

To add to the complexity of this conceptual scheme, it must be remembered that although each medium constitutes a somewhat separate social system in itself, the media are also related to one another in systematic ways. Thus, we may speak of the entire set of communication media, including those which have not been specifically analysed in the present volume, as the mass communication system of the United States.

Maintaining Systems Stability

Within the system itself, the principal internal condition is, of course, a financial one. Most of the components in the system are occupational role structures, which motivate their incumbent personnel primarily through money. To obtain money, they are all ultimately dependent upon the most central component of all the audience. Unless its decisions to give attention, to purchase, to vote, and the like, are made in favourable ways, the system would undergo service strain and would eventually collapse.

Almost any dramatic change in the behaviour of the audience would cause the most severe disruption in the system for any given medium. In an earlier chapter, the swift acquisition of television sets by the movie audience was plotted. The consequences of attention loss to the motion picture theatre as a mass medium was shown to be severe. Such disruptions are infrequent, buy they do occur. The key to heading off dramatic changes in audience behaviour, of course, is to provide entertainment content that will satisfy and motivate the largest possible number of audience members to carry out their roles in accord with the needs of the system. Such content will, in other words, maintain the stability of the system. The ideal, from the standpoint of the system, is content that will capture audience members' attention, persuade them to purchase goods, and at the same time be sufficiently within the bounds of moral norms and standards are not provoked.

The entertainment content that seems most capable of eliciting the attention of the largest number of audience members is the more dramatic, low-taste content. Since the most central media system goal is economic profit, sex and violence or any other attention-getting and attention-maintaining content is functional in the sense that even though it may be of low-taste, it maximizes the size of the audience exposed to advertisements. In general, the larger the audience, the more the distributor and producer can charge for advertising.

The assumption made by many media personnel and advertisers that low-taste content appeals primarily to the relatively uneducated, who still constitute a majority of the potential audience, may be false. In an early study Wilensky found that educated people said that they preferred and exposed themselves to high-taste content more often than did the relatively uneducated. But when observations were made of what the educated and educated actually aid, there was little difference between their levels of exposure to low-taste media content.

There is a great deal of evidence to show that the relatively uneducated spend more time than the educated being exposed to the mass media. It may be misleading to conclude that they do so only because the ureducated relish low-taste content. The relatively uneducated majority also have relatively low incomes, which probably means they have less choice than their more educated and wealthier counterparts in how they spend their non-working hours. The mass media may be more appealing to the relatively uneducated and poor in large part because the media are relatively inexpensive forms of leisure. Moreover, as Baker and Ball point out, it is probably superficial to think that the only reason people in general spend time with the media is because of the inherent appeal of their content.

When all is said and done, however, it is still true that low-taste content sells-and sells big. This fact establishes it as the key element in the social system of the media. It keeps the entire complex together by maintaining the financial stability of the system. Critics who provoke public attention by denouncing media content or by proclaiming that a casual connection exists between media content and socially undesirable behaviour may temporarily receive some recognition. They may also achieve some 'temporary disturbance in the system, or if they are persistent enough, they may ultimately even displace some specific from of low-taste content from a given medium altogether. Examples from the past are quiz shows that were found to be "rigged," and popular disc jockeys who were receiving "payola" (a fee for repeatedly playing a song to make it popular). In such cases the audience may be temporarily disaffected, lowtaste content comes in such a variety of forms that the temporary or even permanent absence of one minor form does not alter the major picture. Critics have been complaining about newspaper concentration on crime news for a century, yet there has been no noticeable abatement in the reporting of such stories. Critics of the soap opera may have breathed a sigh of relief several years ago when these programmes at last disappeared from radio. Their joy must have been short-lived when such daytime serials turned out to be quite popular with television viewers, so popular in fact that soap operas now appear during prime evening hours. Analyses of the level of violent television content show that it goes down slightly after federal government investigations on the effects of television violence or widespread campaigns by voluntary associations (*e.g.*, the P.T.A.), only to return shortly after the public outcry nas subsided.

When a formula is discovered for eliciting attention and influencing purchasing decisions from any large segment of the audience, it will be abandoned by the media only with great reluctance, if at all. The broadcast ballgame, the war movie, the star comedian, the family situation comedy, the western thriller, the detective story, the adventures of the secret agent, the drama of the courtroom all are beginning to rank with such time honoured formulas as the sob story, the funnies, the sex-murder account, the sports page, and disclosure of corruption in high places as attention-getting devices that can bring the eye or ear of the consumer nearer to the advertising message.

In short, the social system of the mass media in the United States is becoming more and more deeply established. Some future change can be expected in the kind of content it will produce to maintain its own stability. At present, however, the function of what we have called low-taste content is to maintain the financial stability of a deeply institutionalized social system that is tightly integrated with the whole of the American economic institution. The probability that our system of mass communication in this respect can be drastically altered by the occasional outbursts of critics seems small indeed. Far more likely than media system change brought about by periodic attacks on low-taste media content is media system change brought about by trends in the economic system such as the emergence of a "post-industrial" society. Because the media system is also a sub-system in the larger economic system, it will have to adapt to such changes if it is to survive. If Bell's forecast that systems in the business of producing, processing, and transmitting information will become increasingly involved in key economic sectors of our society is valid, then we would expect significant changes in the nature of the mass media system. One change would surely be a marked increase in the knowledge and technical information of "nondebated" media content will rise sharply with a corresponding decline in low-taste media content.

DEVELOPMENT COMMUNICATION AND CULURAL CONTEXT

Development Communication

'Development Communication' (or simply 'Devcom') emerged as a field of mass communication studies during the post-World War II years when the countries of Asia, Africa and South America were asserting their right to independence, self-reliance and nonalignment. These very same countries were in a hurry to find solutions to the most urgent needs of their people the eradication of poverty, illiteracy and unemployment. Colonial rule had established massive bureaucracies, skeleton transport and communication infrastructures, few educational and professional institutes, and fewer industries and public services. Centralized economic planning, large-scale industrialisation and the development of the mass media appeared at the time to be the most effective strategies for 'catching up' with the industrialized nations. This indeed was the advice proffered by Western financial institutions, United Nations experts, and foreign advisers to national governments.

Models of Development Communication

Perhaps the most influential work in the emergence and growth of Development Communication as a field of mass communication studies was Daniel Lerner's The Passing of Traditional Society, sub-titled 'Modernizing the Middle-east.' But this study was not the work of an individual but rather part of a large research project of the Bureau of Applied Social Research (BASR), at the Columbia University in New York City. The project was funded by the voice of America (VOA) which was keen on finding out the extent of listenership to this overseas service which was promoted and funded directly by the United States government. The Cold War against the Soviet Union and Communism was a major driving force for the establishment of the VOA, and for supporting such research projects.

Lerner was an Intelligence Officer of the United States army during the War, and was now involved in social research projects. He looked upon the mass media, especially radio, as the means for bringing about development of newly independent nations. They were the forces which would motivate people to turn their backs on tradition and embrace 'modernization', which a close reading of his novelistic account of his experiences in the Middle East reveals, he equated with 'Westernization.' He regarded his model of 'modernization' to be universally relevant and applicable. The media were for Lerner, powerful tools for changing people's perceptions, attitudes and aspirations. At least that was what he argued for in his pane to the 'modern' in the fascinating tale of his encounters in the Middle East.

Diffusion of Innovations

Everett Rogers was an Iowa farm-boy trained in modern agriculture. He found his home community less than impressed with his stock of innovations in agriculture; outside his country he had a marked influence in the field of agricultural extension, through his textbook on The *Diffusion of Innovations*, which over the years has been expanded and updated into the second and third editions.

Rogers developed his concepts and theories of the diffusion of innovations from a synthesis of diffusion research studies in the United States, and in later editions, of diffusion studies in the developing world as well. Rogers defined an 'innovation' as 'an idea perceived as new by the individual.' 'It really matters little, as far as human behaviour is concerned', he added, 'whether or not an idea is 'objectively' new as measured by the amount of time elapsed since its first use or discovery. It is the newness of the idea to the individual that determines his reaction to it.' In later editions, however, an 'innovation' is no more just an 'idea'; it is also a 'practice or object perceived as new by an individual.'

Indeed, by the third edition, Rogers begins to use 'technology' as a synonym for 'innovation', and to urge the adoption of a 'convergence model' that stresses the intricacy of 'interpersonal communication networks' that are in operation during the process of diffusion.

In the mid-seventies, Rogers proclaimed the passing of; dominant paradigm the modernization model though apparently excluding his own 'diffusion of innovation' model, the basic principles of which were derived from the United States experience of agricultural extension, He propagated his model of modernization in developing countries urging that it had cross-cultural applications, Rogers' work was in fact an extension of Lerner's; he adopted Lerner's notions of 'empathy', 'cosmopoliteness', and 'attitude change'; his unit of analysis was the individual, and his main concern was with the 'social mind', and the change of culture, attitudes and ideas.

Magic Multipliers

Wilbur Schramm extended the arguments of Lerner and Rogers in favour of 'modernization' through the mass media which he termed 'the magic multipliers.' His work was part of the efforts of the United Nations and UNESCO for a programme of concrete action to build up press, radio broadcasting, film and television facilities in countries in the process of economic and social development. The survey itself on which the book was base was carried out by UNESCO during a series of meetings in Bangkok, Santiago and Paris.

To Schramm, as to mainstream social scientists of the time, the mass media were 'agents of social change', 'almost miraculous' in their power to bring about that change. Schramm argued that the mass media could help accomplish the transitions to new customs and practices (the 'innovations' of Rogers) and, in some cases, to different social relationships. Behind such changes in behaviour must necessarily lie substantial changes in attitudes, beliefs, skills and social norms'. The process, he elaborated was simple: first, the awareness of a need which is not satisfied by present customs and behaviour; second, the need to invent or borrow behaviour that comes close to meeting the need. Hence a nation that wants to accelerate the process of development will try to make its people more widely and quickly aware of needs and of the opportunities for meeting them, will facilitate the decision process, and will help the people put the new practices smoothly and swiftly into effect. Schramm went further than Rogers in taking account of cultural linkages, in acknowledging 'resistance to change' and in urging 'an understanding participation.' However, his model of communication was still manipulative of behaviour towards the desired end of innovation adoption; it still cited as empirical evidence a strong correlation between high media exposure and development. Schramm argued forcefully that the mass media had the potential to widen horizons, to focus attention, to raise aspirations and to create a climate for development. They also had the potential to confer status, to enforce social norms, to help form tastes, and could affect attitudes lightly held. He was optimistic about the potential of the mass media (and also the educational media such as programmed instruction, language laboratories, electronic digital computers) in all types of education and training. Unlike Rogers, he conceded though that 'the mass media can help only indirectly to change strongly held attitudes and valued practice.'

He therefore recommended that 'a developing country should review its restrictions on the importing of informational materials, should not hesitate to make use of new technical developments in communication, in cases where these new developments fit its needs and capabilities.' The challenge, he concluded, was to put the resources and the power of modern comttlunication skillfully and fully behind economic and social development. He described as fortuitous, 'almost miraculous' that modem mass communications should be available to multiply informational resources. So carried away was Schramm by his messianic role that he observed in a final flourish: 'it is hardly possible to imagine national economic and social development without some modern information multiplier; and indeed, without mass communication probably the great freedom movements and national stirrings of the last few decades would never have come about at all.' Such was the faith of the purveyors of 'modernization' models.

Structuralist Models

By the mid-seventies, however, evaluation reports of 'extension' programmes in the non-aligned world indicated that the consequences of 'modernization' had been disastrous. While there had been some successes in agricultural, health, nutrition and educational extension programmes, the main beneficiaries were the better-off sections of society. There was little evidence of the hoped for 'trickle down' effect; the diffusion of innovations that was believed to have brought about the Green Revolution, for instance, benefitted the richer landowners and farmers, and the expansion of the mass media network was used for political propaganda or for the entertainment of the urban middle-class rather than for development purposes. Indeed, the knowledge-gaps between the haves and the have-nots had widened since access to the mass media was still restricted to the elites. Where serious attempts to use mass media for development were made, bureaucracies and their collusion with the better off and higher-caste groups rendered most projects ineffective. Rural social structures were such that all attempts to reach the poorest of the poor were scotched.

At the international level, the main beneficiaries were the big powers and their industries, the multinational companies and the financing banks and institutions. The harmful effects of 'modernisation' policies were incalculable. Several countries in Africa and South America were turned into one-crop cultures (the single crop was usually a 'cash crop' needed in industrialized countries) and into importers of foodgrains. Further, large scale industrialization and urbanization (the 'hallmarks of modernisation') had led to massive migration from rural areas to the cities, and greater technological dependence on the more advanced countries. This dependence was also increased in the information and cultural industries (both in hardware and software) since the principle of 'free flow' prevailed.

'Dependency' models came to the fore in the early 'seventies as a reaction to 'modernization' models. These new theories were the product of the application of Marxist theories of imperialism, though both Marxists and non-Marxists were instrumental in articulating them. There were in fact various influences at work, such as 'liberation theology'. Freirian thinking on the pedagogy of the oppressed through 'conscientization', Schumacher's advocacy of 'appropriate technologies', popular grassroots movements (*e.g.* formation of 'base Christian communities' in several Latin American countries, and the Sarvodaya Movement in Sri Lanka), and alternative communication strategies (*e.g.* radio schools in Latin America, and people's theatre in India).

The original version of 'dependency and underdevelopment' theory was outlined by Paul Baran and Andre Gunder Frank. The primary concern was finding out the causes of backwardness of the non-allgned countries within the dynamics of the world capitalist system. They assumed that 'underdevelopment' was due, not to some 'original state of affairs' but the result of the same historical process by which the now developed capitalist countries became economically advanced and industrialized. Thus, Baran argued that underdevelopment was the obverse side of development; the capitalist countries had become 'developed' by exploiting the colonies for centuries. Such economic exploitation had left the colonies with a narrowly-specialized, export-oriented primary production structure managed by an elite which shared the cultural lifestyle and tastes of the dominant lasses in capitalist states. This elite continues to perpetuate. the rule of the ex-colonies; hence a kind. of neo-imperialism still prevails.

Andre Gunder Frank elaborated the theory by postulating three 'laws' of motion of the process of development and underdevelopment, and coining the twin concept 'metropolissatellite, to characterize the nature of imperialist economic relations. The ties of dominance and dependency, he explained, run in chain-like fashion throughout the global capitalist system, with 'metropolitan' (or 'centre') states appropriating the surplus from the 'satellites' (or 'periphery').

The Economic Commission for Latin America (ECLA) under the leadership of Raoul Prebisch propounded 'dependency theory' along similar lines. It saw a 'structural' link between development and underdevelopment. ECLA's economists emphasised self-reliant development through industrialization import-substitution though under the aegis of foreign investment. However, the consequence of following this strategy led to greater rather than less dependence on advanced countries for finance, marketing, capital goods, technology design, etc. Indeed, it led to even further underdevelopment, what with the presence of foreign industrial subsidiaries, and the growing balance-of-debts situation, the dumping of obsolete equipment and technologies. Thus 'dependency theories' lost their radical appeal to the peasants and workers.

A structuralist who merits attention here is Emile McAnany, who focuses attention both on the external and internal structures in society and communications in order to explain 'underdevelopment.' He argues that social, economic and political structures enter into the formation of the problems of the poor. He believes that communication has a modest role to play in development, but the necessary condition of this role will be some changes in the environment other than the addition of information.

Alternative Approaches

The eighties have seen a number of critical scholars proposing approaches to development communications that are alternative to both the 'modernization' and 'dependency' approaches. These are in the main non-Marxist approaches; they reject the economism and universal relevance of earlier models. The focus of these 'alternative' approaches is on the social and cultural identities of nations as well as on the external factors that inhibit all-round development. Some of the communication scholars associated with these 'culturalist' approaches include Goran Hedebro, Jan Servaes, Majid Teharanian and Hamid Mowlana.

Other contemporary scholars have underlined the need for 'self-reliance' in any attempt at national development. Non-aligned nations in particular have made demands in international fora like the United Nations for the establishment of a new international economic order (NIEO) and a 'new world information and communication order' (NWICO) so that the domination of the world economy by the big powers is reduced. Self-reliance models attempt to link the NIEO with the need for national development strategies based on autonomous development. No longer is development envisaged to be an externalization movement whose motor of development of trade and technological transfers from outside but as a process of mobilization of local resources with a view to satisfying local needs. The Arusha Programme for collective self-reliance and the framework for negotiations drawn up in February 1979 by the, Group of Seventy Seven, gives expression to this strategy. The Success of the non-aligned movement, China's Great Leap Forward, and the writings of Mahatma Gandhi, Mao Tse Dong and Paulo Freire have provided the inspiration for selfreliant development.

Rajni Kothari, Director of the Centre for the Study of Developing Societies, New Delhi, has been a well-known advocate of the 'self-reliant' and 'humane' development model. However, he stresses the need for looking at self-reliance in 'the context of the rise of new movements and new actors, on the scene.' The new movements are the ecological, the feminist, the movements for peace and for self-determination and democratization. The human rights movement too is gathering strength among bonded labour, the landless, miners, fisher-folk, ethnic minorities and women. But these movements are pitted against governments that are increasingly becoming militarized through arms deals, and against elites that indulge in rampant consumerism. Further, there is a 'transnationalization' of the world's economy; indeed a revival of old paradigms of development through a free market economy, monetarism, export-oriented growth, free trade zones, the adoption of new technologies, and the depoliticization of development. The role of communication in such a situation, urges Kothari, is to be 'part and parcel of the struggle for human liberation, freedom and justice, strengthening the struggles of communities, cultures, and of the marginalized, and to make their voices heard. Communication should be a process that contains the forces of backlash and the forces of transformation and survival. The human rights dimension needs. to be built into the new development paradigm; human survival, and a just, demilitarized and humane society should be the main aims of this development paradigm. Kothari sees human survival as a dynamic force projecting a positive alternative to the theory of progress and the goal of affluence, one that finds dignity in genuine equity and in diverse cultures working out their own strategies in local movements for democracy and autonomy. Global problems, local solutions, he argues, are no mere slogan; it is the very condition of human survival.

Modernization Models

The dominant paradigm of modernisation never really passed. Though communication and development scholars turned their back on it, national governments, the power blocs and the transnationals continued to practise and propagate the old paradigms. 'Catching up' with the advanced industrialized countries continues to remain the ambition of national governments. What is more, the new technologies offered governments greater means of control and surveillance over their large populations.

As the eighties drew to a close, there was a vigorous revival of 'modernization' both in theory and practice, particularly in the aftermath of rapid developments in telecommunications and the new technologies. Rural development was once again the focus of attention but not through the mass media as much as through 'telecommunications.' The term 'telecommunications' entered the field of development communication in the early eighties and came to include not only the broadcast media but also the telephone and related technologies such as tele-conferencing, audio conferencing, and satellite communications. Several rural telecommunications projects were launched in Alaska, India, Indonesia and the South Pacific-mainly with the assistance of international donor agencies.

The evidence from these projects seemed to indicate that there were linkages between telephony and rural development, that telephony was a cause rather than a consequence of development.

The organizations promoting this 'revival' were the International Telecommunication Union (ITU), the OECD, the World Bank, USAID, IBD (the Inter-American Development Bank), and IPDC. The Maitland Commission Report became the bible of this telecommunication approach to development. Some of the assumptions of this approach were: telecommunication use benefits the society and the economy, improves cost-benefits of rural social service delivery, improves cost-benefits for rural economic activities, permits more equitable distribution of economic benefits, and facilitates social change and improved quality of life.

Other 'new' technologies too, such as video and computers, are currently being propagated as tools for quickening the pace of development. The Technology Mission and the Telecommunications Commission launched in India in the late eighties were, for instance, dedicated to development through technology. Urgency has been attached to the modernization of communication infrastructure. In 1981, a Committee on Telecommunication was set up by the Indian

Government. The Committee recommended that digital technology for both switching and transmission be used in future telecommunication networks. In 1984 the Centre for Development of Telematics (C-DOT) was established to develop indigenous digital switching equipment. The phenomenal expansion of telephony, the liberalization of government policy in the area of electronics and computers, and the opening up of the Indian economy to foreign capital, has been the result of the new thrust towards technological solutions. In 1998, the BJP-led coalition at the Centre, established a National Task Force on Information Technology and Software; later, the States followed suit with their own Information Technology committees, to liberalise the sector, and thereby promote private enterprise and foreign investments. Both the Centre and the States went all out to woo telecom and IT multinationals such as AT & T, Microsoft, IBM, Oracle and others to set up shop in India.

Need for National and International Regulations

Telecommunications, computing, video, interactive video, and other new technologies are not necessarily 'appropriate' to all non-aligned countries. In fact, the use of these capital technologies could only lead to further dependence on transnational corporations and the power-blocs that support them. Free enterprise and export-oriented economies in southeast and east Asia, for instance, have succeeded in 'catching up' with the industrialized powers, though at tremendous human cost. Development economists hold them up as 'models' to other non-aligned countries, but socio-economic and geopolitical conditions vary so much from country to country that all talk of 'models' of communication or development support communication seems irrelevant. In the ultimate analysis, the search for grand universal paradigms of development communication is futile; each country or community must find its own path in terms of its values and culture, its resources and ideals, but respecting human rights, basic-needs, social justice, and the world's fragile ecology and its ever-depleting energy and other resources. International regulations on arms trade, the dumping of poisonous wastes, the activities of transnational corporations who are often a law unto themselves, the use of space for surveillance and military purposes, the trade imbalances between and among nations, are imperative for the survival of nations and of mankind itself.

Media, Development and Social Change

From the early stages of the introduction of the mass media in India various attempts were made to exploit their potential for developmental purposes. As early as 1933, rural radio listening communities were formed in Bhiwandi (near Bombay) and rural programmes were broadcast regularly in Marathi, Gujarati and Kannada. Allahabad and Dehra Dun beamed their first rural broadcasts in 1936, and by 1939 there were over a hundred community radio sets for rural listening in the North West Frontier Province alone.

Mahatma Gandhi, the Communicator

The Government take-over transformed Indian broadcasting into a political instrument, highly centralized and controlled. Rural development programmes were broadcast. in the local languages, and community sets installed in rural areas, but the main thrust of broadcasting was political. The World War and the need to counteract enemy propaganda and to hold in check the rising nationalist aspirations under the leadership of Mahatma Gandhi necessitated further expansion of broadcasting, and of stricter control. At independence there were nine AIR stations and a few independent native stations, but providing no access to the leaders of the freedom struggle. Mahatma Gandhi spoke just once over radio, and that was three months prior to his assassination. Yet he was able to mobilize the masses (even in the remotest areas) who themselves had little access to the mass media.

Gandhiji did make good use of the nationalist press and his own journals—Young India, Navijivan, Indian Opinion and Harijan but these were restricted in influence to the urban literates of the country. But he knew that the secret of reaching out to the hearts of the millions in the rural areas was the age-old oral tradition, and the padyatra. There was no substitute for direct, non-mediated communication through meetings and discussion, through song and prayer, and through the folk media.

Role of TV in Promoting Literacy and Social Change

Two experiments in rural television have been conducted in recent years with the prime objective of bringing about social change and development. Both were launched in 1975; the more ambitious programme was SITE-the Satellite Instructional Television Experiment; the second was the more modest Kheda Communication project.

SITE (Satellite Instructional Television Experiment)

In 1967 a UNESCO expert mission conducted, with the cooperation of the Indian Government, a study on the use of a satellite for national development. It recommended that since conditions were favourable such a start should be made. Accordingly, in 1969 the Department of Atomic Energy entered into an agreement with the National Aeronautic and Space Administration (NASA) of the United States for the loan of a satellite free of cost for one full year starting from August 1975. It was the first experiment ever to relay educational television programmes direct (not from relay stations) from a satellite to receivers (with front-end converters) in 2400 villages (some unelectrified) scattered over six selected regions in Orissa, Madhya Pradesh, Bihar, Rajasthan, Andhra Pradesh and Karnataka. Besides, conventional receivers in 2500 villages and towns got the programmes through earth transmitters, which picked up the satellite signals through Receive-only Stations.

SITE Programmes

The four-hour telecast beamed every day from earth stations at Delhi and Ahmedabad concentrated on programmes on education, agriculture, health and family planning. These were planned and produced by AIR at Production Centres set up in Delhi, Hyderabad and Cuttack, with the help of committees which included Central and State Government representatives and experts from universities, teacher training colleges, and social workers. Besides, the ISRO (Indian Space Research Organisation) set up its own Audio-Visual Instruction Division to plan and produce programmes according to schedule.

However, as the satellite had only one video channel and two audio channels it could transmit just one picture at a time with synchronised sound in two different languages. So it was possible to beam programmes to only two linguistic regions at a time.

School Telecasts. Of the 4-hour daily telecast, an hour and a half was aimed at pre-primary and primary school children aged 5 to 12. During this duration, programmes were telecast for 22 minutes each day in Telegu, Kannada, Oriya and Hindi and were watched on community receivers installed in schools, so that TV was regarded as part of the education system. Adults watched social education programmes later on the same sets.

The goals of these school broadcasts were two-fold:

(1) To make school more interesting, and so reduce the drop out rate.

(2) To improve children's basic concepts and skills, promote aesthetic sensitivity, instill habits of healthy living, bringing awareness of modernisation of life and society.

'The observed fact that the school enrolment of the drop-out rate was not affected by the introduction of TV in schools proves that these factors depend primarily on social and economic parameters and not on the attractiveness or otherwise of the school curriculum; the children do not have an independent choice in the matter. So unless circumstances are changed so that parents do not have to make, use of child labour for economic reasons, TV in schools is not going to affect enrolment or the drop-out rate.'

Agriculture. The Ministry of Agriculture set out the following objectives for SITE:

(1) Dissemination information and demonstration of dry land farming etc., advice on poultry and animal husbandry, recommendation of practices for crops and their management, and so forth.

(2) Broadcast of information regarding organisations in districts which are responsible for supply of agriculture inputs such as seeds, fertilisers, implements, and for services in marketing, credit and so forth.

(3) Giving advice and demonstration on pests and their control.

(4) Broadcast of weather forecasts and market trends.

(5) Narration of success stories of farmers, preferably within the region, and other relevant news.

SITE had an ambitious goal in promoting new agricultural practices like dry-land farming and use of fertilisers, pest control, market trends and weather forecasts. It broadcast programmes on agriculture for 30 minutes each day for each linguistic group, plus 30-minute entertainment programmes in Hindi.

The ISRO Report states that there was 'some gain though it is not statistically significant' The Foreword points out that 'some case histories of these innovations indicate that the farmers adopted only those practices, which did not demand additional expense on infrastructure. They were also secretive about their intentions till the time that they achieved success.'

Health. Though one year is too short a period for adopting innovations in health practices, the Report says that SITE gave rise to 'modest gains.' On the practice of seeking medical aid for the delivery of babies, the change brought about was 'minimal', the reason being that 'adoption of this practice depended on the availability of health personnel in the village and also on the ability of the people to afford services.' On nutrition, the social scientists were unable to collect data.

Family Planning. Much was expected from SITE in the area of family planning. The Report, however, concludes that though the adaptation of vasectomy was between two to four per cent higher in the SITE villages, this figure was unreliable, because of over-reporting by males during the emergency. Hence the figure is 'statistically not significant' and the survey admits that a year's time was too brief to change an important social practice. Thus, 'in the practical aspects of nation building on which programmes were telecast during SITE, *viz.*, agricultural and animal husbandry, health and nutrition, family planning and in telecasts for schools we find that the gains were rather meager.'

SITE was a valuable learning experience for both hardware and software people of the media. The hardware people realized that keeping sets in working order for a year was no mean task, even though most of the SITE villages were not very far from cities and towns. During the first month, for instance, only 70% of the sets were in working order, and this figure declined to 33% in some cases in subsequent months. There was a dramatic decline too in the number of people viewing the programmes, particularly among women and children. This was despite the fact that over 50% had never been exposed to other mass media, and over a third of them were first generation consumers of the media. Part of the blame could be put on the low participation of the village level, block level and higher functionaries of development departments in the programmes. The village level workers and the health staff only occasionally viewed the telecasts, and none of them either participated or guided discussion after the telecasts as was expected of them.

SITE Evaluation Studies

It was not surprising therefore, that most viewers considered television a source of recreation rather than of education and development. As the SITE Evaluation Studies by the Planning Commission as well as by the Space Application Centre, Ahmedabad, testify, there were no appreciable gains in the adoption of agricultural practices, or of family planning methods. Children learnt hardly anything from the content of the science education programmes, and women precious little from the programmes on health and nutrition. The SAC study reveals that the programmes were incomprehensible to many viewers, and that inappropriate use of telecast language was the single most important factor that affected comprehension of the programmes especially in the Hindi states. The Planning Commission's evaluation, on the other hand, makes it out that TV played an important role for gain in knowledge in the field of animal husbandry (72%), agriculture (60%) and health (45 %) on the ground that 89% could recall the main message of the programmes. It also discovered that 75 % of the respondents felt the developmental programmes were on the whole useful, and by and large conformed to the local customs, beliefs and practices.'

Soon after the conclusion of SITE in 1986, six terrestrial transmitters started beaming programmes to 40% of the SITE villages. The SITE Continuity Centres-Jaipur, Raipur, Gulbarga, Hyderabad, Sambalpur and Muzaffarpur-were designed to provide developmental support in liaison with the respective State Governments. The scheme envisaged that, as beneficiaries, the State departments should shoulder a major responsibility in the distribution system. But the State Governments were not equipped to take over the responsibility of installation and maintenance of the sets; so the sets were transferred to Doordarshan. Except for Andhra Pradesh and Orissa where the Panchayat Raj departments of the States have taken up the scheme, the SITE continuity project has not been doing well.

Kheda Communications Project

The Kheda Communications Project, on the other hand, has made remarkable progress under the charge of the Space Applications Centre, Ahmedabad. Launched at the same time as SITE, it has over the past 14 years chalked out a path all its own in the use of television for development. (Attempts to wind up the popular project were made in 1986-87, but the local villages resisted the move by 'hugging' on to the transmitter).

Kheda is a small district in central Gujarat surrounded by two predominantly tribal districts and the industrial districts of Ahmedabad and Baroda. 607 Community TV sets have been installed here in 443 villages and are owned by the community, but maintained by the State Government. The sets are kept in the buildings of the Milk Producers' Cooperative Society or the Panchayat Ghar.

The programmes (for over an hour every day) are "produced by Doordarshan and the Space Application Centre. What is distinct about these programmes is that they result from constant interaction with the people. They have their origin in the lives of the local people and are in simple Charotari, a dialect of Gujarati. They are not telecast till pre-testing in the field is done, and feedback obtained. There have been numerous occasions when the programmes have been drastically revised or even dropped altogether.

Take for instance, one of the early serials Chatur Mota on the subjects of dowry and widow remarriage. It proved to be an extremely popular serial. The intention was to highlight the dominance and authoritarianism of the conservative Chatur as head of the family, and to show the growing challenge to him of younger and more enlightened people: However, "the presentation was so realistic, and so habituated were most people to this kind of dominance by traditional ideas that the programmes lulled rather than provoked; the form and presentation drowned the content, and instead of instigating a revolt against the Chatur Motas of the world, only succeeded in further establishing their right to dominate and dictate." It also came to be realized that the problems of dowry and widow remarriage wete basically middle-class problems, not of the poor of Kheda.

The SAC software team scrapped the serial at once, and produced instead a different serial on untouchability, minimum wages, and the need to co-operate to fight exploitation. It proved to be equally popular, as it featured the poorer classes and portrayed their problems. Social researchers stationed in the villages also found that the majority of viewers were from the poorer classes, and women and children were more regular viewers than men. Indeed, in the early months of the Project, over 50% of the audience was made up of children. Accordingly, a series for children was launched.

In the weekend series for women, the most successful were Dadi ma Ni haton (Wise Women's Talks), Hun Ne Mara Ae (I and My Husband), and Jagi Ni Jus To (When I Wake Up and See). The goal of the series was to generate self-confidence, provide a sense of equality and create a realization of social worth and economic importance. The attempt was to wean the rural poor from superstition, wasteful expenditure, evils of child marriage, and to provide new skills. In the majority of the programmes, the format used was group discussion, and where real problems had to be highlighted, dramatization in a studio setting was the preferred format.

Kheda Evaluation Studies. Four evaluation studies of Kheda carried out over a decade indicate that more women than men gained knowledge from TV viewing though their number was small, particularly in the areas of health, nutrition and family planning.

This could be because TV in a community viewing situation provides direct access to information which in most cases is not available to them. After all, women have very little exposure to other mass media and little urban contact too.

The Kheda team's commitment, however, was not merely to be disseminators of knowledge and awareness. They found it necessary and desirable to forge links with 'user' departments particularly the Agriculture, Health and Animal Husbandry departments at the State levels, as well as with the district and village level extension services of these departments and agencies like Annul and others.

So when they produced a series on cottage industries suitable for landless labourers and their families, and involving little or no cost, they worked in collaboration with a training institute, mailed instruction manuals to all interested, arranged for training, for bank loans, and finally even for marketing the products. In their efforts to take an integrated view of development, the Kheda scientists learnt a lot about the bureaucracy and the problems involved in getting people to adopt obviously beneficial trades.

Kheda Credo. The focus of lhe Kheda Communications Project has, however, not been so much on the diffusion of technical innovations, as on *(1)* exposing the oppression and bondages in the present social and economic system in such a way as to heighten understanding; *(2)* mobilising the community and the individual himself to break away from these bondages and *(3)* promoting self-reliance among the individuals and the community.

Development, therefore, to the Kheda team, implied a break from the status quo, from inertia; it implied movement, change. And change required a certain attitude, motivation, and of course, appropriate physical and social infrastructure. It implied, moreover, social change, education, awareness, and of course, economic development which could not take place in isolation.

The Kheda team believed that communication could play a major role in accelerating development, and their attempt in Kheda is to use TV and also to supplement it by other means for development in the broadest meaning of the term.

Power of TV

How powerful then is television as an instrument of change and development? S.R. Joshi, a social researcher in the Kheda team, had this to say at a 1983 Seminar in Baroda: TV is described as a powerful medium. This statement has to be taken with a pinch of salt. The effectiveness of TV depends on a host of factors like infrastructure support, practicability of recommendations, follow-up on the programmes, etc. The choice of the medium, he added, should be determined not by the glamour but by assessing the needs of the situation, people, and experiences of the educator. TV therefore should not be selected only because it is there or because of fancy. The Kheda experiment has been wound up, but an attempt to replicate it is currently under way in the villages of Jhabua district in Madhya Pradesh.

Radio Rural Forums

Very similar in concept to Kheda, were the Radio Rural Forums or 'Charcha Mandals. Started in Pune in 1959 in collaboration with UNESCO, they were based on the Canadian farm forum project. By 1965 the number of Mandals (of 15-20 'members) rose from 900 to 12,000 in various parts of the country, but they reached only the more advanced sections of the rural population, leaving others untouched as the Report of the Study Team on Five Year Plan Publicity (1965) indicated. Membership of the Mandals, says the

Report, shows a fairly high preference for the more advanced sections of the village community, with the small farmers, landless cultivators, artisans, craftsmen and women having only a token inactive membership. More than 70,000 community radio sets were installed all over the country in the early seventies, but the Vidyalankar Committee found that 50% of them were not in working order on any given day. The 'transistor' revolution in the more prosperous villages gradually put paid to the experiments in community listening.

During the mid-1990s fresh attempts were made to revive community or local radio, both by All India Radio and social action groups. This new thrust towards local radio for development is best summed up in the 'Bangalore Declaration on Radio' proclaimed in September 1996 at a Consultation of more than sixty persons representing All India Radio, universities, NGOs involved in development activities, journalists and members of the broadcasting establishment. The organisation that was the driving force of the Declaration was a voluntary social action group VOICES—a unit of Madhyam Communications of Bangalore. The group has now launched the country's first Community Radio in Chitradurga. The radio programmes are broadcast in the dialect of the local people and the focus of news and entertainment programmes is health and family welfare, women's empowerment, micro-credit, watershed management, rural development and non-formal education.

Rural Broadcasts

Since 1966 All India Radio has been putting out Farm and Home Broadcasts to keep farmers informed on the use of fertilisers, pesticides, seeds and new implements. There are 59 such units in the country, but they are inadequately staffed, due to lack of personnel qualified in agriculture. The Rural-urban programmes, and the Intensive Nutrition Programmes introduced some years ago cater in the main to rural elites. All AIR stations beam programmes for rural audiences, but these add up to a nearly 7% of the total transmission time. Moreover, hardly any of the minority castes and tribals figure in the programmes. A 1979 survey showed, for instance, that Punjab

Harijans felt that radio was unfair to them, and that there was no broadcast of exclusive interest to them. They complained that they were often excluded from the community radio centres.

Media and Family Planning

Family planning has been adopted as a national policy since the early fifties. During the sixties, Extension Officers in family planning were posted at select AIR centres. They worked in close coordination with government and voluntary agencies. Radio, films and the press carried the message of family planning to the masses in feverish campaigns that reached their climax during the Emergency. Diffusion studies carried out by the National Institute of Community Development, Hyderabad, demonstrate that 'extensive awareness' among people of the principles and practice of family planning was brought about, but that the gap between awareness and acceptance was very wide. A UNESCO study conducted in 1969 points to the same conclusion, and recommends the use of the oral and traditional media for propagating the message. Writes GN.S. Raghavan, "If the practitioners of traditional media internalise the message of family planning and incorporate it into some of the locally popular tunes, for group singing, or singing accompanied by dance, there will be achieved an interaction and reinforcement of the message, in a pleasant and persuasive form, which can be rivalled by no other means of communications."

And, Dr. Bhaskara Rao found from his survey of the usage of the condom in rural and urban areas that only 6% of potential users of the condom in rural areas used the device, whereas 20% used it in urban areas. He also found that interpersonal communication between health workers and others was more effective in propagating the family planning message rather than any mass media. Indeed, the mast effective canvasser for family planning has been a person sterilized himself who passes on the message by word of mouth. The interpersonal relationship of the opinion leaders with the local people is also of great importance, as also the availability of the devices, the purchasing power of the local people, and the social and religious sanctions of the community.

Traditional Media and Development

What are the clear advantages of using traditional media, of even integrating them into the mass media? In India, such media have played a role in the communication and promotion of new ideas and the adjustment to a new or evolving social or political situation. We know that interpersonal exchanges cannot be dispensed with in the effort to change attitudes and behaviour. The folk media allow for such interactions, for they are essentially participatory, flexible, and familiar. Since they are not usually pure art forms, developmental messages can be introduced through them. A note of caution is necessary here: only those folk forms that lend themselves easily (without shocking the audience) to the propagation of developmental messages must be employed. Care must needs be taken also to see that the forms are not vulgarised (as they often are in the mass media). It is evident that the local people identify most with their own folk forms and the characters in them (the performers, if they are well known, are liked by the audience, and respected for their talent and skills). What is more, the forms-drama, song and dance, religious discourses can be adapted to suit local conditions, local dialects and local concerns and interests.

❐

7

Basic Models of Communication

Interaction, interchange, transaction, dialogue, sharing, communion and commonness are ideas that crop up in any attempt to define the term' communication'. According to Denis McQuail, communication is a process which increases commonality but also requires elements of commonality for it to occur at all. This is an ideal worth striving for, but communication by itself does not increase commonality nor does it need commonality for occurrence. A common language, for instance, does not necessarily bring people together. There are other factors too at play such as a shared culture and a common interest which bring about a sense of commonality and more significantly, a sense of community.

The Sanskrit term. 'Sadharanikaran' in Bharata's Natya Shastra comes closest to the sense of 'common' or 'commonness' usually associated with communication. Sadharanikaran is a social process which can be achieved only among sahridayas, people with a capacity to receive messages. This is an innate ability acquired through culture, adaptation or learning. The focus here is not on the sender but the receiver of the message. Moreover, communication according to this Sanskrit concept is a relationship based on common and mutual understanding and feeling, for sahridaya literally means' of one heart.' The derivation of this ancient Indian concept of communication from the aesthetic theory of 'rasa' will be examined in a later section.

Communication thus presupposes a shared symbolic environment, a social relationship among those who participate.

What it leads to is social interaction, and in combination with a set of other factors, contributes to a sense of community. Since the world of man, bird and beast too possesses and communicates such a social relationship, the need arises to speak of 'human communication' rather, than 'communication' alone in our study, though many communication researchers do not like the distinction.

Denis McQuail sees 'human communication' in linear terms as the sending of meaningful messages from one person to another. These messages could be oral or written, visual or olfactory. He also takes such things as laws, customs, practices, ways of dressing, gestures, buildings, gardens, military parades, and flags to be communication.

Ashley Montagu and Floyd Matson go a step further. In their view 'human communication' as the saying goes, is a clash of symbols, and it covers a multitude of signs. But it is more than media and message, information and persuasion; it also meets a deeper need and serves a higher purpose. Whether clear or garbled, tumultuous or silent, deliberate or inadvertent, communication is the ground of meeting and the foundation of the community. It is, in short, the essential human connection.

W.S. Cardon, a leading exponent of kinesics, the science of body language, develops the argument still further. He stresses that interaction within a culture is governed not so much by language, but by 'body synthesizers' set in motion almost immediately after birth and thereafter conditioned by culture. Communication, therefore, is not a matter of 'isolated entities sending discrete messages back and forth, but a process of mutual participation in a common structure of rhythmic patterns by all members of a culture'.

Types of Communication

Communication has been classified into several types: in terms of the verbal and non-verbal; the technological and non-technological; the mediated and non-mediated, the participatory and the non-participatory, and so on. Most of these typologies, however, are mainly for pedagogic or instructional purposes; in actual practice, there is much overlapping and mixing of the various types. The typologies must be seen as attempts at coming to grips with the apparently simple but really complex phenomenon of communication.

One common typology relates to the size of a social group or the number of people involved in the experience of communication. Such a typology ranges from the intrapersonal and transpersonal to the group and the mass.

Intrapersonal Communication

Intrapersonal Communication is individual reflection, contemplation and meditation. Transcendental meditation, for instance, is an example of such communication. Conversing with the divine, with spirits and ancestors, may be termed 'transpersonal' communication. This is a vital experience in the religious and monastic life, in ashrams and places of prayer, and among aboriginal and tribal communities.

Face-to-face Communication

Interpersonal Communication is direct face-to-face communication between two persons. It is, in other words, a dialogue or a conversation without the intervention of another person or a machine like the telephone or a two-way radio or television set-up. It is personal, direct, and intimate, allowing for maximum interaction and exchange in word and gesture. Indeed, it is the highest, the most perfect form of communication that two persons can attain. It is more persuasive and influential than any other type of communication such as group communication or mass communication, for it involves the interplay of words and gestures, the warmth of human closeness and in fact all the five senses. All interpersonal exchange is, therefore a communion and a sharing at the most intimate and open level. It is total communication for it takes within its compass words, body movements, physical characteristics, body odours, and even clothes. This is not to deny that interpersonal exchanges can be used by confidence tricksters and conmen to throw wool over people's eyes.

A man may smile and smile and yet be a villain for all we know. That perhaps explains, why we cherish our privacy, and are constantly on our guard in face-to-face encounters, much more so than in group or mass gatherings. Only the ones who have our trust, and have proved themselves are allowed to cross the barriers of an intimate relationship. Most are kept at a distance.

In the area of business communication that distance is ritualized. For instance, interpersonal exchanges between a medical representative and a doctor or that between a manager and a clerk, are generally carried out on a professional level. As the saying goes they usually 'talk shop', but on occasions, even business charter can lead to close and abiding friendships. That potential lies in the nature of inter-personal communication; hence the frequent barriers we raise lest people invade our space, our 'territory.'

According to Konrad Lorenz and Desmond Morris, the ethologists, animals and birds often turn aggressive when their territories are invaded by outsiders. This is because of the 'territorial imperative"—the obsession with protecting one's space. The elephant has his herd, the lion his pride, the wolf his pack, and the birds and bees their nests and hives. Any encroachment from other groups is resented, and' fought off, sometimes violently. Human beings react in an equally savage manner when their spatial privacy is encroached upon. In European cultures, it is considered bad manners and bad communication to get too close (literally and figuratively) and too intimate unless you have been permitted to enter the sanctum sanctorum of another. Among Indians and Arabs, however, physical closeness in Interpersonal Communication does not generally imply intimacy, nor does constant gazing into each other's eyes. This is a part of West and South Asian cultures. According to Buddhism, the four social emotions that should guide interpersonal communication are: metta (loving kindness), karuna (compassion), murdita (sympathetic joy) and upekkha (equanimity).

Focussed and Unfocussed Interactions

Interpersonal communication is conducted on the basis of focussed and unfocussed interactions. In his book behaviour in

Public Places, Erving Goffman argues that most interpersonal communication is of an unfocussed nature. It takes place whenever we observe or listen to persons with whom we are not conversing, for instance in buses, trains, lifts or in public places like stations, bus stops, or on the street. It's the kind of activity we indulge in when we are 'people watching' without their being aware we are doing so. And what do we come to know about them? Our inferences may not all be valid or meaningful, but the fact remains that we do make inferences all the time about people. The young man who passes us by in a street dressed in pyjama and kurta evokes different associations from one clad in jeans and a jazzy shirt, depending of course on our own background, and the location of the street. The girl in a simple cotton sari, with her hair tied in a 'plait' say in a city like Bombay, conveys different impressions from the girl in a dress and with her hair bobbed. Additional sources of information about these persons are height, weight, and build. For instance, a well-built tall man is regarded as handsome, a stout fat woman as ugly, a thin wiry figure as athletic. Body movements such as gestures, the manner of standing, sitting or walking too convey certain meanings to us. Very broad gestures and loud talk, for example, are considered uncouth in polite society, but not necessarily so among working class groups. Thus it is that we draw conclusions on a person's qualities, cultural and religious background, socia-economic status, political ideology and Other preferences without ever speaking to him or to her.

Focussed Interactions

Focussed interactions, on the other hand, result from an actual encounter between two persons. The persons involved are fully aware that they are communicating with each other. Sitting or standing face-to-face either close or distant, they know fully well that they are exchanging both verbal and non-verbal messages, though they may not realize how these messages are being interpreted. Also, they are generally not conscious of the meanings they are conveying through 'body language.' An urfocussed interaction usually is set off by eye contact. The meeting of eyes indicates that both parties are willing to have an interpersonal exchange. The turning away of eyes, on other hand, cuts off the attempts to come together and start a conversation. It shows lack of interest. Similarly, reduction in eye involvement during a conversation is a non-verb at signal which indicates that it is time to bring the conversation to a close. Indeed, there is no more effective way of ending a face-to-face interaction than refusing to continue eye contact.

Three Stages of Interpersonal Communication

The Phatic Stage. The initial exploratory stage of communication determines the course conversation will take. This first stage is known as the phatic period (from the Greek "phasis", an utterance). It begins with a "Hi!" or a "Hello! How are you?", "Good Morning" or even a simple 'namaste' or 'vanakkam' or 'Jairam'. The accompanying gestures ate the meeting of the yes, a smile, perhap a handshake, and moving in closer to a talking distance. In a formal encounter, the distance is greater (though not among all cultures) than an informal friendly meeting. The conversation then, may veer to talk about the weather or queries like "How's life?", "How are things with you?" What have you been doing with yourself?', "What's the new's?", "How are the folks at home?"

The Phatic stage is, therefore, a warming-up time during which ritualized greetings are exchanged. In themselves, the words and gestures' exchanged during this period do not mean much. Indeed, the questions asked are not meant to be taken literally. They are on a formalised manner of showing interest and attention. They are a way of saying "I am glad to have met you. Let's have a chat". The answers we give to the queries made are equally formalised. "I'm fine, thank you", for example is a stock reply even if you're not doing too well. No deception is involved at all: what we are doing through words is merely sending signals that we would like to have,a conversation. So at this stage we don't literally mean what we say, but we mean well. It's the meaning after, all, and not the words that really matter. The words are only symbols or ways of getting across. The meaning is more often than not behind the words rather in them. More accurately, meaning lies in a situation and a context, seen not so much in isolation but in a social and cultural environment. This is as true of verbal as of non-verbal communication. For instance, the North Indian's gesture of touching an elder's feet connotes respect and reverence among people of that culture, but is considered a demeaning gesture in the cultures of the south and the north-east. The phatic stage then is patterned according to social and cultural norms and rituals.

The Personal Stage. The second stage, called the personal stage, introduces a more personal element into the conversation. During this period we generally lower our social guard a little and are prepared to take some risk in exposing ourselves and our feelings. Having moved on to this personal stage, we are likely to be willing to talk about personal-matters such as one's profession, the family, health problems and the like. If, on the other hand, we were hesitant to enter this stage, we would have broken off the conversation at the phatic stage itself or continued talking in a formal manner. Professional discussions rarely go beyond the personal stage. Most business communication, therefore, takes place at this level, for it does involve personal interests and we are ready to go along to promote them.

The Intimate Stage. This stage is reserved for friends and relatives, the degree of intimacy depending upon the closeness of the relationship. To some we open our hearts out completely to others, though good friends, we are reluctant to tell all. Nevertheless, it's a stage when social barriers fall and we are at ease; interpersonal communication achieves its highest form in this mode, and words seem inadequate. Says Robert Shuter, "In this period, communicators reveal their innermost thoughts and feelings—their fears and joys, weaknesses and strengths. Marked by intimate revelations, this stage is reserved for individuals who have established a deep union, one based on love, respect and understanding."

Group Communication

Group communication shares all these qualities, though in a much less measure. The larger the group the less personal and intimate is the possibility of exchange. In fact, as the group grows in size communication tends to become more and more of a monologue, for participation becomes problematic. The degree of directness and intimacy, therefore, depends upon the size of the group, the place where it meets, as also the relationship of the members of the group to one another, and to the group leader. Group communication is thus a more complex process than interpersonal communication. The level of mutual participation and understanding among the members suffers as a result. In Interpersonal Communication too understanding and participation may not be complete, especially if the non-verbal cues and the socia-cultural contexts are not paid attention to. However, the possibility of checking up and correcting misunderstanding is much quicker and easier in much interpersonal communication.

Feedback is the key word here. While in interpersonal communication, feedback is instantaneous, it is not so in group communication. What is more, it allows for instant response to feedback received. In Group Communication, on the other hand, feedback is more difficult to measure, and to respond to. It takes time before meanings are clarified and responses assessed. That explains why the art of effective public speaking (an example of one-way top-down communication) is more necessary at the group level than at the interpersonal level. Feedback is a term from cybernetics, the study of messages, particularly of effective message control. When feedback is employed for this kind of social engineering, as in advertising, it is no more communication but propaganda and manipulation.

Face-to-face communication, nevertheless, is more persuasive and influential, particularly in an unequal communication situation. It involves the interplay of words and gestures and above all, the warmth of human closeness. No wonder, advertising people still depend on door-to-door salesmen and salesgirls even where the mass media such as radio, television and the press are widespread. Sincerity and enthusiasm are far easier to convey, and to react to in a face-to-face situation. In Group Communication, particularly where the group is large, deception and pretence cannot be detected immediately.

That must be the reason why 'acting' is associated with Group Communication. The theatre, religious services, dance performances, carnivals, the Kumbh Mela, Ram Lila, Ras Lila and other folk events, are examples of Group Communication. Villag markets, bazars and melas too are instances of informal Group Communication. Then there are' gossip groups and other informal traditional groups that come together either regularly or occasionally for sharing information. These are 'micro-groups' that communicate among and within themselves in terms of their status and the nature of their relationships.

Mass Communication

Group Communication has now been extended by the tools of mass communication: books, the press, the cinema, radio, television, video and the Internet. Mass Communication is generally identified with these modern mass media, but it must be noted that these media are processes and must not be mistaken for the phenomenon of communication itself. Exaggerated claims have been made for the 'power' of the mass media. Daniel Lerner terms them 'mobility multipliers' and Wilbur Schramm considers them to be 'magic multipliers.' Indeed, both the terms 'mass communication' and 'mass media' are inappropriate in the context of developing societies. None of the 'mass media' reach the masses of people in these societies. So in every sense, these are 'minority' or 'elite' media, or even 'class' media, for only those who have the wherewithal can afford to purchase receivers for them. Where access to, and distribution of, the mass media in India is concerned, only the comparatively well-off in urban and rural areas are at an advantage.

Newspapers, transistors, films and televisions are still beyond the economic reach of the majority of our people. Traditional community media like the keertana and yakshagan, and the whole treasure-house of folk song, folk dance and folk theatre are the real organs of mass media in India. They are far less expensive organs, are easy of access, are frequently participatory in nature and communicate much more effectively than the electronic media and at a direct and personal level. Their reach too is far and wide in the country. However, the modern mass media are produced and distributed like other consumer and industrial products on a mass scale.

'Mass-line' Communication

Mao Zedong, who led the Chinese Cultural Revolution, used a type of communication to talk to the masses. He termed it 'mass-line' communication. Mahatma Gandhi too employed a similar type of communication, the essence of which was personal example, respect for the peasant's knowledge, and non-manipulative information. Kusum J. Singh's comparison of the two leaders' use of the mass-line type of communication brings out the relevance of this type of grass-root level communication even today for mobilizing the masses in developmental efforts.

Interactive Communication

Communication via the 'new' media such as video, cable, videotex, teletext, video-on-demand, tele-shopping, computers, and the Internet is usually termed 'interactive communication'. Telecommunication-based services such as telephones, pagers, cellular or mobile phones, electronic mail are also considered to be 'interactive'. They are point-to-point communication systems, and can approximat to the interpersonal (as in the basic telephone and the various 'value-added' services), the group (as in teleconferences and videoconferences) or the mass (as in the Internet's World Wide Web) where companies or people with their own web-sites can reach millions of individuals across the globe at their own convenience. A major characteristic of interactive communication is 'asynhronicity', that is the sending and receiving of messages is at one's convenience, rather than at the same time, as in radio, television. Audio and video recording facilitates listening and watching at a time later than the time of transmission; voice mail, electronic mail and pager messages, can be sent and accessed at times convenient to communicators.

Western Models

Western theories,and models of communication have their origin in Aristotle's Rhetoric. According to Aristotle, rhetoric is made up of three elements: the speaker/the speech, and the listener. The aim of rhetoric is the search for all possible means of persuasion.

Perhaps the most widely quoted definition of mass communication in terms of Aristotelian rhetoric is that of Harold D. Lasswell, the American political scientist. He stated that 'a convenient way to describe an act of communication is to answer the following questions:

Who

Says What

In Which Channel

To Whom

With What Effect?

Lasswell saw communication as performing, three functions: surveillance of the environment, correlation of components of society, and cultural transmission between generations. Such a mechanistic and 'effects' approach to communication was to influence communication theory for decades to come. Essential to this understanding were the notions of transmission and transfer of information for intended effects.

A definition on similar lines was given by Berelson and Steiner: 'The transmission of information, ideas, emotions, skills, etc., by use of symbols-words, pictures, figures, graphs, etc. It is the act or process of transmission that is usually called communication'.

The primary goal of communication, according to Western communication theory, is influence through persuasion. Osgood's definition is an illustration. In the most general sense, he explains, we communicate whenever one (the system), (the source), influences another, (the destination), by manipulation of alternative signals which can be transferred over the channel connecting them.

The Shannon and Weaver Model

The effects-oriented models or approaches to mass communication derive from Shannon and Weaver's Mathematical model of communication. Shannon and Weaver conceived of communication as a system composed of five essential parts plus 'noise': *(1)* an information source, *(2)* a transmitter, *(3)* a channel, *(4)* the receiver, and *(5)* the destination. As engineers during World War II at the Bell Telephone Laboratories in the United States, their primary concern was finding out the most efficient means of using the channels of communication (the telephone cable and the radio wave) for the transfer of information. They, however, claimed that the mathematical model they worked out as a result of their research at Bell, was widely applicable to human communication as well.

Wilbur Schramm, whose theories have influenced much Indian planning on the role of communication in development, adapted Shannon and Weaver's model to human communication, but stressed the encoding-decoding aspects as crucial. He defined communication as 'the sharing of information, ideas or attitudes'. He endorsed the Aristotelian principle that communication always requires at least three elements-source, message and destination.

The encoding and decoding of the message were the most important components to him. As he explained: Substitute 'microphone' for encoder, and 'earphone' for decoder and you are talking about electronic communication. Consider that the 'source' and 'encoder' are one person, 'decoder' and 'destination' are another, and the signal is language, and you are talking about human communication. In a communication model he developed with Charles Osgood, Schramm suggested that communication was circular in nature, where both the sender and the receiver were involved in encoding and decoding, and were equal partners in the exchange.

Berlo, on the other hand, saw communication as a "process' and the events and relationships of this process as dynamic, ongoing, ever-changing, continuous. He argued that you cannot talk about the beginning or the end of communication or say that a particular idea came from one specific source, that communication occurs in only one way and so on. He termed this the 'bucket' theory of communication wherein ideas were dumped from the source into a bucket, such as a film, a lecture, a book, a television programme or what have you and shipped the bucket over to the receiver and dumped the contents into his head.

In sum, Western communication theories and the models (especially of development communication) built on them have been largely unilinear, wrongly postulating a mechanical notion of communication as the transmission of information from active sources to passive receivers. Further, these individual-based models wrongly assume that communication is an act, a static phenomenon privileging the source, not a dynamic process involving all elements in a social relationship.

In recent years, however, the focus in Western communication theory has shifted from mechanistic 'effects' models of communication acts to those concerned with communication relationships and the communication 'experience'. Semiotic models look at communication as 'social interaction through messages.' The focus of attention in these models is language (both verbal and non-verbal) as a sign-system; how 'meaning' is generated and understood is central to this approach. The crucial questions the semiotic approaches address are: What is a Sign? What is the Meaning of Signs? What is the relationship between signs, users and external reality? The user is seen as active, as a creator of meaning, as one who makes his or her own meaning. Meaning is thus not so much in the words, gestures or symbols (the 'text') but in the cultural interpretation of the participants (the 'readers') of the communication experience. The semiotic approaches to communication are based on the work of C.S. Pierce, who stablished the American tradition of semiotics; C.K. Ogden and LA. Richards of Britain; and the Swiss linguist, Ferdinand de Saussure.

Ritual Model

James Carey, the American anthropologist, has been foremost in promoting a 'ritual' model communication. Horace Newcomb, Robert Alley and others also promote this perspective. They base their approach on Victor Turner's extensive anthropological studies of the role of ritual in societies. 'All members of the public, not just message senders, are considered to be actors contributing in some way to the pattern of meaning of a nation or region.' They object to a 'transportation' model which defines communication as the 'transmission of messages for purposes of social control.' Public communication such as television is more closely analogous to the moment of ritual in which myths, values and meanings of life are recalled and re-enacted. Communication is thus a process of creation, representation and celebration of shared beliefs.

As 'Dialogue'

Communication as a dialogic and 'participatory' relationship is at the heart of the South American perspective. The key elements of the perspective are—'liberation', 'participation' and 'conscientization', derived from liberation theology and the writings of the late Paulo Freire, the Brazilian educationist. This perspective of communication challenges the traditional Aristotelian model of communication as 'transmission' and 'transportation'. Much of South American research in communication is based on this model.

As a Power-relationship

In some situations, Communication is an exercise in power-relations, the power of one individual over another, of an individual over a group, and of mass media owners and producers/professionals over audiences. This perspective of Communication focuses on the inequality among people involved in a communication experience: the inequality in class, caste, economic and social power. This perspective has its basis in Marxism which sees 'conflict' and class differences rather than consensus as the function of communication. Communication is a relationship of power in the family, the classroom, the work place, and the mass media situation.

NON-VERBAL COMMUNICATION

We define non-verbal communication as actions and artifactual cues that are not linguistic yet which may have meaningful effects. Like many technical definitions, this one requires further explanation.

Non-verbal communication includes actions such as gestures, vocalisations, facial expressions, and other behaviour. However, non-verbal communication is not limited to actions. The word artifacts is included in the definition because many objects or artifacts have the potential to communicate or to influence communication. Clothing styles, hairstyles, glasses, cosmetics, even our possessions, can communicate. Think of your room. What would it communicate about you to a stranger? Your posters, mementos, even the type of records you have can communicate your interests and can express clues about who you are. We therefore include such artifacts as a part on non-verbal communication.

The definition also uses the word cues to indicate that non-verbal communication is subject to interpretation just as much as words are subject to interpretation. Our facial expressions, gestures, attire, posture, and possessions constantly give cues about us, but they are only cues. They are not unambiguous signs. We can, for example, be mistaken about non-verbal communication from others. Crossed arms may be taken as a non-verbal cue of defensiveness, but it might also mean that the air conditioner is on too high. Because we can be mistaken about non-verbal actions and artifacts, it is best to consider them cues rather than invariable signals.

While the definition indicates that non-verbal communication is not language, the verbal world is not really separable from the non-verbal world. The fact that we use words to talk about non-verbal communication indicates that we need language to express abstract and complicated ideas. However, without the non-verbal world the verbal world would be significantly diminished. Think how dull our story about a fishing trip would be if we could not use gestures to indicate the size of the fish or tone of voice to express our excitement at a bite and our disappointment when we failed to land the big fish. While non-verbal communication is not 'identical with verbal communication, the two are so intertwined that they are separable only for the purposes of analysis. In actuality our messages usually combine verbal and non-verbal communication.

The expression meaningful effects indicates that non-verbal communication may have a variety of effects. Sometimes we express information. For instance, the librarian's forefinger held to the lips expresses a desire for silence. Meaningful effects of non-verbal communication may also include affect displays, or the communication of emotions. Facial expressions, gestures, and tone of voice may express pleasure or pain, happiness or sadness, elation or depression,' or any of the myriad of human emotions. In addition to information and emotion, non-verbal communication may also indicate relationships. For example an acquaintance of mine is deeply involved in climbing the "corporate ladder of success." He is never seen wearing anything other than a three-piece suit: his office is deliberately arranged so that he always sits behind a very large desk. Every chair in his office is a few inches lower than his desk chair so that he is always looking down on visitors. In short, everything about his communicates a superior-subordinate relationship.

Uses of Non-verbal Communication

Non-verbal communication serves a variety of uses in communicating with others; Some of the uses include *(1)* repeating, *(2)* contradicting, *(3)* substituting, *(4)* accenting, and *(5)* regulating.

Repeating is a use of non-verbal communication in which the non-verbal message reiterates the verbal message. For instance, we will often use a sweeping gesture to accompany a request like "Come here." The verbal and the non-verbal messages repeat each other. Sometimes, however, our non-verbal messages contradicts our verbal messages. "How nice? It's just what I always wanted." Expressed in a flat dull tone of voice at a birthday party communicates the exacteopposite of the verbal message. Studies indicate that in cases of the verbal and the non-verbal messages contradicting each other, most people are inclined to believe the non-verbal rather than the verbal message.

Non-verbal communication may serve to substitute for-verbal messages. For example, we often have emblems to substitute for words. A ground-chiefs gestures in docking an aircraft, the circled thump and forefinger for "OK" and the "V" sign for peace or victory are all examples of emblems that substitute for words.

Another use of non-verbal communication is to accent verbal messages. Vocal emphasis, for example, can highlight particular parts of the verbal message. "An apple a day keeps the doctor away" is quite different from "An apple a day keeps the doctor away" because of the accenting function of non-verbal communication.

Regulating is another important function of'non-verbal communication. Sometimes our non-verbal messages serve as regulators to maintain the flow or our communication with others. Our non-verbal messages operate like conversational traffic signals. We often use head nods, eye contact, and body movement to indicate that we would like to speaker to hurry up, to slow down, or to stop so that the other person can speak.

While there are many areas to non-verbal communication including the impact of touch, smell, colour, etc. on communication, we will explore the three main dimensions of non-verbal communication: paralanguage, kinesics, and proxemics. Paralanguage is the area of non-verbal communication concerned with' vocal expression such as the rate, pitch, and other qualities of voice. Kinesics, is the part of non-verbal communication concerned with body movements including gestures, posture, facial expression, and eye contact. Proxemics is the study of space and spatial relationships and their impact on communication.

Paralanguage

Stan Freberg, one of America's most creative advertisers, once produced a recording called "John and Marsha." This comedy routine consisted of two words, "John" and "Marsha." Expressed with dozens of different tones of voice. The changes in voice created a story of growing love and then disappointment using nothing but the two names. Freberg's creation illustrates how meaningful paralanguage can be.

Creating sounds involves a power source in the form of the lungs, the diaphragm a large muscle beneath the lungs. And various muscles around the rib cage. A stream of air is forced through the windpipe and between a pair of vocal folds in the throat. The sound produced by the vocal folds is very thin and requires modification before it can be recognized as speech.

The thin sound produced by the vocal folds is modified by resonators that act like the sound-box on a guitar to fill out the sound of the voice. The resonators consist of cavities, such as the sinuses, the nasal cavity, and the throat cavity. The role of the resonators is well illustrated by how our voices change when we have a cold and the cavities become blocked, To be recognized as individual sounds of speech, however, the sound need to be further shaped and refined, and that is the function of the articulators.

The articulators are the lips, tongue, jaws, teeth, etc. The articulators change the shape of the mouth and allow us, for example, to make the word "nut" sound different than the word "hut." By altering the placement of the articulators and by changing the force and the resonance of the sound, we produce human speech.

Receivers interpreting the messages also engage a physical process of hearing no less complex than the act of speaking. The hearing mechanism consists of three parts: the outer ear, the middle ear, and the inner ear. The outer ear includes the visible ear called the pinna and a thin membrane, the tympanic membrane, which we call the ear drum. The vibrations of air are channelled to the tympanic membrane, which begins to vibrate. These vibrations are in turn transferred to three small bones in the middle ear called the ossicles. These three bones cross the middle ear and transfer the vibrations to a small shell-shaped organ in the inner ear called the cochlea. The cochlea is filled with fluid and bristles with small hair like projections called cilia. The cilia are nerve endings that pick up different movements in the fluid and transform those movements into electrochemical impulses which travel along the cranial nerve to the language receptors in the brain.

The complex coordination of these organs allows us to produce a variety of sounds that our receivers interpret as messages. The characteristics and qualities of the voice influence the interpretation of the messages.

George Trager, a pioneer in the area of paralanguage, identified a wide variety of vocal qualities like timbre and tempo; vocal characterisers like crying and throat clearing; vocal qualifiers, like intensity and extent: and vocal segregates, like hum, err, and other intruding sounds. For our purposes, only a few of the major paralinguistic features will be explored. We will consider four vocal qualities (inflection, timbre, rate, and control) and three vocal qualifiers (intensity, pitch height, and extent).

Vocal qualities are created by the physical process of speech production described above. An important vocal quality is inflection, the changes in pitch and loudness that we put into our voices. We have all been bored by very monotone voices that have no inflection, and we have all become entranced by a very "animated" voice. These reactions are created largely by the inflections employed by the speaker.

Timbre is a second important vocal quality. Timbre is the "fullness" or resonance of the voice. Timbre is best illustrated by recalling the voices of FM radio announcers. They usually have very rich, full-timbered voices unlike most of us who have thinner sounding timbre.

Rate is the third vocal quality to be considered. Rate is the tempo, or speed of speech. Studies indicate that most people talk at an average rate of about 125 words per minute. We can, however, speak as fast as 220 or more words per minute, like auctioneers or the announcer in the commercial for an overnight delivery service.

Control is the smoothness of the movements of the lips and tongue. Over-controlled creates a tense sound, like the way we speak when really angry. Uncontrolled vocal qualities create a "mushy" sound that makes the speaker appear to be mumbling.

Vocal qualifiers are also important paralinguistic cues. Intensity, for example, is the volume, or the loudness or softness, of the voice.

Pitch is the highness or lowness of the voice. Extent involves the enunciation of our words. Extent may vary from very clipped enunciation characteristic of many New England dialects to the very drawn out enunciation characteristic of a southern drawl.

The vocal characteristics and the vocal qualifiers combine to produce important differences in the paralinguistic meanings. For example, consider the differences in the sound of an angry voice and the sound of a sad voice. Angry voices usually have irregular (up and down) inflection, a blaring timbre, a fast rate, considerable control, loud volume, high pitch, and clipped enunciation. Sad voices, on the other hand, typically have a downward inflection, resonant timbre, a slow rate, less than normal control, reduced loudness, low pitch, and somewhat slurred enunciation. Try identifying the vocal qualities and qualifiers of other emotions. Paralanguage is a primary conveyer of emotions, but paralanguage also influences our perceptions of the personality of the speaker.

Experts interested in paralanguage have found a very high correlation among people judging voices in terms of the sex and the age of speakers. Moderate correlation was found for status and occupation (especially preachers) based solely on the sound of the speaker's voices. In addition, D.W. Addington found that listeners tend to have rather stereotyped perceptions of the personalities of speakers based on paralinguistic cues.

Clearly, we need to pay close attention to managing our voices in communication. We need to work consciously on creating appropriate impressions through our vocal qualities and vocal qualifiers. Your instructor or a professor in voice and diction or speech pathology may be of assistance if a severe or pathological problem exists in your speech or hearing.

Kinesics

Kinesics is the area of non-verbal communication that examines body movement. Non-verbal Kinesics messages are processed through the eyes rather than through the ears. Test indicate that most of the stimuli in the human environment are processed through vision; the hearing mechanism is typically able to scan fewerestimuli, and the skin process fewer still and with less subtlety in discriminating features of the stimuli, of course, the ability of the sensory organ can affect vision.

Farsightedness means that the eye can perceive objects farther away more comfortably: near-sightedness means that objects closer to the eye are seen more readily. Of course, there are many other physical factors that can influence our visual perception. Colour blindness, stigmatism, and cataracts are but a few of the typical problems encountered visually.

Interestingly enough the shape, colour, distance and motion of the stimulus are all factors that can influence our perception of the material. A pioneer in the field of Kinesics was Ray Birdwhistell, author of Kinesics and Context. Professor Birdwhistell cited eight different body elements in Kinesic behaviour: the head, the face, the neck, the trunk, the shoulder-arm-wrist, the hand, the hip-joint-leg-ankle, and the foot. Birdwhistell estimated that the face alone is capable of producing over 250,000 different expressions. Naturally, we cannot explore every possible expression of each of the eight areas, so we will focus on a few of the more noticeable areas.

Facial Expressions

Facial expressions are extremely important non-verbal messengers in face-to-face communication. They seem to be especially important as affect displays. The face can express a wide variety of emotions with considerable ease. Unlike other non-verbal behaviours, facial expressions seem to be relatively easy to control, such as when we need to keep a straight face in playing a joke on someone. Unfortunately, we sometimes do not bother to control our facial expressions, or we forget that others may misinterpret our facial expressions. For example, young ladies interviewed in beauty pageants will often tell terribly depressing stories with fixed smiles on their faces. Receivers are quite adept at reading facial expressions with considerable accuracy, and the contest judges interpret the frozen smiles as signs of uncontrolled nervousness.

Perceived Personality Characteristics

Vocal Feature	*Males*	*Females*
Breathiness	Younger, more artistic strung, but shallower	More feminine, prettier, more petite, more, effervescent, more highly
Thinness	No significant characteristics were found	Social, physical, emotional, mental immaturity
Flatness	More masculine, more sluggish, colder, generally withdrawn	More masculine, more sluggish, colder, generally withdrawn
Nasality	Many socially undesirable characteristics	Many socially undesirable characteristics
Tenseness	Older more unyielding, cantankerous	Younger, more emotional, feminine, highstrung, less intelligent
Throatiness	Older, more realistic, mature, sophisticated, well adjusted	Less intelligent, more masculine, lazier, more boorish, unemotional, ugly sickly, careless, inartistic, native, humble, neurotic, quiet, uninteresting, apathetic
Orotundity	More energetic, healthy artistic, pround, sophisticated, interesting, enthusiastic	Liveliness, gregarious, aesthetic sensitivity, proud, humorless
Rate	More animated, more extroverted	More animared, more extroverted
Pitch variety	More dynamic, feminine, aesthetically inclined	More dynamic, more extroverted

The dominant feature of the face is the eyes. As communicators we need to be particularly sensitive to the behaviour of the eyes. Eye contact is especially important as a way of seeking feedback from the other person. Oddly enough studies indicate that if the speaker has disfluencies like stammering, receivers tend to look away rather than at the speaker. This reduces the human contact between speaker and listener and reduces the opportunities for engaging in feedback.

We often use eye contact as a regulating function. We tend to open the channel of communication by "catching the eye'" of the other person. We have all experienced, for example, trying to use eye contact to open a channel of communication between ourselves and the waiter or waitress in a restaurant. Looking away tends to close off communication. Every teacher knows the experience of asking a question and watching the students in the class lower their heads and avoid eye contact, as if to say, "May be if I don't look at the teacher, she won't see me and I won't get called on."

. Eye contact may also indicate the quality of the relationships. We tend to look closely at people and things that interest or attract us. However, we tend to avoid eye contract with people and things that we dislike. There are limits, of course. It has been shown that a stare of longer than 10 seconds can induce discomfort in the other person and may be interpreted as a sign of hostility rather than attraction. Status relationships may also affect eye contact Low-status receivers frequently receive less eye contact than moderate or high status receivers, for example.

Naturally there are many features that affect eye contact. Argyle and Cook, in Gaze and Mutual Gaze, indicated that there may be considerable eye contact when:

(1) people are far apart,

(2) they are discussing impersonal topics,

(3) they are interested in each other and each other's reactions,

(4) they are in love,

(5) they are extroverts, and a variety of other conditions.

There may be very little eye contact when two people:

(1) are placed close together,

(2) are discussing intimate topics,

(3) not interested in each other or in each other's reactions,

(4) dislike each other,

(5) are depressed or autistic, and a variety of other conditions.

Facial expressions and eye behaviour are only two of the many dimensions of kinesics. We should also consider more general body cues like body appearance, posture, and gestures.

The general appearance of one's body makes a definite impression on receivers. Wells and Sieger asked 120 people to rated three different body types. Based only on silhouettes, most people rated endomorphs (soft, round, heavy figures) as older, shorter, old fashioned, more talkative, warmhearted, sympathetic, and dependent. Mesomorphs (bony, muscular, athletic figures) were rated as stronger, younger, taller, mature, and self-reliant. Ectomorphs (tall, thin, fragile-looking figures) were rated as thin, younger, more ambitious, suspicious of others, tense, stubborn, and quiet. Naturally, these are stereotypical responses based on very limited information, but it is important to recognize that a communicator's body type may influence listener reactions.

Height is another influential factor. Interestingly enough, one corporate study revealed that men between the heights of 6 feet 2 inches and 6 feet 4 inches received higher starting salaries than men under 6 feet. One experiment sent out 140 resumes in which the only difference was the listed height of the job applicant. Based solely on a written resume that included in formation about height, only 1 percent of the respondents indicated that they would hire the person listed as 5 feet 5 inches rather than the person listed as 6 feet 1 inch.

Another body behaviour is posture. People communicating with someone they like tend to lean slightly forward in a relaxed posture. On the other hand, people who are communicating with someone they dislike tend to stand with arms akimbo in a slightly backward-leaning and tense posture. Superior-sub rdinate relationships are also cued by posture. The superior, dominant individual will often stand or sit in a relaxed, expansive, backward lean. The subordinate or submissive individual will typically sit or stand with a tense and restricted posture leaning toward the more dominant individual.

Communicators can, perhaps, do little about their body type or height, but they can control posture. A responsive communicator will direct the face and body toward the other individual and will maintain an alert posture with a slight forward lean. All such kinesic cues are marks of high interests and responsiveness to other individual. They open the channels of communication and encourage feedback.

Proxemics

In this section we will explore proxemics, the impact of spatial relationships on our communication with others. Human beings seem to have a definite sense of territoriality. Students in a class will often sit in the same place each day; a sign of growing up is to have your own room; we become uneasy when strangers invade our personal space.

We also have learned certain rules of communication associated with space. We tend to whisper in libraries and churches. We use a different vocabulary in locker rooms than in other places. While there are many dimensions of the subject of proxemics, the two most noticeable areas are the influence of distance and the influence of placement.

Distance

Space influences our communication, We do not, for example, tell secrets aloud in a crowded room; we reserve a more intimate setting for sharing secrets. Edward T. Hall's research into proxemics indicates that we create at least four different zones of communication.

The intimate distance is less than 18 inches from the speaker. The intimate zone is reserved for telling secrets or for very personal topics. Our volume is generally softer when dealing with confidential topics in the intimate zone.

Personal distance stretches from approximately 18 inches out to 4 feet. Personal space is the typical conversational distance for most interpersonal interactions. Hall described this as a neutral zone reserved for persónal subject matter. Typically we speak in a soft to normal voice in this zone.

The social distance is a zone from 4 to 10 feet from the speaker. The social zone is considered a group distance and typically calls for less personal communication. Discussion topics are usually non-personal, and we speak in a full or even slightly loud voice at the outer range of the zone.

The public zone is an area from 10 to 22 feet from the speaker. This is the area used for public address to a group of people. The voice needs to be projected so the whole group can hear. The topics tend to be non-personal ideas to be freely shared with many others.

Of course, there are, many factors that influence our use of distance in communication. F. N. Willis, for example, indicated that speakers typically will stand closer to women than to men in conversations. In addition, it has been noted that people of higher status are given a greater "clearance" space than people of lower status. As might be expected, it is also true that people who are not on good terms tend to stand further apart than friendly peers.

As communicators we need to consider the impact of proximity. Because people feel uncomfortable if we are either too close or too far away, it is important to be sensitive to how our distance affects communication with other people. Appropriate distance are important for effective communication.

Placement

We have rules for placement in communication as well as rules for distance. The head of the table is typically reserved for the hosts at a dinner party, for example. The legend of King Arthur invented the round table to equalize the status among his knights. Clearly, placement has been and continues to be an important matter.

Experts in group communication have noted that people sitting at the two ends of a rectangular table tend to take on leadership roles and to do more talking than people placed at other points around the table. Robert Sommer, a leading expert in proxemics, devoted an entire book, entitled Personal Space: The Behavioural Basis of Design, to this subject. Based on research into the impact of spatial placement on human behaviour and attitude, Sommer's ideas include the following:

1. The nature of the task influences seating preferences. At a rectangular table, most people prefer sitting either across or corner-to-corner from one another for conversing, side by side for cooperating, across from one another for working separately at the same task, and face-to-face for competitive activities.
2. Different environments require different spatial relationships. Classrooms, for example, are usually arranged in rows with the teacher centered at the front of the room. This creates a definite zone of classroom communication with teachers communicating more frequently with students in the front row and the centre aisle of the classroom.
3. Social environments, on the other hand, create quite different interaction patterns. Hotel and airport planners, for example, create spatial situations with rows of chairs locked together in a restricted space to drive people out spaces for communication (lounges and lobbies) and into spaces for commerce (bars and shops).

Artifacts

It is possible to learn much about people through a close inspection of their possessions and clothing. In the case of "The Headed League," legendary detective Sherlock Holmes deduced the occupation, personal habits, travels, and recent activity of a client based solely on artificial clues.

We can, for example, distinguish the sex and age range of individuals based on their clothing. Customs inspectors can often tell the origin of fabrics based on the cut, colour, and fabric weave. Our clothing often gives off clues about our status as well: a cheap suit or dress is usually noticeably different than a more expensive outfit. Other objects are also influential. In Japan, for example, most men wear a lapel pin that indicates their place of employment or the school they attend.

Dress and adornment counselling has become a major business pursuit for John Malloy in Dress for Success and The Woman's Dress for Success and Carole Jackson in Colour me Beautiful. Malloy, for example, suggests that people generally find dark blue solids to be more credible colour and design than bright plaids. While it is far from an exact science, fashion and style consultants can enhance the impression we make through our artifacts.

At one time or another almost everyone has responded to the question "How did this [disaster] happen?" with a statement like "Don't ask me. I just work here." In some cases the excuses is a legitimate one. Someone other than the person making the statement made a decision or took a step which created a problem, but far too often it is a decision, action, or lack of action by the person offering the excuse that led to the inefficiency or failure. Although the performance of every member of an organisation is in many ways influenced by the activities of other members, in the final analysis it is the individuals' choices which decide their destiny in the organisation. It concentrates on communication in organisations because it is through communication that individual employees gain the information on which they base choices and exercise the influence which translates their choices into action. The goal of this book is to give readers a sense of how organisational communication is used strategically, that is, how individual employees analyse the situations they face at work and choose the appropriate communication strategies to use in those situations. The book assumes that all employees are goal-oriented in some important ways and that if they understand how communication functions in their organisation they will be better able to use their communication skills to achieve their objectives and those of their organisations. The book explains when it is appropriate to use a variety of communication strategies, including the denial or responsibility and the claim of ignorance ("don't know. I just work here"), and more important, when not to use them.

The study of organisational communication: One of the most important recent developments in the way people look at organisations has been the increasing amount of attention paid to different aspects of communication. Managers and researchers alike have recognised that businesses must maintain at least an adequate level of communication in order to survive, that increasing the effectiveness of communication within a firm contributes to the efficiency of its operation, and that in some cases highly effective communication can increase productivity and eventually profitability. Perhaps more important has been the realisation that people who understand how communication functions in a business, who have developed a wide repertory of written and oral communicative skills, and who have learned when and how to use those skills seem to advance more rapidly and contribute more fully to their organisations than people who have not done so. As a result the number of college courses and professional training programmes concerned with organisational communication has mushroomed. Of course employees cannot function effectively unless they possess the technical skills that their positions require. But more and more it appears that being also able to recognise, diagnose, and solve communication-related problems is vital to the success of people in even the most technical occupations. Accountants must be able to gain complete, accurate, and sometimes sensitive information from their clients, supervisors of production lines must be able to obtain adequate and timely information on which to base their decisions, managers of different divisions must be able to give their subordinates clear instructions, make sure those instructions are understood, create conditions in which their commands will be carried out, and obtain reliable feedback about the completion of the tasks that they have assigned. In a recent survey of 700 middle managers, almost 85 percent of the respondents reported that it was their subordinates' communication skills (or lack or them) which determined their success or failure in critical situations. Although these managers also noted that factors like their subordinates' job-related expertise and loyalty to their supervisor and organisation also had an important impact on their effectiveness, it was their ability to communicate effectively that was crucial in most cases.

However, being able to communicate effectively at work requires two kinds of knowledge. First, it requires an understanding of the relationships that exit between communication and the operation of organisations. Since communication processes influence the way an organisation operates and are simultaneously influenced by key characteristics of the organisation, neither organisations nor organisational communication can be understood adequately if they are examined in isolation of each other.

Second, effective communication depends on employees' understanding how to choose appropriate communication strategies in different situations. This book intends to provide readers with an understanding of strategic communication skills—the ability to analyse a situation, select an appropriate communication strategy from a number of available options, and employ that strategy in an optimal way. However understanding strategic communication demands that an individual understand how communication functions in organisations, how it creates and solves problems, how it makes some situations occur and how it prevents others, how it makes some outcomes more probable and others improbable. This chapter will introduce these two most important concepts: the role of communication in organisations and the characteristics of strategic organisational communication.

Role of Communication in Organisations

Historically, formal organisations have been examined from two very different perspectives. One view has depicted them as the combination of a number of different components, each of which is linked to each other on the basis of some carefully planned and clearly articulated design. People who accept this perspective believe that organisations are designed in three distinct steps. Designing an organisation begins with an analysis of a potential market and a decision about what products goods or services, the organisation should produce. Designers then decide which tasks must be performed in order to produce the desired output and determine how each of these tasks can be completed most efficiently. Finally, designers organise the various tasks into structures and sequences which are intended to maximise the efficiency of the total operation. Since many of the components of the organisation are people, someone must be assigned the job of seeing that all who are involved in each part of the production process understand the tasks they are to perform, how they are to accomplish those tasks, the fact that they must accomplish them in a timely and efficient manner if the organisation is to function properly. In this perspective, communication is important for instrumental reasons. It functions in ways which allow members to share the information necessary for the successful completion of a complex array of interdependent tasks. Although the end products, task requirements, employee skills, or relationships among these components may change when market conditions or technologies change, this perspective assumes that the rational design of an organisation will stay relatively constant. At least, the organisation will stay stable enough so that the designers can draw a picture, usually in the form of an "organisational chart," which accurately reflects its operation.

Another viewpoint describes organisations as complex, interdependent matrices of ongoing process, not as a rational, carefully planned combination of interrelated static components. This distinction is important for two reasons. First, it leads to a view of the members of an organisation as actors, not as relatively inert components of the organisation. Employees constantly are making choices about how they will act in the variety of situations they face. Second, organisations are networks of interdependent, human actors whose actions both create situations they face allow them to respond to those situations. Although organisations can be designed by objective, outside planners, their designs constantly are in a state of change. Businesses are composed of large numbers of people who constantly are monitoring their own actions and the actions of others, processing that information, and choosing those courses of action that they think are appropriate. This description of organisations does not imply that their members are either manipulative or Machiavellian although it would admit that some of them are. Instead, it suggests that people are active agents who have their own reasons for acting as they do. They are not mechanical components of the production process, doing only what they are designed to do in precisely that way in which they are designed to do it. They are choice-making members whose actions are part of a complicated array of ongoing processes.

Within this perspective, communication is important to an organisation for two reasons. First, communication is the means through which people acquire the information and develop the criteria by which they decide how to act. Second, communication is the process through which they put their choices into practice. That is, through communication members of organisations learn that there are precedents in their organisation which constrain their choices, and they learn what those precedents are. Through communication with others, they develop and express the purposes which guide their actions. They are able to consider the potential effects of different actions only because they are capable of communicating. In addition, it is through communication that members of an organisation are able to coordinate their actions with other members of the organisation.

Because the complex array of tasks that must be performed in an organisation are independent, each member of the organisation can perform only if other members do also. In almost situations, only a small proportion of the activities of anyone employees will be necessary preconditions for the successful action of other employees. However, for each member of the organisation, there are some actions that must be taken if the organisation is to operate. And, because all members must depend on the actions of some other member(s) in order to do their jobs, they must be able to predict accurately what those other people will do in different situations. Being able to do so requires employees to understand why they act as they do and to recognise that they regularly respond to certain situations in predictable ways. Communication is the process through which people make sense out of the actions of other people, it is the means by which they are able to understand how they can coordinate their actions with the actions of others. Human action is contextual, it is the result of the choices people make within the situations they perceive themselves to be.

Unfortunately, these two views of organisations and communication often are seen as being mutually exclusive. Scholars who focus their attention on the design or structure of organisations and the functions of communication in organisation that have been described in this chapter often overlook the complex processes through which people decide how to act at work. Conversely, when scholars concentrates on understanding the relationships between processes of communication and processes of organising, they often deemphasise the tasks people perform at work and the function communication plays in the completion of those tasks. Understanding strategic organizational communication requires an analysis of both the functions of communication in organisations and the processes through which communication guides the actions of members.

❐

8

Technological Development in Communication

History provides insights into developments apt to occur as the age of information begins. Contemporary circumstances provide further hints as to the future. In combination, these elements go far toward painting a clear picture of what lies ahead, toward defining the shape of post-industrial information technologies and the changes that will occur in mass communication.

Viewed concurrently, current conditions and historical trends can generate projection that should enable communicators to avoid pitfalls capitalize on opportunities as the age of information takes shape. Projections at best are tentative. They nevertheless can help planners avoid misconception and missteps that otherwise might occur.

The age of information is *supplanting* the industrial age in the United States and other industrialised nations. Necessary hardware exists and link are being forged among communication systems to create and all encompassing integrated electronic grid. Communicator's concerns, however, are more focused on. the nature than of the timing of the post-industrial society's development. Neither the nature of the transition to the age of information and the wired society nor the potential impact can be precisely calculated. Astute observers, however, will be able to detect change in time to develop appropriate responses.

Relatively complete and current information is necessary to accurately assess prospective changes in society and mass communication. The evolution off the computer and the development of the integrated grid, for example are critical to the age of information. The speed with which they evolve will determine how rapidly the nation and the world make the transition from the industrial age to the age of information. The primary characteristics of information societies also must be considered.

These characteristics determine the future of emerging and existing channels of communication.

Finally, anticipated changes must be viewed in their historical context. Much of what is about to transpire has occurred before, although perhaps in less radical form and at slower speeds.

Communication Phases

Human communication has progressed through four distinct phases. A fifth now is beginning. Each phase is associate with a specific form of communication. During the first four phases, or stages, humanity proceeded from speaking to writing and then to printing and telecommunication. In the fifth phase, which now is taking shape, the emphasis will be on interactive communication systems.

The era of verbal communication began with the development of language. Language, which probably came into use about 35,000 B.C. in the Cro-Magnon period, enabled humans to more readily communicate with one another. Enhanced communication produced greater efficiency in food gathering and facilitated the development of complex tribal societies.

Five thousand years later, the area of writing began. Sumerian writings on clay tablets dating from 4000 B.C. mark the start of the period. Writing became humanity's dominant communication technology for must of the ensuing six centuries.

The printing era began with Gutenberg and his Bible in 1456. Printing remained the most sophisticated of communication techniques until 1844, when Samuel Morse invented the telegraph. The age of telecommunication began with Morse's telegraph and was perpetuated by Marconi's wireless. Telecommunication predominated among forms of communication until the advent of the computer in 1946.

The impact of each of these developments was greater than many now consider to have been the case. The development of writing for example, led to ability to maintain historical records and develop libraries. Generations were freed from having to relearn that which had been learned before and could dedicate themselves to adding to the knowledge of humankind. The printing press and the other technological developments were no less momentous. Printing destroyed the clerical monopoly on the bible and led to growing literacy, which in turn enhanced ability to learn. The telephone and telegraph were no less significant and history probably will proclaim the computer as the pre-eminent scientific advance of the twentieth century.

The University of Pennsylvania's ENIAC, which used eighteen thousand vacuum tubes, marked the beginning of the computer era. ENIAC's offspring in six primary forms: microcomputers, teleconferencing, teletext, videotext, interactive cable television, and satellite communication.

Most individuals knowingly have come in contact with no more than one or two of the six forms. The word knowingly is necessary in that most off today's mass media are dependent in large part on satellite communication. Television is most dependent, but newspapers and radio stations also are extensive users of satellite signals.

Other than unknowingly in the form of satellit etransmitted information, relatively small percentages of the United States population have had occasion to use a computer or to come in contact with one of the early teletext, videotext, or interactive cable systems. These circumstances cannot be taken, however, as meaning that little progress is being made toward the age of information. A close look at the process of assimilation suggests, in fact, that the information age is closer than many believe.

Assimilating Technology

The impact of interactive communication on contemporary society and on the mass communication disciplines will be a function of the speed with which the technologies involved are assimilated into society. Assimilation follows a well-established path described by J. R. Right as a "process of technological innovation". Bright's eight steps are scientific suggestion, theory or design concept laboratory verification of theory or design, laboratory demonstration or application, full scale or field trial, commercial introduction, widespread adoption, and proliferation.

Interactive communication channels already have made considerable progress along this continuum. All have proceeded through field trial to commercial introduction. Some trials, as in the case of the Qube system in Columbus, Ohio and Knight-Ridder's experience in Dade County, Florida, bave been less than successful. Their successors, in the process of installation in the late 1980s remain to be proved, but widespread adoption and eventual proliferation appear inevitable.

The microcomputer has made greater progress and probably stands between Bright's widespread adoption and proliferation stages in the assimilation process. Diffusion processes tend to progress more rapidly than most perceive to be the case, as the microcomputers has demonstrated. A 1980 study suggested computers were in about 5 percent of the 80 million United States households and that penetration would increase to more than 25 percent by 1990. Four years later, the estimates already had proved inadequate. Multiple 1984 studies showed that 15 to 16 percent households then had computers and that the total might reach 40 to 50 percent by 1990.

Household penetration, however, cannot safely be equated with computer use, more than a few computers will be underutilised although the reasons doubtless will differ, from those that prevailed during the 1970s. Early microcomputers lacked the capacity to perform functions claimed for them in much of the advertising of the day. Disappointed buyers often relegated the machines to attics or closets rather than buy more equipment.

Underutilisation during the 1990s is more likely to be a product of relatively steep learning curves. Learning problems often are encountered in complex applications software even where user friendly operating systems are used.

A companion issue to Underutilisation arises out of variety in application. Computers are as readily used for recreational or vocational purposes as for acquiring or information. Computer utilities such as CompuServe probably are as often used for one purpose as the other, although published data on this point are lacking. Lack of information in areas such as these, and the complexity of the interactive media, will render efforts to assess the extent to which the information age has arrived rather difficult.

The Integrated Grid

While microcomputers are proliferating, technolog's largest strides toward the age of information have occurred with little fanfare and beyond the eyes of casual observers. As the 1980s drew to a close, the United States stood at the brink of completing what has been called the integrated grid, a network though which the nation's communication systems would be brought together into a cohesive whole. The grid in 1989 consisted of telephone, cable television, electronic mail, and voice mail systems, all soon to be linked directly or indirectly to satellites, data banks, and to one another.

The major breakthroughs of the 1980s occurred late in the decade in two forms: unification of electronic mail systems and development of bridging mechanisms to permit movement of information across system boundaries. The unification process was a sort of "shotgun wedding" arranged by the Aerospace Industries Association (ALA), whose members send almost a million electronic mail messages annually. AlA's message to the seven sisters of electronic mail (Easy Link, Telemail, Dialcom, MCI mail and AT&T Mail) was this: develop a uniform system or we will take our business elsewhere.

Within months, because a technological standard had been established in 1984, the uniform system was installed and operating. The technological standard earlier had been permitted to languish only because each of the players apparently felt that adoption might cost more subscribers than it produced.

The electronic mail systems change to the uniform standard was the latter-day equivalent of the linking of the nation's independent telephone companies. The more recent change was especially momentous, moreover, in that bridges already existed between electronic mail and computer systems. CompuServe Information Service (CIS), a computer utility, already had linked up to MCI Mail and also was offering facsimile services to its customer. South Central Bell concurrently was installing its. T.U.G. gateway system, which offered direct access to CompuServe. Only cable television systems were still to be tied in and telephone companies were moving in that direction as rapidly as legislative and regulatory constraints permitted.

Information Bridges

All that will remain to be accomplished with completion of the network is comparable development in systemic content, which appears to be occurring as well. The value of the grid to users will be limited only by the quality and quantity of accessible information. The information exists in two basic types. One type, already reduced to electronic form, is readily entered into the system. Information in print or on tape is another matter.

Evolving technology already address the growing volume of information existing in electronic form and soon will also be able to handle the bulk of printed and taped information. Information in electronic form is contained in the nation's data bases. In 1980, some three hundred data bases existed and communication scholars were predicting they would more than double in number by the end of the century. In 1989, less than ten years later, more than three thousand data bases existed, and the total by the year 2000 was expected to be at double or triple that figure.

Many of the new data bases will contain information that once existed only in mechanical form, information once believed to be beyond reach of economical data entry techniques. Three technological devices in 1989 appeared to evolving to a point at which this obstacle would soon be overcome. One was the optical scanner; the second was a growing collection of software capable of translating documents from one language to another. The third was the voice activated computer.

Optical Scanners. Optical scanning systems appeared in relatively crude from in the mid-1980s. Like many computer-relate technologies, they consisted of three parts: a mechanical scanner, an accompanying software package, and a microcomputer. Early scanners accepted images only in "bit mapped" from. Alphanumeric characters could be loaded into computers via scanners, but only as graphic images. Resulting computer files could not be edited, because characters were handled by computers as drawings. Content of printed or typed pages could not be converted to conventional computer file form for handling as for example, word processing or data files.

The "bit-mapped barrier" as it might be called was overcome for most users by 1990 as optical character recognition (OCR) software started to appear in ever more sophisticated and progressively less costly form. OCR software package enabled scanners to produce conventional computer files suitable for further manipulation in word processor or data base programmes. Accuracy rates in reproduction were in excess of 99 percent. Accuracy rate refers to numbers of errors typically appearing in scanned computer files. No more than one character in one hundred, in a file that is 99 percent accurate, would not conform to the original document.

Accuracy rates of 99 percent were acceptable in most applications because resulting word processing files then could be manually or automatically edited. Computer spelling an grammar checkers both could be used to eliminate misspellings. The latter processes were imperfect in that programmes could not differentiate between, for example, farm and form because both are valid words. Resulting documents nevertheless were sufficient to most information user's needs.

Scanners Applied. Scanners equipped with relatively accurate optical recognition software represented a major breakthrough in information management. The technologies involved enabled computer user to easily and rapidly load masses of information that had not been created in electronic form, thus completing state-of-the-art banks of information.

Scanner loading ultimately can be expected to be used, for example, in creating comprehensive professional libraries for organizations such as the Public Relations Society of America (PRSA). The society in 1987 set out to document and bring together in a single repository the body of knowledge underlying the practice of public relations. The first step was a year long effort by a team of academic researchers and practitioners to specify books and documents to be made part of the collection. The following year was dedicated to abstracting the material involved, creating brief summary statements that could be entered into a computer.

Abstracting work carried but on multiple university campuses was done on computers. Resulting documents thus were readily gathered and indexed in a central location. PRSA had no immediate plans to load the underlying documents. Legal complexities would make this a time consuming process. Availability of optical character recognition software made the process practical, however, and many in the profession anticipate that the task soon will be undertaken.

The only substantive barrier to creating the sort of comprehensive data library that would result for PRSA is economic. Data loading would be labor intensive even with legal obstacles removed. Costs involved could be justified only if PRSA or an alternative sponsoring organization could establish the data base on a self sustaining basis.

Self-funding would require a volume of user revenues adequate to cover data base maintenance costs and recapture all initial expenses. A cash flow of that magnitude, in turn, would require a larger user base than immediately was in prospect. Best available estimates in 1990 indicated that fewer than two thousand public relations practitioners were using on line data bases. The user base was growing but neat term growth rate did not appear adequate to justify the investment required.

Translation Programmes. A further quantum increase in user potential was possible, however, with the advent of computer programmes that could translate from one language to another. Programme developers by 1989 had met one of the most difficult translation challenges a programme would translate Japanese to English and vice versa. Such a programme requires computer recognition and translation to and from symbols as well as alphanumeric characters. Programs to translate virtually very other major language were expected to quickly follow the Japanese-English programme.

While superficially a minor step forward, translation programmes imply a quantum increase in data base usage.

Depending on programme size, translators could be stored, in either mainframes housing data base or in personal computers. Data base uses could instruct mainframes to translate before downloading or could download and then translate. Benefits to the academic world and resultant increases in database usage in that sector would be unprecedented. Computer, data banks, and translation programs will have reduced by years or decades the time that otherwise would elapse before papers published in obscure academic journals in Japan could be read in the English-speaking world.

While most in the academic world are computer users and comfortable with the technology, lay person are another problem. Computer phobia is a common although curable aliment in contemporary society. Curses occur as users learn that *(a)* they are dealing with dumb machines that require specific directions and that *(b)* no error on the part of the user can harm the machine. At worst, the process involve must be abandoned and restarted.

Voice Activation. Unfortunately, cures historically have been unlikely where prospective user manage to avoid physical contact with computers. Physical contact soon many be unnecessary, however, as more, and more computers are equipped with voice activation systems. If computer phobia is the last major barrier to universal computer usage, voice-activate systems may prove to be the climate antidote.

Computer that respond to the human voice rather than to keyboards became available in simple form during the late 1980s and promised to quickly come into common usage. While a novelty when first introduced, voice activation offered considerable promise for equipment vendors as well as users. Potential for manufacturers and vendors in the form of increased attractiveness in the market-place and, consequently, grater sales suggested that voice activated equipment might proliferate at an unprecedented rate.

The first generally available commercial development in voice activated computers was a simple translation device designed for use by English-speaking international travelers. Users simply turn on the machine and speak clearly into a self-contained microphone. The machine plays back the phrase or sentence in the designated language.

While prospective user of the translation device were few in number, 1989 also saw the introduction of another voice-reading device aimed at a broader market: a voice activated telephone that could be programmed to dial the numbers of any of fifty individuals or firms after receiving appropriate verbal commands.

Neither of the voice activation systems was highly sophisticated. Developers of the translation device experienced difficulties in coping with difference in user voice and inflections. The telephones were programmed to respond to their owners voices and did not perform as reliably for other household members. There appeared little doubt, however, that voice activated equipment would be quickly refined and more generally applied. As this trend develops and the technology is applied to databases, their use can be expected to increase.

Integrated Systems

Collectively, technologies of the types described above will permit development of highly integrated systems that will accept and deliver information in any form. The basic language probably will be computer code, but "translators" quickly will bridge gaps between systems.

Optical characfer readers and voice recognition equipment will be the primary bridges. The optical character readers will translate written or printed material into computer language, while voice recognition equipment will do the same for humans or their transcribed messages. Where appropriate, scanners and electronic "cameras" also will be tied to the combined telephone-voice mail cable television electronic mail systems to transmit drawings and photos.

The flexibility of these systems will produce massive growth in informational resources. Complexity off systems used in information retrieval also will increase, however, contributing to the complexity of the interactive media so complex, pervasive, and potentially rewarding can these systems become that efforts to assess their potential impact are especially difficult. Close examination of a number of factors nevertheless may suggest how future trends may develop and, by implication, the responses that may be necessary on the part of professional communicators.

Perhaps the strongest governor of speed and scope of change will be the relative complexity of the interactive media. Although necessary to handle the volume of information that soon will be available for public use, systemic complexity can discourage use. The responses of individuals and organization to the arrival off the interactive systems also require consideration.

The nature of information societies also will play a role in acceptance of interactive media. Computer literacy already is required in most schools and is fast becoming necessary in most occupations. These condition may pave the way, at least in part, for the arrival of interactive media. Some insight it no potential public response also may be gleaned from earlier experiences with television, although television, it must be remembered, was and remains primarily an entertainment rather than an informational medium.

Media Complexity

Interactivity, most researchers agree, is the primary characteristic of the new media. Definitions of interactivity are difficult to come by, however, and no two come close to full agreement as to the meaning of the term. Most definitions incorporate a half dozen variables present in most interactive media. The variables, according to Michigan State University's Carrie Heeter, are the following:

1. Complexity of choices available to users
2. Level of effort required of users
3. Media responsiveness to users
4. Extent to which media monitor users
5. Extent to which users can add information to sources
6. Extent to which interpersonal communication is supported

Heeter's list is not all-inclusive. It does, however, provide multiple bases for comparing interactive media.

User Choices. The extent to which interactive media enable users to be selective is important in that audiences tend to fragment as selectivity leaves increase. In television, for example, individuals channel audiences shrink as numbers of channels increase. Addition off interactive channels will produce further audience fragmentation.

This phenomenon will be of special interest in that the content of some new channels may be wholly informational, as in the case of Cable News Network, while others may consist entirely of entertainment, as with HBO or Cinemax. Entertainment channel audiences, to the extent that their members avoid information, will become a challenge to communicators.

Effort Required. Ease of access also has always been a factor in the extent to which mass media are used. Newspaper circulation for example, tends to be better where home delivery is available than elsewhere. Magazine circulation levels climb where publications are available on newsstands as well as by mail.

Accessibility of information varies to a greater extent among the new media. Cabletext system, for example, need only be turned on. Pre-programmed material scrolls up the screen automatically, requiring no effort on the part off the viewer. Electronic data bases such as CompuServe and The Source provide access to more information but require much greater user involvement in retrieval.

Responsiveness. Higher levels of effort seem to be better tolerated. Where systems are highly responsive. A number of researchers have defined system responsiveness as the extent to which interactive media function in human fashion. In phone mail, for example, systems give callers exhaustive sets of options (buttons to push) as they obtain information or organizational responses. Phone mail, in the late 1980s, probably came closest to this definition of responsiveness in that computer responses were delivered in "human voice."

Interactivity, then in part is measured by the extent to which media can react responsively to users. The key word here is responsively. The ultimate is reached in this dimension of Interactivity when the modicum's second, third, and subsequent responses are functions of earlier human input.

User Monitoring. Where interactivity exists, user monitoring also is usually present. While included by most scholars as a dimension of interactive media, user monitoring along is a marginal attribute. Telephone companies for years have been able to monitor the extent to which their services are used. Origin, destination, time of placement, and elapsed time of telephone calls long have been recorded for billing purposes.

User monitoring of interactive media differs from telephone company practices only as to *(a)* level of user privacy and *(b)* application of resulting data. Telephone companies historically have been protective of customers privacy. Whether media will be equally protective is open to question, especially since collected data conceivably could be both sold to advertisers and used to fine tune content for maximum commercial value.

Interpersonal Communication. Privacy also can be an issue where interpersonal communications exists. The degree to which systems facilitate interpersonal communication is a major variable among media. Traditional media offer no potential for interpersonal exchanges CompuServe, The Source, and other computer utilities also offer electronic mail, bulletin boa d, and in some cases, facsimile services. Bulletin boards are, open systems, but user privacy is protected in electronic mail and facsimile systems.

Collectively, Heeter suggests, the six attributes of interactivity create a broader range of user options than ever existed before. The existence of these options, she said, suggest four propositions concerning popular concepts of mediated communication:

1. Information is always sought or selected rather than merely disseminated.
2. Media systems require different levels of user activity.
3. Activity varies with users as well as media.
4. Person-machine interaction is a unique form of communication.

The first and last of these propositions are especially important to communicators, although the others are noteworthy as well. There appears to be little doubt that the information that individuals assimilate in the age of information will consist primarily off that which has been sought or selected. So great will the total amount of available information have become that individuals will have little choice but to establish formal or informal screening mechanisms. These may include more frequent changing of television channels, limiting computer based information gathering services to select information on specific topics.

Person machine interact on inevitably will be necessary in the latter circumstances, and more and more of this type of communication is to be expected. The trend is apt to be stimulated by growth in available information in the context of more demanding occupational circumstances. To extent, at least, variation in types of user will produce variation in information use and in level of communication activity.

The Television Experience

What can communicators anticipate with the one set of the age of information or as the interactive media become part of individuals daily lives? Individuals information gathering patterns inevitably will change. Those who can apply the interactive media in ways that will make their lives easier, more enjoyable, or more productive inevitably will do so. Just how their usage patterns will develop, however, is open to conjecture.

Some sense of direction might be gained by examining changes is media use patterns that developed in the wake of the introduction of television. A 1955 study published by the United States Department of Health, Education, and Welfare showed massive shifts in individual use of time subsequent to acquisition of television sets.

The increase in television use was based on the amount of time respondents previously had spent viewing television away from home (an average of 12 minutes daily) compared with time they subsequently spent with television at home 9267 minutes daily). More important in the overall, however, was the fact that the average individual increased by 41 percent the amount of time spent with all media.

Where did the additional time come from? Research by J.P. Robinson indicates that the public appetite for television was satisfied by sacrificing the following activities:

* 13 minutes of sleeping

* 12 minutes of social time away from home

* 8 minutes of radio time
* 6 minutes of reading listening
* 7 minutes of housework
* 5 minutes of travel
* 5 minutes of conversation

Television induced user, in other words, to sleep less, stay home more, spend less time with other media, and converse less the they had before. Other than in the case of radio, media usage patterns showed little immediate change. Change that did occur, moreover, apparently involved the entertainment rather than the informational component of the new medium.

The broad impact of television cannot, however, be assumed to have created uniform results. An analysis of sources of voter information during the 1984 election and earlier, for example, showed that television progressively became more popular as a source of national political news. Voters continued to depend on other sources, however, for information on state and local issues.

The Information Society

To what extent will the television experience be repeated with the onset of the age of information? The question is difficult if not impossible to answer at this juncture. The age of information, according to Rutgers University's Jorge R. Schement, can be identified generally though the presence of six characteristics:

1. Information exchanged as a commodity
2. A large information work force
3. Inter-connectedness among individuals and institutions
4. The special status of scientific knowledge
5. A social environment with many messages and channels
6. Widely diffused information technology

All of these elements, to a greater or lesser extent, exist today. The issue of magnitude then becomes paramount in determining whether the age information has indeed arrived. The best answer probably can be structured in keeping with the extent to which the interactive media have become pervasive in the society. What is pervasive? Some suggest that telephones, television, and automobiles, for example, are pervasive in our society. Pervasiveness, they contend, implies that the element in question would be missed were it absent. The telephone, for example, is pervasive in that it would be quickly missed were it suddenly to disappear.

By the Pervasiveness standard, microcomputers remain in their juvenile years. While proliferating at rates greater than anticipated by many early forecasters, they have yet to appear in half of the nation's households. The mechanics of the information age, however, are quietly putting the finishing touches on a system that will leapfrog the microcomputer into the lives of very individual. That system is the integrated electronic grid, an amalgamation of telephone, electronic mail, and computer systems that soon will reach into virtually very household in the nation and much of the industrial and postindustrial world.

The electronic grid readily could provide all the convenience of a computer at negligible cost by enabling individuals to access and use mainframes by telephone or cable systems. Futurist dream of computers in very home thus may remain far away while at the same time standing much closer to realization than many believe. With the electronic grid, homeowners will require nothing more than many keyboards attached to their television sets to access mainframe computers. Microcomputers, in many of their applications, may become unnecessary in home applications.

Information for Profit

All of these changes will take place in an essentially capitalist society populated by media organisations that have no intention of yielding the dominant positions. All are engaged in what for years has been a simple and lucrative pursuit: selling information for profits.

The sale of information for profit underpins all of the communication disciplines. Advertising, marketing, public relations and sales promotion all add value to information that in the end is disseminated by the mass media. All of the costs ultimately are paid by consumers.

Neither the businesses nor the disciplines involved, from the largest of publishing or broadcasting organizations to the single professional advertising consultancy, necessarily want to change the ways in which they have been generating profits for years. Neither corporate nor personal preference, unfortunately, will exert any real influence in the marketplace. Change inevitably will reship all media and all communication disciplines.

Preparedness Lacking

While the media have been preparing for change, and while those involved in advertising have been on the front lines in preliminary economic skirmishes, most communicators have yet to feel the cutting edge of the information age. Advertising, marketing, public relations, and sales promotion all have evolved in concert with change in society an technology. Recent experiences among members of the communication disciplines leave them ill prepared, however, for changes yet to come.

Members of the communication disciplines-advertising, marketing, public relations, sales promotion, and related fields-experienced little difficulty in adjusting to contemporary circumstances. Many, perhaps most, practitioners readily adapted to using computers, videotape, facsimile systems, and electronic mail. Too many have concluded that, in adjusting to these technologies, they have mastered the ability to manage change. They tend to assume, as a result, that the 1990s and the 2000s will be similar to the 1980s. Those assumption are tenuous at best, dangerous at worst.

The United States and other developed nations have been caught up in what Peter Drucker described as an age of discontinuity, a turbulent era of transition from industrial to postindustrial society. The 1980s saw the traumatic weaning of the economy from dependence on the nation's industrial base. The 1990s will see the equally difficult onset of the postindustrial age of information. Problems that accompanied the decline of industry during the 1980s were met with relative ease among the communication disciplines. Clienteles and their needs changed, but few practitioners or counseling firms found themselves in dire straits as a result. The 1990s and 2000s promise to be less comfortable. Communicators will be called on to cope with basic structural change occurring at an accelerating pace. The change involved, moreover, will be fundamental to the communication disciplines rather than to the organisation communicators serve.

The latter distinction is important. Counseling or otherwise assisting organisations caught up in discontinuity is a relatively easy task. Professional detachment permits dispassionate problem analysis and prescription of logical and rational remedies. Coping with change that threaten personal economic survival requires identical procedures in emotion-laden environments more conducive to panic than logic.

As the name itself implies, new communication technologies are those which are of more recent origin. Interactivity is their distinguishing feature. For the purpose of this unit, new communication technologies can also be understood as those which are capable of a much higher degree of interactivity than that offered by the traditional communication technologies.

Writing, printing and electronic media like radio and television are examples of traditional technologies which are essentially one-way in nature. Therefore, their interactive capabilities are very limited. Besides, this limited interactivity occurs after considerable delay. For example, a newspaper which depends on the traditional technology of print can, be said to be interactive to the extent that it publishes readers, letters in its, 'letters to the editor' column, Similarly, a radio station too is interactive in that it broadcasts programmes which carry responses to audience queries. We can, therefore say that interactivity is at best a marginal property of traditional communication media.

In the new communication technologies, on the other hand, interactivity is the main property. The use of computer in one form or the other, as an integral part of their system, is what enables them to be interactive. In the following sections, we will take up for study some of the main technologies under this category.

The idea of interlinking and communicating with the aid of computers was as old as the mainframe computers of the 1970s. Owing to their prohibitive price, the mainframes came to be owned only by mega-establishments like government, big business house, universities, etc., Individuals could not afford them for personal use. At the same time, the high cost of the mainframes required their owners to find ways and means to maximize their utilisation in order to make them cost effective. The networking of computers, it was found, allowed simultaneous access to a single mainframe by any number of user. Naturally, this development suited owners and users alike.

Computer networks thus emerged as a kind of public utility to help users communicate with a central computing facility such as a database, and retrieve information too. In the decades that followed computer of much smaller computer that displayed greater capabilities at just a fraction of the price. At present the use of computer network of various specialised and general purpose has become quite common, even in the less developed parts of the world.

In our own country, computer network are widely used by public sector organizations, big business houses, government department etc., for their day-to-day transactions. Indian Airlines, Indian Railways and a few state under taking own computer network dedicated to managing their operations. The National Informatics Centre (NIC) has set up a special purpose computer network known as NICNET which has its headquarters in Delhi. Spanning district headquarters across the country, this network facilitates real time exchange of information on various aspects of the development process.

Such real-time flow of information enable planners and other decision makers at the headquarters to decide on appropriate policies, taking into consideration the latest statistics. In the absence of such computer net working in the past, it is said that vital decisions at the national level had to be taken with the help of data which were at least a decade old. Apart from helping administrations, NICNET is also said to be regularly used for other application like exchange of expert medical advice by specialists to doctors working in remote areas.

On a global scale, INTERNET is the largest computer network which permeated almost all parts of the world, Composed thousands of interconnected networks initially in the united state. INTERNET. can offer you an immense range of information services such as electronic mail, file transfer, data bases and multimedia. INTERNET also provides connectivity to mobile receivers through a wireless broadcasting service operating on satellite links.

Computer networks have several advantages over interpersonal communication. Asynchronocity, that is flexibility inherent in the system to enable information exchange without the need for the sender an the recipient to be present simultaneously, is one such advantage. However, it also suffers from various drawbacks like the lack of human touch. Communication engineers constancy endeavor to improve the so-called user friendliness of the system concerned by approximating in to interpersonal interaction.

Teleconferencing

Teleconferencing is a means by which individuals or group located at different places can exchange date, speech visual materials like graphs or diagrams, or moving pictures of themselves and any other relevant information. Teleconferencing is made possible by the integration of computers and communications in such a manner as to form a holistic system which can work in real-time.

Depending on the particular application, scope and complexity involved teleconferencing can be classified under the following types:

— **Computer Conferencing.** In this case, only computer data can be exchanged among multiple locations. Real-time interaction among the locations is possible, but only to the extent of computer data. The physical linkages among the several computers can be in the form of telephone wires or through wireless means as in the case of microwave or satellite.

— **Audio Conferencing.** In this, the participants can actually talk to one another as if in a face-to face situation. Facilities are provided for anyone location to talk to any another or all of them simultaneously. In addition, audio teleconferences also enable exchanges of computer data on the same physical link (telephone cables or wireless). Audio Teleconferencing enables real-time exchange of information without losing the human touch.

— **Audio-Graphic Conferencing.** This is more advanced form of audio teleconferencing in which in addition to audio and computer data, still graphics like drawings, maps, etc., can also be exchanged. Further refinements in technology enable even slow-scan video pictures to be exchanged as a part of audio teleconferencing system. The same pair of telephone wires would suffice to carry all the above by Bandwidth Compression techniques which are technically . known as ISDN (Integrated Services Data Network).

— **Video Conferencing.** This is the highest form of teleconferencing in which a two-way exchange of moving pictures is possible without any restriction, in addition to aüdio and data.

The telecommunication links required for such a conferencing system prove to be very costly because of the fact that moving pictures need very wide bandwidths. Hence, a lower version of video teleconferencing which is called one-way video and two-way audio is gaining currency.

In the latter case, the main location (typically the headquarters of an organization) will have facilities of sending audio as well as video which are received by all the remote locations. But the remote locations will have facilities for sending only audio, and not video. Another words while the remote locations can receive both pictures and voices they will be able to respond only through voice. Teleconferencing of this kind has been widely experimented with by many organizations in India using satellite links.

Already, Teleconferencing is an accept form of technology in advance countries, especially for business communication. It is only a matter of time before this technology becomes popular in countries such as ours, because the necessary infrastructure like telephone links and satellite are already available. Teleconferencing is gaining popularity due to the minimal physical travel demanded of its participants. The time-saving involved in this process is also significant factor. The experience of advanced countries has been that, apart from economizing on time and travel, teleconferencing also helps in improving corporate efficiency and participator management.

Teletext

Teletext is form of broadcast technology by means of which several 'pages' of textual information (say, latest weather reports, stock exchange figures, airline/train reservation etc.) can be transmitted on an already existing television channel. The teletext information is encoded in the so called 'vertical blanking interval' of the television screen which is invisible in the normal course of television viewing. However, when activated by a teletext 'decoder' at the receiving end the television screen starts displaying the teletext information in lien of the normal TV programmes. Facilities exist in teletext to enable viewers to choose a particular page of teletext containing relevant information which serves their needs, and recall the particular page. Thus, a business man wanting to know the latest trend in the stock exchange can press his decoder for the particular page containing stock market news, and get the display on his TV screen instantly. He will be also to view that page as long as he wishes or he can turn over to some other page or revert back to the normal TV programme as per his wish.

TV station equipped with a teletext service, normally update the information in regular intervals, say very half an hour, for the benefit of the viewers. About 300 teletext pages (a page means one TV frame containing information) can be accommodated per TV channel and a collection of these pages goes by the name of 'teletext magazines'.

The Delhi Station of Doordarshan provides a teletext service on the second channel; access to it is possible with the help of a diecoder. The magazine contains specific pages earmarked for national and international news, travel information, sports, local announcements weather reports etc. A few main pages of the magazine are also putout in the 'picture mode' *i.e.* on the main chartnel itself for the benefit of those not equipped with ctecoders. It is possible to extend this service to other Doordarshan stations for the benefit of viewers all over the country.

Teletext is a simple technology which can be used to advantage for public communication. The advantages in hornet in broadcast media such as instant and widespread reach, to an unlimited clientele, are applicable to teletext as well. Different countries have teletext services which confirm to different technical standards, and a universal code of transmission is yet to be invented. Its essential simplicity, instantaneous dissemination of messages and ease of updating information make it a worthwhile technology with myriad applications.

Radiotext

Better known by the term 'Radio date system (RDS), Radiotext is a technology similar to Teletext but with the important different that it works in conjunction with FM Radio (Frequency Modulation) while Teletext works on television.

While conventional radio broadcasts on mediumwave and shortwave bands have the advantage of larger service areas for a given radio station, the severe congestion of radio stations in these bands in recent years has forced the use of higher frequency bands for radio transmission. Use of these higher frequency bands as in the case of the FM Radio, however, would mean restricting the reach of a radio station essentially to line of sight range which is about 30 km radium. FM stations are ideal as local radio station, as they can offer programmes of local community interest, high fidelity music, local news etc., to the public.

Radiotext is to be seen as a value-added service on FM Radio. This technology essentially consist of transmitting data and other textual material piggy-back on the FM carrier so that the listeners/ viewers who are equipped with a radiotext 'decoder' can extract this signal from an ongoing FM transmission and watch the same on a computer screen which forms a part of the radio text receiving system. Facilities are available in a decoder to select either the radiotext or the normal FM transmission at will. In addition, the listeners or viewers, as in the case of teletext, will be able to select the particular page of information of their interest and hold on to it for any length of time. Audio signal of speech quality (*i.e.* of restricted bandwidth) can also form part of a radiotext signal. This would mean that institutions like Open Universities can transmit their audio lessons or radiotext, while simultaneously transmitting portion of their print material.

Experiments of this kind are already underway with the joint collaboration of All India Radio and Yaswantrao Chavan Maharashtra State open University, Nasik. An important deterrent for widespread use of Radiotext for such application, however, is that the receiving system works out to be several times costlier the FM Radio set itself. Moreover, FM Radio is still in its infancy in our country and the availability of FM radio sets in rather. Under the circumstances, the widespread use of Radiotext in our country is unlikely in the near future.

Videotex

Videotex (please note the absence of 't' at the end of the word) is another form of interactive communication technology which is inside usage in several advanced countries. While the teletext operates on television and radiotext in FM radio, videotex work with the help of the public telephone connection an the domestic TV set/ computer screen form integral components of a videotex system. Customers provided with videotex facilities can make use of it for such varied applications as electronic shopping, access to data bases, tele-banking, or exchanging messages with friends.

As videotex is essentially interactive it has much more to offer than teletext or radiotext in terms of selective information exchange and retrieval. However, a well developed and reliable telephone network is essential for operating a videotex service.

For this reason, as of now, videotex services are popular only in advanced countries. With gradual improvements taking place by way of digital telephone exchanges and replacement of conventional telephone wires with optical fibres, the reliability as well as capacity of telephone systems everywhere are bound to increase in due course. Value-added services like the videotex too are expected to gain in popularity alongside such developments. Dissemination of television programmes via cable to a community of households started in the '50s. To begin with advantages of cable distribution was seen as improving the reception conditions of television in isolated mountainous regions. Later on, TV signals received via satellite were put out incurable distribution systems, thus offering many more TV channels for the viewers. With this, the popularity and spread of cable distribution systems grew dramatically. Concurrently with the distribution of satellite channels, facilities like 'pay TV' in which individual viewers have the choice of receiving programmes of their preference at a price, have also been introduced. In other words, the cable systems have been endowed with interactive properties.

Advancements in digital technology and fibre optics have resulted in further improve version of cable distribution. For example, viewers in advanced countries can now make use of the cable for receiving programmes of their choice at the press of button. The selected programme is then down-loaded by the cable company into the viewer's terminal as a compressed 'digital packet' in a matter off seconds. The programme is the held in the electronic memory off the receiving terminal which can be viewed straightway or some time at leisure. The asynchronocity of interactive cable distribution systems is a unique advantage in the gamut of new communication technologies. Transnational television, *i.e.* transmission of television programmes from one country to another, became a reality with the development of Communication Satellites. These satellites are satellites in an orbit above the earth's equator at a height of about 36,000 km. called the geo-stationary orbit. All satellites parked in the geostationary orbit have a period of rotation equal to 24 hours and hence, appear stationary to an observer on the earth. Besides, the great distance of the orbit also offers the advantages for the satellites to 'see' as much as one-third of the earth's surface thus enabling it to cover such a vast area.

Communication Satellites are owned by various individual nations as well as collectively by group of nations to cater to several applications like broadcasting, television and telecommunication. INTELSAT (International Telecommunications Satellite Consortium) is an international body consisting of more than 90 member countries of which India is one. The satellites commissioned by INTELSAT cater to the collective needs of the members countries as per as mutually agreed tariff structure. Ground terminals (these are known as earth stations) for receiving/sending signals from/to the satellites are located in several places in the member countries. In India, two such earth stations have been established for the INTELSAT network—one near Pune an the other near Dehradun. Most of the international telecommunications traffic and exchange with other countries of live coverage of events takes place via the INTELSAT network.

India is credited with taking several major initiatives in the field of satellite communications. The famous SITE (Satellite Instructional Television Experiment) during 1975-76, In which about 2400 remote villages in the country were served with television programmes via satellite, is a case in point. The experiment has proved the efficacy of satellite communications as a cost effective means for countrywide dissemination of educational and developmental TV programmes.' Gradually, our country has developed its own satellite system, INSAT (Indian National Satellite System).

INSAT is a multi-purpose satellite service catering to telecommunications, radio and TV transmission an weather forecasting. The second generation of INSAT satellites which are currently in operation, have a larger number of transporters which can be used for further expansion of satellite communications. In particular, regional telecasting can be extended in all language zones new services like teleconferencing introduced.

Mushrooming of satellite-based transnational television in recent years is a cause for concern as well as hope. The sudden spurt in the availability of satellite channels all over the country from across our borders would mean a potential threat to our own national broadcast media. The virtual absence of any legal mechanisms to check or control these transmission of external origin can jeopardize our own priorities in the communication sector and divert the attention of the populace away from important information on development activities. On the other hand, the competitive presence of external channels can motivate the local broadcasters to become more professional and quality conscious.

Direct Broadcast Satellites (DBS) are specially designed for broadcast applications so that the signal transmitted from them can be directly received by home receivers equipped with a small dish antenna (typically half a meter diameter) and an interfacing unit. Use of such satellites obviates the need for land based retransmitting stations (called LPTs). DBS are in extensive use in Europe, the USA and Japan.

As mentioned earlier, the application areas to which multi purpose satellites like the fact become that we take them for granted. Whenever you dial a long distance telephone call, say from India to the USA your voice and the person you have called travel via some satellite route or the other, most probably via the INTELSAT network. You may notice in such cases, a very small but clearly discernible deal of a fraction a seconding receiving the respond of the other person. A similar delay will be by the person at the other end while receiving your voice. This is because of the extraordinarily long journey of thousands of kilometers which the voice signal have to travels on the satellite route. Of course, such delays are common not only to telephone conversations but all other traffic taking place through satellite communications.

Many national newspapers which are published simultaneously from multiple location take advantage of satellite communication for instant transmission of their pages from the publishing center to another. For example The Hindus has arrangements for publishing its Delhi edition by transmitting pages from Madras to Delhi through INSAT.

In the foregoing sections, we have surveyed the salient features of some of the new communication technologies individually. It is to be noted, however, that real-life situation often employ the simultanous use of more than one technologies individually. It is to be noted, however, that real life situations often employ the simultaneous use of more than one technology in a given situation. For example, the STAR TV programmes that you receive on your home TV set, reach you by means of satellite communications up to the point of your cable operator's terminal, and from then on via cable. Similarly, a long distance telephone call may get connected via microwave or a submarine cable for part of the route and via satellite for the rest of its journey. Such combinations, however, usually do not affect the technical quality of the communication in question. So the user of the most part remain unaware of the details of the technology mix involved. Nevertheless, every technology has its distinct attributes advantages an disadvantages, because of which an optimal technology selection is possible for any given application. Some of these have already been discussed in the concerned sections earlier; what follows is a relative assessment of the various technologies with regard to communication parameters like Interactivity, asynchronocity and demassification.

Interactivity. While Interactivity is a property in which the new communication technologies, as a rule, excel over the traditional ones, some of them are evidently much more interactive than others. Tele-conferencing and video tele-conferencing can be cited as the most interactive while, teletext or radiotext can be placed at the other end of the interactivity scale. Even in the traditional communication media, the ordinary telephone is a very good interactive device. The strength of the new technologies in this regard, is that their Interactivity is much more extensive and is not necessarily limited to just two individuals as in the case of telephone.

Asynchronocity. The term asynchronocity refers to that property of the medium whereby the simultaneous presence of all the participants in a communication exercise is not compulsory. For example, in a computer network, facilities like "store & forward" enables the message to be retrieved at a convenient time other than the one at which the message has actually been sent. Thus while real time exchange of communication is possible though such a technology, it offers the added flexibility of asynchronocity. The degree of asynchronocity varies from one technology to the other. It can be said to be the highest where only computers are required to intact without live human intervention, as in the case of Electronic Mail, or computer data are only kind of tele-conferencing. It is least in a two-way video tele-conferencing.

Demassification: Traditional media like press, radio or television are instances of one-to many kind of communication. Therefore, they are unsuitable where the communication needs are more individualized. Demassification refers to the extent to which a given technology can lend itself to such individualised communication. The normal telephone system is an ideal example of a technology endowed with a high degree of demassification. New communication technologies in general possess this characteristic while at the same time enabling communication among large group or individuals dispersed over large areas. In other words, the new communication technologies are the reverse of the traditional technologies. Tele-conferencing or computer communication are high in their demassification while teletext is at the lower end of the demassification ladder. The new communication technologies have not yet penetrated sufficiently in Third Word countries like ours. Therefore, we will not be able to determine their likely impact on our society with any degree of certainty. What we can conjecture in this regard is by studying the experience of developed countries like the USA which have been using these technologies over a considerable period any by extrapolating the impact of some of the present technologies like television, Noted communication scholar. Everett Rogers, says that the new communication technologies have a marked social impact in the following respects, especially during their adaptability stages.

As the new technologies are relatively costlier and knowledge-intrusive, they will be adopted only by the higher echlons of society at fist, who can really afford them. Thus ironically, communication gaps would widen among several sections of society because of the new communication technologies. This phenomenon is, of course, not unique for the new technologies. When television was intruded, a similar thing has happened as only the rich could embrace this medium in the beginning. As the ownership of TV sets gradually increased, the initial imbalances too have become less pronounced. A similar situation is expected in the case of the new technologies. Despite initial imbalances, however, overall information flow in the society is bound to go up. What happens by way of information imbalance within a society is also true of situation among at large. Advanced countries which are already information-rich tend to become richer, thereby widening the information gap between countries. This may lead to an unfavourable situation for the Third World countries which are already at the receiving end of the technological supremacy of the First World. Information overload is likely to happen, which in turn poses problem of coping with selective retrieval of required information, from heaps of randomly accumulated information. Here again, the new technologies themselves are likely to come to our rescue, as for example special computer software which may enable users to obtain such selective display of information as is relevant to them. Unemployment may abound in certain sectors as the new technologies would eliminate or render surplus certain traditional jobs and occupations. Some new jobs and new occupations may be created in their place, but not in numbers sufficient enough to compensate the loss of traditional jobs. Displacement of jobs may be felt more acutely during the introductory phase off the new technologies, than when the technologies in question get integrated fully into society. The universal presence of computers and easy access to them via network is likely to raise problems concerning privacy and security of communications. Use of special passwords and the like are of course an obvious protection, but they too have their limitation. Clever use of special software may also enable computer miscreants/hackers to break the secret passwords and get at the classified information straight away. Great use of the new technologies may enable the organisations concerned to become more decentralized in their diction making and other functions. Here again, an exact opposite may be possible as the new technologies permit much tighter monitoring on the movements and performances of subordinate staff thereby bringing about a 'Big-Brother" kind of centralized control. Much depends on the way the managements want to use the new technologies. It is feared gender inequality will increase. Though unfounded, the apprehension is prevalent that boys rather than girls will adapt themselves faster and more easily to things like computer programming, due to their supposedly inherent superiority in mathematical skills. This is of course a debatable point. However, in the initial stages of adoption of the new technologies, social pressures may be generated because of gender inequalities.

From the above discussion, you may be inclined to think, that since these new technologies have certain undesirable effects on society, they might as well be avoided entirely. Such thinking. however, would be to short sighted and technophobic to be true. The history of technology is replete with instances of social instability and resistance upon introduction of major technological innovations. Eventually, however, as the society adapted itself to these new innovations and assimilated their full impact, the initial resistances were found to have melted away. Not, only that the new technologies themselves were found to be instrumental in finding solutions to the very problems what they had generated in the first place. In case any particular technology was found unable to conform to the above pattern, sociological forces would automatically tend to relegated such a technology into oblivion. The case of the new communication technologies that we have discussed in this unit, can be no exception to this overall trend.

❒

9

Mass Media in Practice

Prasar Bharati

After it assumed power in 1989, the National Front government came out first with a Cabinet Paper and then introduced the Prasar Bharati Bill in December 1989. According to P. Upendra, the Minister for Information and Broadcasting, the Bill borrowed from the Prasar Bharati Bill of 1979 and took into account the changed circumstances and the present ethos. Many, however, felt that the bill was put before the nation in a hurry. A national debate was initiated, in many cases with the active encouragement of the government to arrive at a consensus on the framework and the modalities of media autonomy. The Bill, after incorporating some amendments, was unanimously passed in both Houses of Parliament. But following a change of government in October 1990, the lack of political good will to translate the concept into a working proposition was apparent. While there was no official pronouncement, the interim government headed by Chandrashekhar continued to maintain the status quo. The dissolution of the Lok Sabha in April 1991 signed the death warrant of the Prasar Bharati Bill, which then had needed only the Presidential assent for becoming Law. The death of Rajiv Gandhi and the advent of Congress rule in June 1991, under P.V. Narasimha Rao, put an end to any hopes about the issue. Meanwhile, the question of broadcasting autonomy has become irrelevant as other sources of information and entertainment *viz.*; STAR TV, CNN and BBC have burst into view in the wake of the Gulf War. The invasion from the skies has begun.

Today, the rapid expansion of television in India in terms of availability (7 channels) and sheer expansion (545 TV stations) speaks of unqualified success by any standards. TV has often reached a high degree of professional excellence in its news coverage. The 32-hour continuous election telecast in May-June 1991 involving on-the-spot reporting from the counting booths even in the remote corners of the country and the swift shuttling between the national network and the local centres was a refreshingly dramatic experience for the viewers. But barring occasional and isolated instances, it has steadily developed an urban bias and an elitist approach, popularising, in the process, an alien life style and culture far removed from the realities of Indian life.

Policy Versus Practice and Performance

The Doordarshan has always suffered from the dichotomy between policy pronouncements (which emphasize the use of the mass media for social progress) and the continuous drift and departure from them in actual practice. In a developing and democratic country like India, access to television and the social benefit accruing from it, is a crucial test of the social relevance of such an expensive medium. The reason to the establishment of the Doordarshan in India, according to official statements, is to create a sense of participation in our efforts to usher in a new social order. As early as February 1973, a seminar on software objectives sponsored by the government recommended that, "Television must be used in the development process as an instrument of social change and national cohesion by unhesitatingly upholding progressive values and involving the community in a free dialogue. Indian TV has to shun an elitist approach and consumer value system and evolve a truly national model."

Officially the task assigned to the electronic media is three-fold. First, "the AIR and Doordarshan should inform people about happenings in India and the world, objectively, fairly and without any bias, as adequately and quickly as possible." Second, "the electronic media should get across to the people the policies and programmes that the government has framed for accelerating the process of socio-economic transformation." And finally, the broadcast media should pursue "an open policy and a policy that does not shirk issues and the responsibilities connected to these issues in order to develop an informed and participative citizenry; so. that people know and think for themselves what is good for them and for the country." There can be no serious difference of opinion on these objectives. The reach of the electronic media together with the high percentage of the illiterate population make the broadcast media the most appropriate vehicles of national communication.

Mrs. Indira Gandhi, who played a leading role in the growth of TV in India, saw its role primarily as a promoter of development and education in a backward country. She repeatedly affirmed the national importance of utilising TV not just for the idle entertainment of the elite but for the uplift of the poor, especially in the inaccessible rural areas. But in effect and in actual practice, the purchase of a TV set is seen as wholesale investment in entertainment which obviates the bother and expense of going to an auditorium or a stadium. Even a cursory examination of its programmes during any week makes it clear that the order in which Doordarshan fulfils the three functions of the medium are entertainment first, information second and education third. This is true even after the introduction of the five Metro channels.

Even a casual viewer cannot but notice that the Doordarshan does not practice what it preaches and evidently such guidelines are honoured more in the breach then in the observance. The official media, despite occasional airs of openness, are generally identified as the propaganda wing of the party in power. These media do not present a balanced and non-partisan view of the events and happenings, which an average citizen so badly requires in order to arrive at an informed judgement. India may demand free and balanced flow of information at the international level. But at home, the distinction between the ruling party and the government, between the party interest and the national interest often gets blurred. In addition to the lack of objectivity and frankness, the news on Doordarshan also suffers from an overdose of elite and urban values.

From inception, broadcasting in India has been looked upon as a public service for the promotion of social objectives. The concept of advertisements for the promotion of consumer's goods was also considered incompatible with the prevailing philosophy of the "socialistic pattern of society." What causes alarm today is the proliferation in the mass media of these very advertisements for consumer goods.

In a developing country like India, radio and TV should be viewed as a national resource for the uplift of the masses. It is only through a strong media network that the right kind of information and education can be imparted to the people. But the media in our country, like elsewhere in the world, have buckled under the pressure of commercial interests. As a result, besides discrimination of information or the 'haves' from the 'have nots', there is erosion of regional and cultural identities and ethics. Mindless entertainment with little or no educative value defeats the very purpose of building up a strong media network. For one, it is definitely not in the interest of the people to provide them with unproductive media fare. For another, it is nothing but unjustifiable use of invaluable resources.

The question that inevitably arises is whether we should use TV for promoting a humane social order or to create synthetic needs.

Under the existing system Doordarshan has become a tool for the promotion of class consumerism. It is a strange paradox that this public investment, which facilitated the rapid expansion of the TV network in a poor country, is now being exploited by the big businesses for building their own corporate images. While it is conceded that ad revenue makes a network viable and independent, the same advertising also dictates the nature, form and content of the media software. Every noble intention to arouse social consciousness through the media gets traded for unhealthy programming. Here is an example.

Advertisers would always prefer to sponsor those programmes which create the proper mood in the viewers to buy their products. Their choice, invariably, falls on entertainment programmes. On rare occasions when serious programmes on topics like environment preservation, public hygiene or any significant social issues like land reforms br minimum wages are telecast, no sponsor is usually available. This is in stark contrast to the situation when advertisers lined up to spend a total of Rs. 35 crore on the serial 'Mahabharat' alone. To play the role of communicator-cum-educator in developing countries, broadcasting media have to provide software that would enrich the lives of the people. A communication policy would have to specify some guidelines to our communicators regarding balanced programming. Here, 'balanced' would mean the right mix of entertainment, information and education.

Performance of Indian Press

The press in a democratic country plays a vital role in creating, moulding, and reflecting public opinion. It is a fundamental institution of our society.

Though the press in India is free, it suffers from many ills. It has yet to identify its true post-independence role so as to ensure against haphazard growth and directionless expansion.

There are a few in-built handicaps such as vast geographical area, illiteracy, poverty, multiplicity of languages, and absence of adequate communication facilities. Some other bottlenecks exist, like the linking of ownership of newspapers with other industrial or commercial enterprises; limited newspaper ownership with closely held 'share interest'; urban-oriented expansion of newspapers leaving the vast country side population untouched, inadequate and expensive newsprint, and the lack of local advertisement support.

Eminent journalists have pointed out several drawbacks which stand in the way of making the press in India an independent and impartial instrument of communication of news and views. Some of these drawbacks are: the present system of accreditation of journalists; the government's allocation of newsprint; fixation of advertisement rates; favours to journalists in the form of perquisites such as subsidized housing, medical facilities, etc., heavy dependence of the press on official releases.

For a comprehensive and an in-depth examination of the state of the Indian press and the steps that need to be taken for its development on sound and healthy lines, the Government of India appointed the second Press Commission on 18 May, 1978, headed by Justice K. M. Mathew.

The appointment of the Second Press Commission had become necessary as the Indian Press had undergone several changes, had taken new strides, and acquired an added significance with an ever-expanding readership.

One of the recommendations of the Second Press Commission was to include both positive and negative aspects of an event in development reports. This implied that these reports should investigate the reasons for success as well as failure at different places and under different conditions of various development programmes affecting the lives of the common people. But most of our newspapers merely carry official handouts giving statistics of man-days of employment provided, persons made literate or area brought under irrigation.

The reporting of non-official initiatives in rural development, education reform, struggle against superstitious beliefs. Evil practices like dowry and Sati or other areas of social campaign, is even less extensive than in-depth reporting of the implementation of official development programmes. The Commission says: "our newspapers usually become aware of such non-official activities only after they have been honoured by a Jamnalal Bajaj Foundation award or Magsaysay award."

Another long standing criticism of the press is that it carries too much bad news at the expense of the good. To gain maximum readership, the press emphasizes the exceptional rather than the representative; the sensational rather than the significant. Many activities of the utmost social consequence are not considered reportable incidents. But, as Indira Gandhi never tired of pointing out, "the meek may one day inherit the earth, but never the headlines." This brings us inevitably to the question of social responsibility. Certainly, the press has travelled a long way from the arrogant attitude of the newspaper owners who said, "A newspaper is a private enterprise owing nothing whatsoever to the public, which grants it no franchise. After all, responsible journalism is journalism with a conscience." Nikhil Chakravarthy, an eminent journalist, had said that, "Even if you don't like someone or disagree with him ideologically, you must be fair." A journalist is confronted with ethical decisions almost daily. Should a news source go unnamed? Should a "leak" possibly affecting national security be used? Does the public interest override individual privacy? Should a rape victim's identity be disclosed? Should communities be identified in a communal clash or gory details of violence reported? General professional codes call for truth, accuracy, impartiality and fair play. Unlike most countries where a free press exists, there is no universally accepted code of conduct in enforcement in India. Even the professional bodies have not been unanimous in developing any. Nor has any serious effort been made by the press to find out what the society thinks of it let alone identify the possible areas of disagreement.

The Indian press had always been known for its sanity over sensitive issues like communal disturbances. But on the threshold of the nineties, it appeared that a large section of the press lost its sense of balance and fairness while reporting such highly explosive issues and events. Barring a few glorious exceptions, most of the newspapers betrayed a distinct and dangerous slant in reporting the Ram Janmabhoomi-Babri Masjid controversy.

For all this, the absence of a code of professional conduct in our country is more or less made up for by the adherence of the press to the social responsibility theory. And the performance of the press can be evaluated on the basis of this single criterion. Such accountability to the public serves as a self-regulatory mechanism in place of an explicit policy.

Future Role

What is the role of the government in making the mass media truly effective vehicles of culture, creativity and expression? Whatever the nature of media ownership-whether government, public corporation, or private enterprise-it is the government which is ultimately responsible for ensuring the use of broadcasting frequencies in the public interest.

Programme content is based on the objectives of the medium, these objectives form the basis for media policies. In our country, the Ministry of Information and Broadcasting monitors the content of the print and electronic media to ensure that all the mass media serve their noble purpose; to be tolls in the process of development and change. The improvement and expansion of the media network is directly linked to this goal.

From time to time various Committees and Commissions have been set up for the purpose of evaluating the working of the communication network. Attempts have been made to formulate a mass media policy based on their recommendations, whether or not these suggestions will be incorporated to the working of the media system depends on the authorities. In response to some of the policy considerations the government may decide to make resources available through direct budgets, or grants or provided fiscal advantages to quality productions, or offer preferential customs duties when importing hardware or software, etc. Alternatively, the media policy itself may be the outcome of such decisions and regulations.

Public participation in the formulation of national mass media policies may be achieved by setting up Mass Media Policy Council, with representatives from among media professionals and others concerned with the role of communication in society.

To implement policy initiatives, institutions may be started or existing ones improved for training and research in the media of film, radio and television broadcasting, printing and book production, etc.

It is of utmost importance to chalk out a detailed communication policy to guide the growth of the communication networks. Piecemeal initiatives only harm the functioning of the media system. A comprehensive policy would help bring about more effective and purposeful communication.

For effective mass communication it is essential that mass communications have as much information as possible about the audiences or receivers. Although mass audience for each medium is seen as a large group of unknown people, there are also specific audience for particular contents.

Information technology has advanced so much in the years that it is now possible for people, while sitting in their drawing rooms, to witness the events taking place in any part of the world or even in space. We can watch the live coverage of sports events or music concerts taking place thousands of miles away. Indira Gandhi was able to talk to Rakesh Sharma in the space shuttle and the whole of the world could watch them in conversation. The war in Iraq was shown live by CNN. Tele-conferencing makes it possible not only to watch events far away but also to participate in the action.

Technology has expanded the audiences manifold. Today we think in terms of audiences spread over the whole world, a phenomenon which Marshall McLuhan called global village. National boundaries hold no barriers for mass communication.

Still communication cannot be without targets. Mass communication is effective if it is produced for specific groups people. Thus, on the one hand, audiences of mass communication are spread across the national boundaries; on the other hand media content has to be target oriented.

We have seen that each of these media has certain advantages over the others. We have also seen that different people exhibit different preferences for media use.

Meaning of Mass

The term mass in used to denote different things. In physics, the word mass refers to the quality of matter or material contained in an object. It may also mean a quantity of matter of indefinite shape and size a lump.

Sometimes the word mass is used to refer to common people, specially the lower classes. Mass also has both negative and positive meanings. In the negative sense, it refers to the ignorant and unruly mass. Mass implies a lack of culture, in telligence and even of rationality. In socialist tradition, mass has a positive meaning. It connotes the strength and solidarity of ordinary working people when organised together for political ends.

In general usage, the word mass refers to people in a large number. If we say masses are ignorant, we mean that a very large proportion of the population ignorant. Similarly, when we say mass destruction means destruction on a very large scale. Mass awareness programme refers to a programme that aims to create awareness amongst a very large number of people. In fact, the important feature of mass is its very large size in terms of the number of individuals. It will be appropriate if we say that mass refers to an infinite number of individuals. The size of mass is very large and unknown.

Secondly, masses are geographically distributed. Very large number of large of people may be attending a public meeting. They are physically present anywhere and everywhere. When we say masses in developing countries are poor we refer to the people living in Africa, Asian, Latin America and perhaps some other and perhaps some other parts of the world as well.

Since the masses are very large in size and in physical terms the people are distributed all over, they are anonymous to each other. They are not even conscious of the presence of one another. There may be a vague feeling of others like us but it is not well defined. Since the people are anonymous to one another, the masses are unorganised. Unlike the people in a public meeting, there is not organisation and therefore no leadership or hierarchy in mass. Further, the masses are not capable of behaving as one unit.

We can conclude that for our purpose that mass to an infinitely large number of people who are physically located at different places and are not organised at all as a group. In fact scholars like Roymard Williams have summarised that masses actually do not exist, it is only a way of conceiving large groups of people as masses.

Society is a large and complex system. With modernisation the complexity of the society further increase. The traditional society has a well defined social system in which individuals are closely tied to each other, mainly through kinship ties. But industrialisation and urbanisation lead to the formation of society where interdependence of numbers in economic terms increase manifold but kinship ties gradually fade away. The individuals become more self-centred. The socially, economically and politically isolated. The modernising societies experience an increase in individuality. The individuals develop a strong alienation with the community as a whole. There is an increased growth of segmental and contractual relationships. Such a society which is very large in size but where members are isolated and relationships are contractual is called a mass society.

However, the concept of mass society is not to be equated with of massive society. It is more than the massive society. There are many traditional society that are very large in a numbers but are not necessarily mass societies. The individuals in a traditional and Selznick have explained the concept of mass society as follows.

"Modern society is made up'of masses in the sense that there has emerged a vast mass of segregated, isolated individuals interdependent in all sorts of specialised ways. Yet lacking in any central unifying value or purpose. The weakening of traditional bonds, the growth of rationality and the division of labour, have created societies made up of individuals who are only loosely bound together. In this sense, the mass society is something closer to an aggregate than to a tightly knit group.

In fact, as stated earlier, mass society has no continuous existence, except in the minds of those who want to reach as many people as possible. It will be useful to further understand the concept of mass society using a set of contrasts with other kinds of units in social life, like group, crowd and public.

In a small all members know each other. They are aware of their common membership, share the same value, have a certain structure of relationship which are relatively stable. The members of a group interact other for a purpose.

The crowd is a spontaneous collection of individuals. It is temporary and never reappears with the same composition. Members of a crowd may strongly identify with each other. More important, they share the same mood. But there exists no order or structure in the crowd. In many cases the actions of the crowd are emotional, sometimes irrational also. Crowd is physically present within observable boundaries, that is, at a particular place.

Unlike crowd, public is widely dispersed. Its size may be small or large. Generally public is identified with some cause, purpose or activity. Public may be quite heterogeneous and members may not be aware of each other. Usually public is identified by the people who want to perceive a large of people as targets.

Let us illustrate each of the above discussed concept with example from our day to day life. Each one of us belongs to many groups simultaneously. Family is the primary unit and basis for all social life. We are all members of our families. Along with this we are also members of class, team, peer group, club etc. On a railway platform we are a part of the crowd. A crowd is also formed when we together to protest against the non-availability of goods.

Political parties treat us as public when they tell us about their policies and plans. We are public for public for police, when it informs us about the imposition of curfew. We move in small group of friends or families in a mela. In the mela, we become apart of the crowd but for those displaying their items we are a public.

Concept of Audience

The commonly used meaning of the term media audience is the aggregate of persons forming readers, listeners, viewers of different media, that is, the content of different media. In other words, audience is a group if individuals with a common pattern of media consumption. Such individuals share common access or exposure to the same mass communication products.

There are four different ways of looking at media audiences. These are media reach, media access, media exposure and media exposure and media effects. We shall discuss these approaches one by one.

Media Reach

The owners and producers of the mass media conceive the total population whom their communications can reach. The signals of All India Radio are available to about 85 percent of the population living in about 85 percent of country's area. So the total population of India may be treated as audience for All India Radio. Similarly, Doordarshan can claim more than 80 percent of the population as its audience because its signals can reach that many people. For a newspaper, audience would be defined in terms of all individuals who are within the distribution range of the papers. For a cable TV system the audience reach will include all residents within the wired area.

Media Access

Mass media may be available but the capacity or willingness to us the media may not be there. A large section of the population does not have the radio receivers or television sets. Thus, only those who own the radio sets may be treated as audiences of All India Radio. But access may not overlap ownership. In fact, there are many people who watch television programmes at the houses of neighbours or friends or in community centre. Groups watching a popular television at television shop is a common sight.

Many families do not buy newspapers but their members may read newspapers at various places like teashop, barbershop, library or even at neighbours' or friends' house. This, those who have direct access by virtue of ownership along with those who are non-owners but get exposed in other ways accessible audience. Who are non-owners but get exposed in other ways constitute the accessible audience.

Media Exposure

Everyone who has access to radio or television does not necessarily use them. In a family that subscribes to a actually expose themselves to the media audiences. Again, no one is exposed to the total content of any medium. No one listens to all the programmes broadcast by All India Radio. Similarly, it is impossible to watch all the programmes of Doordarshan. Many people do not even glace at the commerce page of the newspapers. There are many young people, specially students, who read only the sports page. So audiences can also be seen as programme specific or content specific, that is,. populations actually exposed to specific media contents.

Another important aspect of media behaviour is that all users of media content are not uniformly exposed. There are people who listen to news everyday without fail. Others may listen to news, says on an average of five days a week. Still others may be people whose exposure to news or radio is nil.

Media Effects

Another way to think about audiences is in terms of individuals who have been exposed to mass communication products and have undergone a change in their knowledge, opinions, attitude or behaviour. A person may not recall anything of the person, after watching an advertisement, may immediately rush to buy the advertised products. Voters generally do not change their voting preference after listening to election broadcasts by the representatives of political parties.

Duality of Audience

The most interesting feature of a mass communication audience is its dual nature. At one level media audience is a collectivity formed in response to media content and defined by attention to that content. When a new newspaper is launched, people gradually start reading it. MTV, STAR TV, and ZEE TV have created their own audiences.

Alternatively, audience may be conceived as collectivity that exists already in the systems and mass media may begin to cater to its information and entertainment needs. Krishi Darshan may aim to cater to the needs of the farmers. Yuvvani attempts to cater to needs of the youth. Femina is meant for the women whereas seminar is meant for the intellectuals.

In the first case, media or its content is the cause of the creation of the audience, but in the second case, the audience become the cause of the creation of the media content.

In many case, it is very difficult to determine whether audience is responsible for creation of the media content or the media content has created the audience. The fact is that the audiences are both, the cause as well as the response to the mass communication process. A new newspaper creates its own readership but at the same time it tries to the needs of the targeted readers.

Rise of Audiences

The original audiences were the sets of spectators for games, stage plays or dispension of justice by the king. Such pre-media audiences existed in all cultures in one form or another. Audience for religious discourses have played a very significant role in the spread of social and political ethos.

Invention of printing revolutionised the whole character of audience. This was the beginning of mass audience. The most important change that the took place was that the audience participation as a private act became possible. People could now take the printed materials to secluded places and undergo a totally private experience. This led to another important change. The audiences become delocalised. It was no more necessary for all members of the audience to be present at one place. A book had readers spread all over the world.

The advent of newspapers created mass audiences in the real sense. Newspapers also converted mass audiences into potential receivers of commercial message or advertising. The advent of electronic media further delocalised the audiences. The information carried by electro-magnetic waves could ross the national boundaries. The audiences were now spread over the whole world. The members were separated from each other and their distance, physical and social, from the communicators also increased.

The audiences now not only took the form and character of masses but they also acquired the features of a mass society. The satellite communication, coupled with cable network on the ground, has brought a situation where the Whole world population can be treated as one audience.

Audience Types

The types of audiences can be distinguished based on their demographics characteristics and mental make up.

Elite Audience

Elite audience are composed of the people who are decision-makers and trend-setters in the society. They are economically well to do and are highly educated. They have high status in the society. Their numbers is very small but their influence is very strong. They may also be the owners or controllers of the mass media institutions. The members of the elite audience are the early adopters of communication technologies. Their actual media consumption is generally low.

General Audience. They are Very large and highly divers groups that represent the broad-cross-section of the society. Majority of the people to this category. The media content is generally targeted at them. Their participation determines the suecess or failure of content or medium.

Specialised Audiences. These audience are composed of individuals who possess similar characteristic. They are relatively small in number. Mass media generate special contents for these audience groups. Programmes for tribals, for housewives, for college students, etc. are example of programmes for specialised audiences. Similarly, journals like Mainstream, Femina and Economic and Political Weekly have limited but known readership.

Audience as Markets

Rise of consumerism has led to a situation where audiences are treated as markets. The media products is a commodity or service offered for sale to a given body of potential consumers, in competition with other media products. Their potential or actual consumers can be referred to as markets.

With the commercialisation of broadcasting and telecasting in our country, the audience are being treated more as markets. There is competition between Doordarshan, STAR TV, ZEE TV, MTV to capture as big an audience as possible. Drastic changes in the programme content of Doordarshan main and Metro channels is an indication of the fact that even the state controlled medium is forced to view audiences as markets. Audience, according to the market concept, can be defined as an aggregate of potential consumers with a known socio-economic profile at which medium or message is directed.

Audience has a dual significance for the media. Firstly, as set of potential or actual consumers of media content and secondly, as the audience for advertising message. Thus a market for media content is simultaneously a market for other products; media serve as advertising vehicles for delivering messages to the potential customers of other products. Advertising is the largest source of revenue for all media. In fact, no medium can survive if not supported by advertising or some other sources. Till the time AIR and Doordarshan were not commercial, the government used to subsidies their services. The most popular programmes of radio and television attract the maximum advertising. Not only that, advertising rates are the highest for prime time programmes. The treatment of audiences as markets has social and moral implication as well. First, when the relationship between the media and audience is that of producer and consumer, the character if relationship become manipulative. The aim is torn sell as much as possible.

Secondly, the members of the audiences are markets and are treated as passive receivers. The audience are lured by cleverly designed message, Thirdly, the success of the media is measured not in terms of needs fulfilled but in terms of sales of the products. Lastly, the market view is that of the media owners and media producers. Audiences never see themselves as markets.

Nature of Audience Experience

Audience is the single most important element in any conception of mass communication. The development of the relationship between the mass media and the audience can be seen in two contrasting ways. We may consider the availability of a large number of media units as media explosion. In this conception, the media occupy the central position and information from the various media is seen as acting upon the audience.

But if we observe the media audience relationship carefully, we find that the audiences actually exercise their choice as to which medium is to be used and also which content they would like to be exposed to. Marshall McLuhan saw the audiences at the centre of the numerous attacks by different media. He referred to this as media implosion as against the media explosion.

The efforts required for attending to mass communication may be considered in terms of the availability of the media and the ease with which we may use the media.

Expense involved and the time required are also important factors in "the effort required." Watching a film on television is less expensive, less time consuming and little efforts is required for it as compared to watching a film in a cinema hall.

The uses and gratification theory of the media effects proposes that basic human needs motivate individuals to attend to particular forms of mass media and to select and use messages in ways they find personally gratifying. Thus, audience members make a conscious and motivated selection amongst the various mass media and also amongst the various item of content.

Audience Feedback Systems

The producers of mass communication keep a hand on the pulse of their audiences in order to make their products more and more acceptable. Audience feedback systems are the mechanisms through which information regarding audience reaction is taken back to the owners, controllers and producers of the media. There are two distinct feedback system; market-based feedback system and research based feed-back system. Mass Communicators receive the following information through the market-based feedback system: *(a)* audience access to the media; *(b)* audience exposure to the media.

The above mentioned information is received by the communicators by three methods:

Audiences decision to subscribe to newspapers or magazines is a direct feedback about the popularity of the publication. Rise and fall of circulation is a very important feedback that the market provides. More and more houses paying for cable TV connections indicate the increased popularity of the satellite channels. At the same time, it may also indicate that the audiences are not very happy with the Doordarshan programmes. Increased circulation of a newspaper implies endorsement of the style and editorial policies of the new paper. Sales at box-office is a good feedback about the popularity of a film.

Sometimes, audience reactions to, mass communication are very actively solicited. Coupons, rebate offers, bring-this-and-get-a-discount and similar practices are used to measure the impact of particular promotional efforts.

For books, magazines, papers, video and audio cassettes, film and cable TV connections, the audience behavior has a direct bearing. More consumers mean more revenues. In case of radio and television and even news papers and magazines, the largest share of revenue comes from advertising. But again the advertising rates are determined by audience size, and thereby audiences exert their influence, through indirectly.

Direct Feedback. Mechanisms of direct feedback are provided in each media system. Newspapers and magazines have columns reserved for letters to the editor sent by the readers. Similarly, radio and television networks have programmes reserved for comments, reaction, suggestion from the audiences. Unsolicited letters and telephones also provide important feedback. In some cases, casual conversation between employees of mass media and members of audience may provide important feedback.

A careful observation of the media in our country over the last two decades would reveal the felt needs for direct feedback from the audiences increasing. Space devoted to the letters to the editor column in newspapers and magazines has increased. Similarly, more and more air time is being given on radio and television for programmes where representative of the audience are allowed to give their reaction and suggestion.

Media Reviews. Media give the greatest importance to the feedback through the reviews. Every news paper and magazine has media review column written by a media critic. In these columns, the media critics examine the mass communication of radio and television. Similarly, there are regular review of films, audio and video cassettes published in newspapers and magazines.

The role these media reviews is two fold. One, the owners, controllers and specially the producers of radio and television programmes take the comments very seriously. Secondly, these reviews provide information to the audiences. They, in fact, provide expert opinion and influence audience to notice and use particular mass media content. A radio or television programmes or a film or book or a song sequence commented favourably becomes acceptable to the audiences. Many people buy or read a book after reading its review.

In our country, there were no reviews of the print media except in academic journals till recently. Now, some newspapers have introduced these. For example,. The Pioneer has a weekly column Blue Pencil by G.S. Bhargava. It appears on very Sunday and critically comments on the coverage in different newspapers.

Firstly, the critic acts as a link between the producers and the audience. At this point, the critic performs the role of calling attention to the availability of information and recommending responses. Secondly, the critic may provide his expert comments to the producers. At this point, the act is an interpretation of how and why the audiences reacted positively or negatively to the content. Various functions performed by the reviewers can be listed as follows:

(a) Informing audience what is new and interesting.

(b) Raising the cultural level of the community.

(c) Advising the audiences on how to use their time and money.

(d) Helping artists and performers to understand how their efforts are being received by the audiences.

(e) Recording the history of mass communication.

(f) Entertaining audiences with their articles and reports.

Research-based Feedback

The market-based feed back and the reviews are more or less passive systems. Feedback information gets generated without the producers making efforts for it. They leave many questions unanswered. A newspaper will get information that its circulation is decreasiring but it is not known as to who are the people who have stopped subscribing and why have they done so. Similarly, media critics may not comments at all on a programme or their comments may be considered subjective. Research based feedback systems are created to provide systematic information about audience response to a particular mass communication products of services.

Many media organisations have their own audience systems. For example, there are Audience Research in All India Radio and Doordarshan. These units keep on collecting audiences responses to various programmes. Based on the research finding, the producers may improve their programme; some programmes may be discontinued or their timings may be changed.

Reliable and systematic information collected about the listenership or viewership leads to ratings of different programmes. The use of the media by advertisers and made to reach the desired audiences in a more cost effective manner. It is hoped that soon it will evolve into an authentic and reliable system.

Audiences of Various Media

Mass communication does not mean communication for everyone. The media and their audiences come together through a process or natural selection. Media tend to select their audiences by means of content. The audiences also tend to select among and within the media primarily on the basis of content.

Different media may different audiences but there is a considerable overlap between the audiences of one medium with those of the other. Researchers have shown that persons who are above average in exposure to one medium to other media as well. A person who: reads a news paper is likely also to read magazines, listen to radio and watch television. Lazarsfeld and Merton called this phenomenon as all-or-non principle. A person interested in escapist entertainment will find it in books, magazines, films and televisions. Anyone who has little opportunity to use one medium because of poverty, illiteracy, ignorance or lack of time or interest will probably have little opportunity to use any medium.

Newspapers attract very heterogeneous audiences. Children and young people generally do not read newspapers. Most of the readers read only the headlines or at the most read the introductory paragraphs. The finance page has a special readership composed of businessmen and those involved in economic and commercial activities. Sports page has an audience of predominantly young people. Editorial and edit page contents have a very small readership.

Magazines are generally read by people with more education and those belonging to higher economic strata, in general, young people are likely to use newspapers and magazines for entertainment, older people for information and views on matters of public life. Adults do more news reading than young people; the latter pay more attention to photographs and visuals like cartoons and comic strips.

More males read newspaper and also at greater length than females. Higher economic status is generally accompanied by increase in the reading of public news, sports news and society news. People belongs to low and very low socio-economic strata generally read local newspapers or they more attention to local news in regional or national news papers.

Middle-class readers to read national news papers. Highly educated and rich people tend to read international newspapers and magazines or the newspapers and publications of other countries.

Radio Listeners

Before the advent of television, radio was the medium for all classes. However, many people neither owned radio sets nor did they have access to radio in any other way. Transistor revolution spread the ownership of radio receiving sets very widely. But in our country at no time more than 60 percent of the families owned radio sets.

Not-so-poor people and belonging to lower middle classes generally owned single band or two band radio sets. As a consequence, their exposure was mostly confined to local radio station or medium wave stations. People with efficient receiving systems listened not only to AIR but also to foreign systems like BBC, Voice of America, Radio Moscow.

After the advent of television, radio listening in television owning households has fallen drastically. Many television owning households do not use the radio sets at all. The predominant use of radio today is for music in the background while people are engaged in other works. Many people use radio as an announcer or time. Unlike in U.S and other western countries, radio is not much used in motor vehicles in our country. Audio-tape players have become more popular in cars, buses and trucks.

Young persons use radio to listen to film and non-film music. Adults also listen to music but they tend to use radio as a source of news and information. Housewives may use radio as a companion during the day when they are alone. Young men and women appearing in competitive tests use radio as an important source of information, specially news and current affairs programme. Spotlight and Samayaki are very popular among those sitting in civil services examinations.

The tremendous popularity of television is at the expense of radio. With the advent of television, total time devoted to the media has increased. All sections of the population wish to watch television. Many have their own sets. Others watch telev ;ion at neighbours or friends houses or at community centres.

News and current affairs programmes of Doordarshan are seen by more educated section of the society. Common people tend to watch entertaining serials. Ramayana on Doordarshan had the largest ever largest ever audience. DD Metro is more popular than the main channel of Doordarshan. Generally, people now subscribe to cable network systems. ZEE TV has a wide audience in Hindi-speaking middle and lower classen. The audience of STAR TV is restricted to middle and upper middle classes. MTV has an audience of young and rich who are relatively more exposed to western culture and values. Research has shown that programmes like Krishi Darshan have very small audiences even among the farmers. It is important to note that the viewers of television also become the audience of the films. A number of films are shown on various channels of television. Besides there are many programmes that based on films. The television and films industries have become closely related and there are films now produced only for television.

Till television spread its networks, films were the most widely used mass media. All sections of the population, very poor to very rich, went to cinema theatres to watch films.

With the advent of television, VCR, VCP, satellite transmission and cable networks, the films watching in cinema halls has decreased considerably. But the total exposure to films has perhaps increased.

Different types of films have different audiences. Common people generally like to watch masala-films that have an adequate mixture of emotions, comedy, violence, dance, music, sex etc. The new-wave films, the art films and low cost films have an audience that is composed of more educated, socially conscious and intellectual section. Religious films based on epics have an audience composed mainly of rural people, women, illiterate poor etc. Similarly, informative films or films with social messages have different audiences.

Book Readers

Books attract people who are above average in education and also in their use of the serious contents of other media. Books are more likely to attract young adults than older ones, people living in urban rather than in rural areas, people or high income rather than low income. Readers of English books attract audiences more from highly educated, well-off people. Books in Hindi languages are read mostly by the people belonging to these ", language groups. Generally, book-readers have a high exposure to other media.

Communication is one of those human activities that everyone recognise but few can define satisfactorily. Communication is talking to one another, it is television, it is spreading information, it is our hair style, it is literary criticism: the list is endless. This is one of problems facing academics: can we properly apply the term 'a subject of study' to something as diverse and multi-faceted as human communication actually is? Is there any hope of linking the study of, say, facial expression with literary criticism? Is it even an exercise worth attempting?

The doubts that lie behind questions like these may give rise to the view that communication is not a subject, in the normal academic sense of the world, but is a multi-disciplinary area of study. This view would propose that what the psychologists have to tell us about human communicative behaviour has very little to do with what the literary critic has.

This lack of agreement about the nature of communication studies is necessarily reflected in this book. What we have tried to do is to give some coherence to the confusion by basing the book upon the following assumptions.

— assume that communication is amenable to study, but that we need a number of disciplinary approaches to be able to study it comprehensively.

— assume that all communication involves signs and codes. Signs are artefacts or, acts that refer to something other than themselves, that is they are signifying constructs. Codes are the systems into which signs are organised and which determines how signs may be related to each other.

— assume, too, that these signs and codes are transmitted or made available to others: and that transmitting or receiving signs/codes/communication is the practice of social relationships.

— assume that communication is central to the life of our culture: without it culture of any kind must die. Consequently the study of communication involves the study of the culture with which it is integrated.

Underlying these assumptions is a general definition of communication as 'social interaction through messages.'

The structure of this book reflects the fact that there are two main schools in the study of communication. The first sees communication as the transmission of messages. It is concerned with how senders and receivers encode and decode, with how transmitters use the channels and media of communication. It is concerned with matters like efficiency and accuracy. It sees communication as a process by which one person affects the behaviour or state of mind of another. If the effect is different from or smaller than that which was intended, this school tends to talk in terms of communication failure, and to look to the stages in the process to find out where the failure occurred. For the sake of convenience we shall refer to this as the 'process' school.

The second school sees communication as the production and exchange of meanings. It is concerned with how messages, or texts, interact with people in order to produce meanings; that is, it is concerned with the role of texts in our culture. It uses terms like signification, and does not consider misunderstandings to be necessarily evidence of communication failure they may result from cultural differences between sender and receiver. For this school, the study of communication is the study of text and culture. The main method of study is semiotics (the science of signs and meanings), and that is the label we shall use to identify this approach.

The process school tends to draw upon the social sciences, psychology and sociology in particular, and tends to address itself to acts of communication. The semiotic school tends to draw upon linguistics and the arts subjects, and tends to address itself to work of communication.

Each school interprets our definition of communication as social interaction through messages in its own way. The first defines social interaction as the process by which one person relates himself to others, or affects the behaviour, state of mind or emotional response of another, and, of course, vice versa. This is close to the common-sense, everyday use of the phrase. Sometimes, however, defines social interaction as that which constitutes the individual as a member of his culture or society.

The two schools also differ in their understanding of what constitutes a message. The process school sees a message as that which is transmitted by the communication process. Many of its followers believe that intention is a crucial factor in deciding what constitutes a message. The sender's intention may be stated or unstated, conscious or unconscious, but must be retrievable by analysis. The message is what the sender puts into it by whatever means.

For sometimes, on the other hand, the message is a construction of signs which, defined as transmitter of the message, declines in importance. The emphasis shifts to the text and how it is 'read.' And reading is the process of discovering meanings that occurs when the reader interacts or negotiates with the text. This negotiation takes place as the reader, brings aspects of his cultural experience to bear upon the codes and signs which make up the text. It also involves some shared understanding of what the next the text is about. We have only to see how different papers report the same event differently to realise how important is this understanding, this view of the world, which each paper shares with its readers. So readers with different social experiences or from different cultures may find different meanings in the same text. This is not, as we have said, necessarily of communication failure.

The message, then, is not something sent from A to B, but an element in a structured relationships whose other elements include external reality and the producer/reader. Processes is that they occupy the same place in this structured relationship. We might model this structure as a triangle in which the arrows represent constant interaction, the structure is not but a dynamic practice.

At one time or another almost everyone has responded to the question "How did this [disaster] happen?" with a statement like "Don't ask me. I just work here." In some cases the excuses is a legitimate one. Someone other than the person making the statement made a decision or took a step which created a problem, but far too often it is a decision, action, or lack of action by the person offering the excuse that led to the inefficiency or failure. Although the performance of every member of an organisation is in many ways influenced by the activities of other members, in the final analysis it is the individuals' choices which decide their destiny in the organisation. It concentrates on communication in organisations because it is through communication that individual employees gain the information on which they base choices and exercise the influence which translates their choices into action. The goal of this book is to give readers a sense of how organisational communication is used strategically, that is, how individual employees analyse the situations thy face at work and choose the appropriate communication strategies to use in those situations. The book assumes that all employees are goal-oriented in some important ways and that if they understand how communication functions in their organisation they will be better able to use their communication skills to achieve their objectives and those of their organisations. The book explains when it is appropriate to use a variety of communication strategies, including the denial or responsibility and the claim of ignorance ("I don't know. I just work here"), and more important, when not to use them.

❐

10

Media for Mass Communication

DEVELOPMENT OF PRINT MEDIA IN INDIA

Print media in India has undergone revolution in last 20 years. Their role, layout, visual display and reading material have advanced and this has resulted in to flourishing of print media industry and beooming more challenging and competitive in nature. It has grown enormously in quantity and variety Consequently the print media in regional languages has also developed.

There is marked advancement in printing, composing, layout and visual display with the advancement in printing technology. Print media are constantly trying to compete with electronic media although their nature and characteristics are different. The various print media include newspapers, magazines, books, booklets, pamphlets, other periodicals and so on. Journalism has emerged as modern profession. It has also become a branch of study by itself.

Today's print media face the challenge of educating and entertaining their readers so that they can participate fully in the affairs of the country. Apart from this they face the challenge of electronic media too. It is obvious that they can not compete with electronic media but they have an important role to play as a social watchdog, social monitor, constructive critic and stimulator of new ideas. Thus, they occupy a prestigious position among the media of today. During British period, there was an early demand for free press made by Raja Rammohan Ray and British Journalists in India like James Silk Buckingham. As a result, newspapers were rooted in the British territories by the administration, not allowing any criticism or inconvenient or embarassing news irrespective of the professional quality of the newspaper. The 19th century marked the emergence of two other categories of newspapers. One started by the Serampor Missionaries as the cultural arms of British imperialism, attacking Indian religions and their philosophies and Indian culture. The other category consisted of newspapers started by Indians.

Gradually these news papers became the tools of freedom movement and played an active role in India's cultural rennais-sance and reformation in the country. Indian newspapers grew in both quality and quantity since the information and news needs of the people also grew due to socio-cultural controversies of that period. Raja Rammohan Ray ceased publishing his paper later in protest against the Government's Press Regulations.

The Bombay Samachar, a Gujarati Newspaper, appeared in 1812. By 1850, other vernacular papers also started. By 1885 The Times of India, The pioneer, The Madras Mail, The Statemen and the Amrit Bazar Patrika came into existence—all except the last edited by Englishmen and serving the interests of English Educated Readers. In 1910, The Indian Press act clamped further controls due to which vernacular press suffered the most. World War I introduced still more severe press laws, but there was no let-up in nationalist agitations. During 2nd World War, Indian press played key role in reporting the struggle for freedom.

According to Kumar (1989), "It opposed communal riots and the partition of the country, and when partition did take place in the glorious year of independence, lamented it. Indeed, it could, be said that the press played no small part in India's victory to freedom."

Free India constitution provided the citizens right to freedom of speech and expression, which included the freedom of the press. However, unlike Pandit Jawarharlal Nehru, Mrs. Indira Gandhi was always at unease with the press. Even during emergency in 1975 when pre-censorship was imposed, underground presses were active. Today print media have grown enormously both in terms of dailies and periodicals and their circulation which is known as the periodical or magazine explosion.

In the Western World, the explosion of newspapers came with the passion for power.

In India, popular journalism grew from the revolt of the subject class. Newspapers were a vehicle of the freedom struggle. Most media owners of the 50's had their roots in the freedom struggle. Indian journalism after independence continued to carry the hall mark of missionary work, as though the social responsibility associated with publishing outweighed all commercial considerations. The need for systematic changes in the format or design of the newspapers was not felt for a long time. However, there were global technology shifts. In the '70s, hot metal printing gave way to offset technology and the color printing became cheap. The big changes took place in '90s. with the increasing consumerism, press advertising volume grew three times over, from Rs. 800 crore to Rs. 2,600 crore in the first five years of the decade. The national dailies sectionalised their editorial offering, adding gloss and glamour with the purpose of drawing advertisement from the white goods and services sector. Looks and readability wise, the quality of newspapers and magazines have improved. The publishing industry in India has moved a long way from its, socially committed roots. All this does not mean that, investigative journalism is dead. Newspapers and magazines are indeed breaking far more stories on corruption than ever before. This forces the print media system to become increasingly accountable. Publishers have understood the fact that truth can be reported only if message and medium are market driven.

The number of dailies have steadily increased in India. The number of daily newspapers in 1994 increased to 4043 from 3740 in 1993 thereby registering an increase of about 8.1 %. Between 1985 and 1994, the number of dailies increased by 124.36%. During 1994, newspapers were published in as many as 99 languages/dialects including few foreign languages. Hindi newspapers constitute the largest group in the country.

CHARACTERISTICS AS MASS MEDIA

The invention of print media has not only accelerated the culture of mankind, but also brought in cultural revolutions resulting in rapid scientific and tcchnological advancements.

It is expected that the use of print medium will increase significantly with the increase of literacy and purchasing power of the people. Media experts did fear that the print media usage will decline with the increasing use of television as mass medium, but it has proved wrong. Print media used for mass communi-cation are powerful sources of bringing about attitudinal change and motivating people for action. They have a unique place in conscientizing people as well as in their continuing education.

Newspapers have been the leading print medium ever since Johann Gutenberg started his press in mid-fifteenth century. Newspapers provide place for debate. For example, the topics like political participation of women and civic affairs, discussed in series of articles in Times of India provided a very effective platform to debate on these topics, by the people from a cross section of the society. These national debates in newspapers analyse and mould the culture and influence the government.

Print media such as newspapers, magazines, journals etc. also play a role of watchdog and present a true picture of the events to the people many times. For example, the role newspapers played in scanning the animal fodder scam in Bihar, Hawala case, Shahbano case have enlightened people with many unknown facts and series of events. Thus print media play an important role in connecting and adequately informing people about the events and developing understanding of the social realities especially in a society consisting of different ethnic, linguistic and religious communities. But the way some of the major events of the country and reported in the press also indicate that sometimes press fails to be a truthful informer. For example, at the time of Operation Blue Star or demolition of Babri Masjid, press could not play a positive role in attitude formation.

News papers as mass media today do not just observe and report but ask, pursue, investigate, doubt and demand. It is true that they cannot compete with radio and television as far as fastness of the news is concerned, but they serve independently as a supplement to these media by offering details of the news with thorough reporting and coverage.

News papers and magazines offer wider variety of reading material and viewpoints of many people and thus provide better comprehension of the affairs and issues. They provide space for expression of their views and grievances in reader's columns. Thus providing for feedback component of effective communi-cation process. This generates debates on various social and other issues. Thus, print media serve as social vitalizer.

It is observed that newspapers report tension creating news and their editorials keep on emphasizing harmony and need for cordial community relations. Newspapers try to show that they are with the people. The Press Council of India has often appealed to the press to exercise due care and caution while reporting matters where sentiments of communities and castes are involved.

Like television and radio, newspapers also have built their base in certain important cities and towns which have occupied eminence as printing and publishing centres from the time immemorial. The immediate impact of television pictures cannot be equalled by press reporting. But television can not match the extensive, in-depth coverage of news that the printed page can provide. It would take a television news reader ten hours to read out the contents of an average newspaper.

TYPES OF PRINT MEDIA

There are variety of print media available for communi-cation. Newspapers, periodicals, journals, books, booklets, pamphlets, newsletters are the various types of print media. The discussion in this chapter will mainly focus on those used for mass communication purposes.

> ***Newspapers.*** A newspaper complex package of news, comment, information and entertainment, and the combi-nation of these contents varies from paper to paper. Most people choose their daily paper to match their specific tastes, and individuai newspapers have developed in different ways to provide for these. The 'tabloids' are the popular

papers, printed on half the broadsheet size. For example, Mid-day, in India, Sun and Daily Mirror in Britain.

There are newspapers which are called national newspapers or national press. Such as, times of India or Indian Express in India or Observer in Britain or USA-Today in United States of America. These newspapers fulfil the role of national newspapers, with their nationwide and international circulation. These national newspapers provide readers with a serious and comprehensive coverage and analysis of the national and international news of the day, with informed comment on social and political issues.

The local newspapers or local press has also developed strongly in India due to the multifarious languages of the country. The national newspapers may be the prestige newspapers, but local newspapers are read just as avidly. Many people get their news from the vigorous regional or local publications. They cover the issues concerning regional and local people and cover the interesting activities of the people. The readers get the news which is close to them and may have involved people they know. These newspapers also serve as a focus for the local community, bringing people together, for support or fight for any common cause.

Recent Developments in Newspaper. Over the period, many changes have taken place in the news papers. They have many pages now and are filled with advertisements. Today journalism has become one of the prosperous professions. Some of the newspaper houses in India are among the most affluent industries.

The number of news papers has risen sharply and profits have also boomed. Development of information technology has made the work of news paper publi-cation easy and less laborious. The journalists' range of coverage of news and other items remains increasingly limited to the wired world of computer and telephone. This leaves agriculture ignored by the national news-papers, except for occasional sponsored features. The race for advertisement revenue is also eroding news coverage.

Bhattacharjea (1997) says, "Multi-colour printing and arrays of types and designs, all programmed on computers, enable newspapers to compete with TV in trying to titillate the urban palate."

Todays newspapers are being criticized for serving the consumers and not the readers. The press today is facing various pressures such as technological, financial, professional and so on, which affect it's credibility. Some of the well-established newspapers still resist pressures and temptations. They still show their concern for credibility and society.

As pointed out by Bhattachareja (1997), "In other countries, newspapers are realising that they cannot compete with TV in impact or glamour. They can, however, provide backgrounding and informed comment to be read at leisure. But for that they must retain credibility. The TV viewer must continue to turn to his paper to validate what he sees on the screen".

Most of the dailies devote space for advertisements ranging from 40% to 60%. Income from advertisements is an important factor in the economic structure of news papers. Out of 254 dailies, which supplied data pertaining to their advertisement, 32 dailies (9 big, 6 medium and 17 small) derive more than 75% of their income fnom advertisements.

Another change in the press is the gender revolution. Many women journalists are either employed in the press or they work as freelance journalist. Many of them come with academic background and qualifications in journalism.

Today's newspapers have lots of investigative stories/ reports. This contributes to bringing in light big scandals and scams resulting into fall of a person.

Jeffrey believes that demand for news papers will grow. Firstly because exposure of television or any single medium leads to the consumption of other media. The regional language newspapers will be able to adapt to it and ride on it. Secondly, the growth of literacy, slow though it may be, is steady and unstoppable.

Magazines. There was a 'Magazine boom" in India in 1980s. Magazine publication grew in both English and major Indian languages. The trend started with the launch of India Today in mid seventies and the new look of Illustrated Weekly of India under the editorship of Khushwant Singh. In early eighties other magazines, like Gentleman, Fashion Quarterly, Onlooker, New Delhi, Bombay, The Week, 'G' were started.

Magazines appeal to an expanding range of reading tastes and interests. They are designed for homogeneous or special interest groups. Despite their design for special groups, they developed as a mass medium because they appeal to large numbers in a national market that cut across social, economic and educational class lines.

Mainly there are two types of magazines. General interest magazines and special interest magazines. General interest magazines attempt to cater to a wide variety of reading interests. D'souza points out, "Increasing affluence, education and leisure time had fragmented the mass audience and enabled people to persue a variety of interests to which hundreds of specialized magazines responded".

Pointing out the functions performed by the magazines, DeFleur and Dennis said, "The magazine as a contemporary medium continues to serve surveillance functions, monitoring what is going on, transmitting the culture, and entertaining the population. Its most notable function, however, is correlation—that is, interpreting the society by bringing together diverse facts, trends and sequences of events. Magazines in essence, are the great interpreters of what is happening in society."

Kumar notes that the magazine boom continued in India in 1990s despite the closure of longestablished magazines like "The Illustrated Weekly of India" and "Bombay". The growth was spectacular in the case of special interest magazines, especially those dealing with business and finance, computers and electronics. Several special interest periodicals such as Parenting, Auto India and Car and Bike were launched in 1993.

Magazines have been much more visually innovative than newspapers. Their covers blaze from news stands and market racks, thus attracting the readers' attention with colour and allure of advertisements besides their articles. These are basically news magazines but they include sections on arts, culture, sports, films, business, politics, industry, environment and so on. There are about 500 such general interest magazines focusing on news and current affairs, having largest readership. For example, India Today, The Week, Frontline, 'G' etc. These are opinion magazines, which set agendas, shape ideas and start trends. These are read by government officials, business leaders, educators, intellectuals and others who affect public affairs.

Special Interest Magazines. These magazines cater to the interest of a specific profession or group. Such as Business India or Business Today, women's magazines such as Femina, Women's era, Savvy, Gruhshobha etc., Children's magazines such as Safari, Chandamama, Target, etc. There are many other special interest magazines for readers interested in interior decoration, literature, architecture, sports, medicine, etc. Advertisers use these magazines as medium for publicising their products to the special target groups. For example, products for women in women's magazines or products for children in children's magazines. They get people in and out of them easily and quickly.

The number of magazines and periodicals in 1994 increased to 31,264 from 29,597 in previous year. It indicated the increase of 5.63 per cent. They are brought out in all the principal languages of the country.

Compared to television news or immediacy and impact of daily newspapers, magazines serve the function of informing modestly. Even in case of fictions or feature stories, newspapers have stolen the market. The advantage that magazines have is that they have the luxury of expressing their biases and 'they can make long investigations and present their findings in lengthy form. The magazine business has become very competitive and dynamic. Many varieties of magazines are started every year and many fail also.

Activist Journals. The alternative press has emerged as a result of the need of some of the groups such as feminists, environmentalists, ethnic minorities or political activists, etc. to permit their point of views. Many such groups feel that their voice is not heard and mainstream press is complacent and biased. So they publish their own papers and news sheets. Many such newspapers have grown into profitable journals. But many find it difficult to attract advertising or to have good distri-bution because of their radical views. They perform a valuable function in offering a platform for a wide spectrum of opinion.

There are magazines and journals which are started by individuals or groups or organizations which are involved with the serious issues of social concern. These journals have created distinctive niche in the print media. No data is available regarding the number of such journals, their frequency, circulation, financial viability and so on. No systematic content analysis of these journals has been done.

Sethi points out, "Last decade has been one of many booms from concepts like development, popular participation, to now organising the poor, concern about environment and ecology, medicare, gender equality, and one can go on in this vein—all as part of a search amongst, 'concerned intelligentia and citizens' for 'a viable, just and humane' alternative to an oppressive present".

Some of such journals published in English are—Voices, Manushi, Dalit Voice, Muslim India, Other India and so on.

These journals/magazines provide space for the ideology or viewpoint of the concerned activists, academicians or policy makers. These journals are produced by NGOs, academic institutions, or mass organizations, who want to communicate their specialised interests and viewpoints to others, more so, since each activist group is convinced not only of the correctness but the centra-lity of its ideas. Few of these journals have been able to maintain their frequency and status, which are the one brought out by reasonably funded institutions.

These journals have contributed to raising new ideas, refining them and raising the level of both academic and activist debate. Many such journals disappear from print world for many reasons. Such as, lack of funds, followers, dedicated team of workers, and lack of market or death of the pillar person or founder member.

Other Print Media. Textbooks, other books, booklets, pamphlets, brochures, folders, periodicals, wall newspapers, publicity and promotional literature also constitute media for mass reading, information and enlightenment. They less extensively used as compared to the newspapers and magazines.

Books are non-periodical printed publication of at least 49 pages excluding the cover page, published in any country and are made available to public. Today India is among the ten largest book producing countries in the world and ranks third, after USA and UK in the production of English Titles. It is estimated that, there are over 11,000 book publsihers in the country. The largest number is that of Hindi publishers followed by those in English and Bengali. India, as a large producer of quality books, has a growing potential for exporting books, and our books reach over 80 countries.

The National Book Trust plays an important role in the promotion of books in the public sector, produces books of good quality at moderate prices. It publishes reading material for children and rural masses.

Central and state governments also publish dailies and perio-dicals. Administration of Andaman and Nikobar and government of Bengal publish one and two dailies respectively. Language wise largest number of government publications appear in English followed by Hindi and other principal languages. More than 700 periodicals are published by the government on the subjects like news and current affairs, animal husbandry, commerce and industry, social welfare, banking and co-operation, films, radio, sports and so on. The Publications Division of the Union Ministry of Information and Broadcasting is one of the leading publishing houses in the country. It sells its publications through a network of booksellers and the Division's own sales section. It brings out journals such as Yojna, Indian and Foreign review, Kurukshetra and Employment News. The Directorate of Advertising and Visual Publicity (DAVP) is the Central agency of the government of India for undertaking advertising and visual publicity campaigns on behalf of various ministries and departments through press advertisements, printed publicity materials and outdoor publicity items of various forms. Apart from these, NCERT, Universities, public relations departments, tourist departments, produce pamphlets, brochures, folders, posters, reports, speeches and other informational literature.

There are publications which are not studied by press in India, but they have definite periodicity. They do not contain news or comments on public news. There are astrological magazines, fictions, market reports/bulletins, publicity journals, school/college magazines and so on. These are published as weeklies, fortnightlies, quarterlies, annuals or dailies. There are bimonthlies and half yearlies also.

IMPACT OF PRINT MEDIA

Marshall Mcluhan was in no doubt about the revolutionary effect of mass use of print. Print created individualism and rationalism in the sixteenth century. No person exposed to it can resist being changed by prints'subliminal charge. Reading he argued created individuals. Print broke down reality in to discrete units, logically and casually related, perceived linearly across a page abstracted from the wholeness and disorder and multicensory quality of life. Print, he concluded created Henry Ford and the assembly line and standardized culture.

Increase in the use of print media indicates that literacy is spreading and communications are improving and it is affirmed that the communication revolution has in no way subtracted from the influence of the press and printed media. It has proved that the telecommunications explosion have actually substantiated the permanence of the written word.

The impact of print media depends on their credibility among readers as well as on how the content is presented, understood and interpreted. How different people or groups will read the same content depends on their social background. Thus, sometimes print media only reinforce widely held beliefs and status quo rather than bringing about change and development. The period of emergency showed how the credibility of the press could suffer due to lack of freedom.

Many times newspapers, activists' journals or so called grassroots print media have played the role of watch-dog and acted as a catalytic agent to hasten the process of social and economic change. For example, dialogues generated by news papers on women's political Participation, urban development, new education policy, new economic policy have contributed greatly as a catalytic agent. They have been playing the role of watch-dog when they report about scams, scandals, corruption, improper implementation of development schemes, programmes or projects.

The editorials of the newspapers and periodicals have contributed to steering public opinion in a particular direction. For example, when editorial criticizes the action taken by the Governor in Uttar Pradesh or Gujarat or appreciates aloud the action taken by the president or discusses the scam or scandal from its various angles or justifies war between two countries, it contributes to the knowledge and understanding of the people of a given situation. Although people tend to resist newspaper influences, it does certainly exist, particularly in the long term sense of reinforcement of opinions already held.

Chakravarty discussing the impact of newspapers on opinion building, says, "It is amongst these relatively knowledgeable readers that the newspaper is most likely to influence opinion. Over a long term period, the newspaper's influence can be very pronounced (especially, as has been seen in the sphere of foreign affairs), the process by which readers' opinion is eased along in its natural direction may not only take the form of very strong reinforcement, but many also border on the formation of new ideas, in that it sows seeds and implants suggestions on points to which people have upto now given next to no thought. Provided that these are, at least superficially, compatible with the reader's own outlook, they stand a good chance of being incorporated amongst his attitudes and opinions."

As far as the news values are concerned, people have become aware that all the newspapers are same with minor differences, though they bring out more editions in terms of content and ideological bias. That is, the criteria used by all newspapers in selecting the content for publications is the same.

In India, print media have been the active participants in the political process right from the days of Jawaharlal Nehru. It has frequently set the national agenda on domestic and foreign policy issues. They have provided indigenous enrichment. They have served as valuable check on executive power in the absence of a strong opposition.

With the globalization, foreign media also entered into the country. Foreign newspapers and magazines are, happily visible and available all over the country, but there is surely a difference between mere availability and being published in India. A New York Times editorial on the Indian political situation will not have the same weight as one written by its own Delhi edition.

Majority of the newspapers and magazine houses are located in big cities and the editors and writers are mostly the elites of the cities. This results in to almost negligible reporting on rural affairs or development. Even urban slums and lower strata hardly get coverage in the print media. Press Commission has also pointed out that there is a need to give news values a different orientation in the interest of higher professionalism and national development. Newspapers in India have not taken up dynamic journalism because of which the impact of the development programmes is not known to many of the country people. This is hampering the process of social revolution. Today's journalism is more of pragmatic nature and business oriented. Therefore, the kind of impact that print media could create during the pre-independence period, can not create today.

Poornananda blames Indian press for playing a significant role in promoting commercial attitudes and practices. He says, "It has been an important input into the steady deterioration of the communal climate in our country to the extent where our democratic system is threatened as never before. The newspapers in Indian langauges and English have worked for an ill-informed and biased public opinion instead of an integrated and enduring social order." The reports of many inquiry committees on communal riots indicate that the press has contributed to the escalation of tension between the communities.

As far as development or extension work is concerned, print media such as booklets, pamphlets, folders, leaflets, circulars, wall news papers have played important role in communicating with target groups of farmers, homemakers, rural groups, etc. These media have helped development workers in making their advisory work more interesting. These are either read or listened to by their target groups. They help in convincing and motivating people about the new ideas. For example, new varieties of crops, new ways of farming, water shed management, environment protection etc. Printed material such as circular and pamphlets have helped development workers to communicate quickly, inexperiencedly and effectively. Moreover, these media help them to maintain communi-cation with the client system in a regular and friendly manner.

In eighties, Arun Shourie's writings had demonstrated this type of journalism. Newspapers and magazines are indeed breaking far more stories on corruption than ever before.

Newspapers today have acquired strength in features, photographs, graphics and quality of paper used. The newspapers have been able to stand with magazines by publishing supplements in areas of general interests along with their regular editions. This is due to revolution in printing technology.

Print media like magazines are affected adversely due to onslaught of television. The news stories of magazines become obsolete, when published fortnightly or monthly. Magazines are required to constantly try to create new identity for themselves.

There are hardly any studies conducted on the impact of print media except the readership surveys, which throw light on what people prefer to read.

For last four centuries, printed world has ruled unchallenged in shaping and expressing public opinion. That monopoly has not ended with the development of radio, television and video. But the printed word still plays an important role behind the curtain in the form of the scripts or software for these media.

Availability of various types of printed media has provided readers with wider choice for selecting the printed medium as well as the content. However, it has also resulted into people browsing through newspapers and magazines in order to go through all those available to them. This has reduced the concentrated reading on part of the readers.

With the wider choice available in print media, readers have become so much 'want' conscious that the front pages of daily newspapers are dominated by politics, conflicts and tensions and development news gets hardly any coverage. It is true that since a newspaper is a marketed commodity, it will naturally carry what the readers want. But should that be the sole consideration?

Mass Media in India (1992) report mentions that English newspapers which are read by the middle classes in the cities denote as much as 17.4 per cent of space to development while Hindi newspapers denote only 14.1 per cent.

The role of the press in a developing country like India is to aid in the process of economic and social transformation and to accelerate it. It can do so by being more relevant by reaching out to the vast multitude living in the countryside. The print media in India has yet to make attempts to reach out to the large population of neoliterates whose number is growing fast and to convert them into readers. Development and social content is the first priority for these groups rather than sensational and selling political news and articles.

In distance education programmes also print media are the most important medium. This applies to all conventional correspondence courses as well as courses of open university. Print media have proved largely effective in the cognitive, affective and psychomotor domains.

The functions served by the print media in earlier times were limited, but nowadays newspapers have shown impact in persuading people to support particular candidate, policies and programmes. They get coverage in their front or editorial pages. At the same time some newspapers provide favourable or unfavourable coverage of institutions, candidates and issues. There is great impact of the information function performed by the newspapers. This function is alive and well served by the various parts of the newspapers which are devoted to news. Advertise-ments in print media also perform this function. Newspapers and magazines today are performing the function of entertainment also by including human interest stories, puzzles, comics, recipes, advice columns, sports, film and television and so on.

Malhan criticised news papers for three reasons:

1. News papers in India continue to be largely urban phenomenon. They are either published in metropolitan cities, big towns or state capitals.
2. Plagiarism has entered Indian print media. Reporters or editors do not read public documents properly and add a few words of their own and publish, which is not interpretive, educative, expository and promotional in nature.
3. Newspapers in India have not adequately taken up development journalism or reporting which is based on field work or direct observation or participant observation.

Advantages of Print Media

The multi-channel television has not led to a fall in the number and circulation of newspapers in the country. this is because of the special advantages of these media. When compared to other news media such as radio and television, buying a newspapers is extremely cheaper and provides a wide variety of information.

These media are portable without causing any incon-veniences and provide good company when traveling alone or on long distances. It is possible to read and re-read them at one's own pace and convenience. These media cater to the intellectual needs of the serious section of the population. As they report an item at any length, people look for details of the event in news papers even after watching television or listening on radio. Apart from these the production of print media is inexpensive as compared to production of programmes on electronic media.

In India, where illiteracy is a major problem, outreach of print media is limited but even reading aloud by literate person helps in gaining general knowledge simply by listening. It is also possible to read again if the listener has missed out, which may not be possible in case of radio.

Newspapers provide information and analysis of other media such as radio, television, books and so on. The daily schedules of radio and television, new books published in various areas, theatre activities as well as critical analysis of radio and television programmes, books, any other theatre activities such as play, folk drama or dance and so on. Thus, newspapers provide publicity to the other mass media.

Newspapers and magazines carry advertisements as their important part. Many people buy the paper to search through the classified advertisements for a job, a second hand car, a plumber or residence. One can find out from the advertisements about the latest restaurant, bargain sales, and holiday offers.

Limitations

The country like India where almost half the population is illiterate, the spread of print media and their utilization remains limited compred to other mass media. Thus, the advantages of print media are enjoyed by literates only. Moreover, due to increasing prices of papers and printing processes and advances in printing technology the prices of all kinds of print media have also gone up considerably. Thus, except newspapers the circulation of other print media remains restricted to the elite group who can afford them. The content of print media like newspapers and magazines go out of date soon. Lastly, the mistakes in the printed materials can not be rectified once printed.

RADIO AS MASS MEDIUM

Radio is widely used mass communication medium and has a great potentiality in dissemination of information as radio signals cover almost entire population. More than 177 radio stations are there across the country. About 97 percent of the population is reached by the radio.

Radio being a convenient form of entertainment caters to a large audience. With the advent of transistors this medium has reached the common man in urban and rural areas of India, though the utilization of radio is more among rural elites. It has advantages over the other mass media like television and newspapers in terms of being handy, portable, easily accessible and cheap. It is the most portable of the broadcast media, being accessible at home, in the office, in the car, on the street or beach, virtually everywhere at any time.

Radio is effective not only in informing the people but also in creating awareness regarding many social issues and need for social reformation, developing interest and initiating action. For example, in creating awareness regarding new policies, developmental projects and programs, new ideas etc. It can help in creating a positive climate for growth and development. It widens the horizons of the people and enlightens them, thereby gradually changing their outlook towards life. Research have shown that radio is an effective medium for education when it is followed up with group discussion and question-answer session.

In India, radio with it's penetration to the rural areas is becoming a powerful medium for advertisers. It gets 3 per cent of the national advertising budget. Radio is still to cheap alternative to television, but is no longer the poor medium in advertising terms. Because radio listening is so widespread, it has prospered as an advertising medium for reaching local audiences. Moreover, radio serves small highly targeted audiences, which makes it an excellent advertising medium for many kinds of specialised products and services. As far as commercials are concerned, no one is able to tune out commercials easily as is possible with remote control devices and VCRs. It is thought that radio's ability to attract local advertisers hurts mainly newspapers, since television is less attractive to the small, local advertiser. As far as audience is concerned radio does not hamper persons mobility. As a vehicle of information for masses it is still the fastest. For instance, it would take less time for a news reporter for radio to arrive on the spot with a microphone and recorder than the same for TV along with a shooting team and equipment.

Another important feature of radio as mass medium is that it caters to a large rural population which has no access to TV and where there is no power supply. In such places, All India Radio's programmes ccntinue to be the only source of information and entertainment. Moreover, AIR broadcasts programmes in 24 languages and 140 dialects.

"Radio should be treated akin to newspapers in view of the fact that it is local, inexpensive, linked to communities, has limited band width and operates through simple technology". Feels Arora (1997 : 5).

The economics of radio does allow tailoring programme content to the needs of small and diverse audiences. Thus it is economically viable to recast a programme for broadcast to audiences in different sub regional, cultural and linguistic context. This enhances the value of radio as a medium in networking developmental programmes. Thus, it offers many possibilities in networking, from locally or regionally co-ordinated broadcasts and interactive exchange of queries and data.

It can serve as a stand alone medium of information dissemination or a support medium for curricular learning, jointly with print material or with fieldwork.

Kapoor, Director General of AIR (1995) said, " Radio is far more interactive and stimulating medium than TV where the viewer is spoon-fed. Radio allows you to think, to use your imagination. That is why nobody ever called it the idiot box".

ADVANTAGES OF RADIO

Like other electronic media radio duplicates one-to-one communication thousands of times. A large section of receivers can be communicated quickly through radio. In case of emergencies, for examples, warnings of floods and other weather disturbances can be repeated every 15 or 30 minutes on radio. It can convey the message with speed and immediacy.

Due to many local radio stations as compared to television stations, radio is the major source of local news for many people. Local radio stations are targeted at specific audiences youth, rural, housewives, ethnic groups and so on. Thus, it becomes a valuable medium for development workers.

Radio needs relatively low infrastructure and overhead costs. It is easier to get on radio than television since radio programme is cheaper to produce and not much preparation is required. News, programmes and advertising for radio need little preparation. It can accommodate the last minute news story and sudden change in advertising messages. Radio can stay ahead in all message areas. This is also not possible with time consuming procedures.

It has greater audience reach. Even in the physical sense of 'reach', radio lends itself to a greater diversity of receiving situations. It does not demand undivided attention. It permits receiver mobility. A radio broadcast can be followed while going about various activities and chores, indoors and outdoors. It is inherently versatile medium, as it offers wide range of programme and frequency choices to its audience. It offers variety of programming slots. Transistors can continue to communicate even in case of power failure. In India, radio caters to a large rural population which has no access to TV and where there is no regular or limited power supply.

In such places, All India Radio's programmes continue to be the only source of information and entertainment. Moreover, radio brings programmes in 24 languages and 146 dialects.

LIMITATIONS OF RADIO

Radio has many inherent limitations. It provides one way channel of communication. Therefore, no feedback regarding the messages can be received. Since the listener's attention is held only by the sound, messages communicated through radio can reach only those people who listen carefully and intelligently. One has to be very attentive to receive the messages from radio otherwise he misses a part of the message. Radio lacks the pictorial quality provided by television and motion pictures. Moreover, no visuals can be used with radio to support the messages. Radio is not suitable for all types of commercials as some require illustration or demonstration.

Since radio conveys messages through sound only, it demands a habit of skillful listening which generally people lack. Mohanty (1992) rightly pointed out that radio may broadcast a well developed lesson, but cannot develop a lesson with the audience. With many people to receive a complete detailed lesson or a programme through radio becomes very taxing or boring as it tends to become monotonous at times.

Rahman (1977) said, "Radio broadcast is evanescent, impermanent and rarely sufficient in itself for the case of illustration. intended in educational broadcasting. It cannot be turned to, studied or re-read at leisure".

A wasthy has aptly said that in radio the artist and his audience are nowhere near each other. In the physical sense they are non-existent to each other.

Television as Mass Medium

Amongst all the mass media today, television attracts the largest number of viewers. Its audience is greater in size than any of the other media audiences. This is because television is able to attract the audiences of all age groups, literate and illiterate and of all the strata of the society.

In India, from the beginning *i.e.* 1989, television has been used more for education and information purposes than for entertainment. It has performed different functions as compared to the television in west. Even today, though commercials have entered Indian television in a big way, it's basic purpose has not changed. It continues to perform it's function of national integration and development.

Dr. Rajendra Prasad. while inaugurating India's Television Service on September 15, 1959, hoped that television would go a long way in broadening the popular outlook in line with scientific thinking.

There is no doubt about the fact that the technology has given us a major tool in television. It is a very powerful persuasive mass communication medium. How and why we make use of this tool will determine the effectiveness of this tool to enhance the development process.

In India uptil now, television is government owned medium. Therefore, it has to further the cause of development and spread the message of people's participation in development programmes launched by the government. The Indian model of television programmes is unique as it is expected to pass on the culture from one generation to other and persuasion.

Doordarshan, India's national network, has 41 major Kendras (stations) with studios, production facilities and regular programmes originating from the stations and 921 transmitters. Today, Doordarshan is competing with all cable TV networks in meeting the entertainment needs of the people.

Television in India, through it's programmes presents a composite national picture and perspective of India's rich cultural heritage and diverse thinking. They represent various religions and cultural expressions and activities of people, belonging to different parts of India, thus it reflects the Indian society. Television has been able to influence the people living in a remote areas of our country as its outreach has covered the remotest villages and tribal pockets. It is ushering information explosion.

The growth in television both in technology and reach in the last three decades has been phenomenal. It was basically conceived as a mass medium and a mass educator for its large population scattered in remote and culturally diverse areas. It is supposed to disseminate the message of development and modernization to create awareness for generating public participation. It is expected to support government plans and programmes for bringing about social and economic change and to protect national secutity as well as advance the cause of national integration.

Television, being an audio-visual medium, brings us into contact with events in an exciting and clarifying way. For example, a live telecast of a national event such as celebration of golden jubilee year of independence, or launching of a satellite, offers meaning to the events that no amount of reading or still pictures or even films could match. However, this incomparable quality of reality and immediacy is not found in all television programmes, especially those programmes which are prepared specifically for education purposes. Television is considered as a mirror of a national's personality. It can recall the past, dwell upon the present and peep into the future of a society. This role of television is all the more relevant to a country like India, having continental dimensions and innumerable diversities. It has the capability to reach simultaneously millions and millions of our people. Since it can transmit not only words but pictures as well, the significance of television as a medium of mass communication has universally been realised and recognised.

In a country like India where population and illiteracy are the burning problems, electronic media provides tremendous reach for disseminating audio-visual information even in remote areas. India has diverse cultures, religions and traditions. Therefore, medium like television can play a very important role in developing common understanding among the people and bringing them closer. It opens up the prospects of educating villagers in the remotest areas, in the affairs of the nation and associating them in the task of development, along with creating wider vision of the world.

Television provides masses a common experience at the same time, in a verifying degree. A telecast can use combination of various audio-visual materials and methods, such as, objects, models discussion, demonstrations, plays, exhibits, chalkboard and so on. This helps in clarifying the messages to audience varying in their comprehension level. Thus, it makes mass communication more effective and appeals to the groups of varied nature. Television, like radio, is also primarily a one way channel of communication.

There have been developments in television medium so as to make two way communication possible, but in India this technique is used occassionally only. For example, at the time of elections we are able to watch communicator and receiver communicating on TV from a distance. Normally the communicator on a television screen can not enjoy the rapport with his audience which makes difference between a one-sided performance and a true interaction of communicator and receiver.

Like film, television also stimulates and reinforces ideas, beliefs and tendencies already possessed by the viewer. For example, television repeats and thereby reinforces the messages on family planning, importance of girls education, marriage age, environment protection, energy conservation etc. Thus, it serves persuasive function.

Television has more flexibility and mobility in its coverage due to audio-visual presentation. This is the reason why it has become a family medium. Family members receive messages in their own environment. It can show what happened and how it happened. It can show landing of a man on mars, functioning of heart or division of cell through animation. Above all, it can provide entertainment also. Thus, television as a mass medium informs, educates, inspires and motivates.

As far as educational messages to the masses are concerned, television can be the most powerful educational medium because it combines speaking, writing and showing. You not only talk to the masses at one time but you show them what you mean. Thus, TV presents mass demonstration to thousands of viewers at the same time.

Discussing the importance of television as mass media. Saxena says, "Television in India has acquired today newer dimensions, greater popularity and a much wider reach. The moving images of television fascinate people, demand attention and eventually influence their thoughts and behaviour. The small screen has indeed turned out to be large enough to compress, within itself, India's tremendous cultural diversity over a rather broad social spectrum. Television has become part of our popular culture-part of our life itself".

TELEVISION AND DEVELOPMENT

Television aimed at disseminating development information and foster the process of modernization and encourage public participation and support in developmental programmes, protecting national security and advancing the cause of national integration.

"Perhaps we have ascribed inappropriate expectations to the medium, or perhaps the medium has its own limitations."

The primary purpose of television in India is development through education, information and enlightenment, to improve the quality of life of the largest masses of the people, to bring communities and societies, regions and the states together as one nation through mutual awareness and sympathy while preserving their cultures, customs and traditions. The secondary purpose is entertainment.

Ever since the first five year plan was launched in 1951, the role of communication for development support has been stressed in every five year plan. Funds allocation especially for television also increased in the sixth plan. Massive expansion of Indian television took place during this period. Seventh plan aimed at television reaching the remotest part of the country.

The only example of using television exclusively for development communication was the Kheda Communication Project (KCP), which not only aimed developing and demonstrating a new approach to the use of television for development and education but also to try out a more meaningful direction for Indian Television, KCP succeeded in demonstrating effectively that TV could be used for development and social change. It received world-wide recognition and it was awarded a UNESCO prize for rural communication effectiveness. (Bhatia and Kamic,1989). After commissioning of Ahmedabad transmitter and with the increase of individually owned television, there was the pressure to close down PIJ transmitter and had no transmission between August 1985-May 1988. Community Television sets were left unused. Programme quality also deteriorated after it's restart in May, 1988. There was commercial pressure on professionals, more government guidelines to be followed for programme making. Finally, by October, 1991, Ministry of Information and Broadcasting, decided to stop it's transmission.

According to Sinha, "The premature death of this development communication experiment leaves many unanswered questions. Those who believe that television can play a meaningful role in developing the community at large must carry out a postmortum on the successes, the failures, and the lessons to be learned from the demise of this model of development communication".

SITE and KCP evaluation studies have rendered that development depends on many factors. Television can disseminate information supportive of development, but unless a development project has strong support from powerful groups and proper infrastructure to match the demands generated by that information, such information soon becomes superfluous. Thus, the Indian Television's dilemma is—should it continue with it's original objectives and commitments to development or join race of entertainment with other channels?

The commitment of Indian television is to support the formal and non-formal education systems. However, the impact of television transmission for primary school students, for higher education, and for distance education is being questioned by society at large and by educational policy makers. indian Television stands at a crossroads in the role it has to play in improving the quality of life. However, the increasing dependence on sponsored commercials a source of revenue required for its functioning and growth and the competition it faces from other open channels attracting audiences with entertainment programmes have presented considerable threats to Indian television. In the beginning it was successful in its role of development communication to the deprived masses, but slowly the nature of its role as an agent of change seems to have disappeared.

While describing television an agent of social change, Saxena (1996) expressed that the process of change in a developing society has generally been slow. All the more, in a highly tradition bound country like India. Our people generally resist change. So, mass media strategies have first to create in them a general awareness of what all is going on elsewhere. There to motivate them to 'accept' and 'achieve' some thing new. And eventually, to let them decide how best and fast could that be done. At different stages of this transition, television, being visual, played a more dynamic role. Take, for instance, Doordarshan's very first major project, a citizenship through Television, introduced by Delhi TV. A number of teleclubs were established in and around Delhi to let the viewers take advantage of the social messages, beamed through TV. The UNESCO in a report also commended this project.

At the time of introduction of television, the official policy stressed that TV was to be used as a medium of social education as well as an instrument to support programmes specifically it was stated that TV would be used as a weapon against illiteracy and ignorance. It would bring about awareness among the people of sociological problems and make them conscious of national goals; it would create a sense of participation in India's efforts to usher in a new social order; it would play a vital role in cultivating civic consciousness and respect for law and order, public morality and so forth and, in the field of entertainment, it would mould public taste to higher aesthetic levels.

In reality, TV has turned out to be a family entertainment medium. Doordarshan audience research has also shown that the development programmes do not have large viewership. However, the programmes on health, nutrition, environment protection, energy conservation, pollution, adult education, consumer education, agriculture, animal husbandry, and family planning are being telecast by Doordarshan. Rural programmes are one of the most important target specific programmes of Indian television. Nearly 80 percent of Indian population lives in villages, and India is an agrarian country. The basic objectives of rural programmes of television in India are:

(a) To familiarise rural viewers with the latest technical and scientific know-how about farming, agriculture implements, fertilizers, good quality seeds, cottage industries, rural development, weather forecasts etc.

(b) To provide healthy entertainment (Folk music/plays/puppet shows).

(c) To acquaint the audience with the importance of education, personal hygiene, health and family welfare.

The rural programmes have been criticized for not reflecting the ruralness in their approach and content. Development practitioners have attributed it to the following factors.

1. All production centers are located. in the urban areas and programmes are being developed and produced by the urban professionals who do not have rural orientation or experience of rural problems. Thus, rural problems, needs and aspirations do not get reflected in the rural programmes of television.

2. Compared to urban viewers, rural viewers are less in numbers. Therefore, the impact of programmes on the expected size of rural population is not seen.

3. Many rural families are still not able to afford a television set.

An Audience Research Unit of Doordarshan conducted a study in 1993, covering 420 villages from 15 states. The study revealed that the development oriented programmes do not have large viewership because of:

— lack of local specificity

— unavailability of regional programmes

— variations in TV ownership patterns

— viewing by many viewers perset.

The telecast of Krishi Darshan - a programme on Agriculture and Rural Development (ARD) was started in Delhi in 1967 and now all the 41 Doordarshan Kendras telecast similar programmes. When the reach of television was limited, Doordarshan had made special efforts to reach the rural audience. It was through SITE experiment, Kheda communication project, and INSAT scheme of Area specific programmes from 1982, which included ETV programmes, programmes from all production centres.

The Joshi working group on software for Doordarshan also observed : The trouble with many development programmes, like Krishi Darshan is that they are produced within the studio often with urban men in rural garb. It is often an urban view of rural programmes, or a view of problems of urbanised villages. Considering the immensity of the task of fighting poverty, we recommend that more than half the time of Doordarshan must be related to the development.

Findings of several studies confirm that rural development programmes on TV need to be given sharpness, and thrust so as to make them more useful and relevant. According to Doordarshan study there are many schemes of providing community TV sets to rural areas - some centrally sponsored, some by state governments and some by local community organisations.

There is a need to evolve extension departments, agricultural universities, departments of agriculture and other allied institutions in producing effective and appealing television programmes for rural development.

It requires development of scientific attitude, inculcation of values for modernization and support from the leaders of the groups, communities and society to foster the multi-faceted process of development through television. No one agency or medium can do this. It requires the support of the suciety as a whole.

Thus Indian television is at a cross roads as far as its role in the development of a nation is concerned. Sinha, analysing the role of television in development today, pointed out, "It is unfortunate that despite the best intentions, development communication projects with a participatory approach rarely get beyond an experimental status because of social, political and economic constraints. Development communication cannot be treated 'normal' television and probably requires separate training for those who produce rural media and separate standards for judging its quality and success. The social use of development communication in India is not only lopsided in terms of distribution between the rural and the urban, but is also grossly inadequate to meet even the needs that exist in the metropolitan sector."

Nowadays television is concentrating more on earning revenue through sponsorships and advertisements. This has pushed aside the purpose of developmental communication and encouraged consumerism. This has resulted in to domination of entertainment programmes on Television. The dilemma before Indian television today is who will take care of development communication. Sinha suggests that Doordarshan, can have seperate television for achieving developmental objectives. Thus, high cost entertainment TV could earn its revenue while low cost development communication could be the state's responsibility.

IMPACT OF TELEVISION ON THE SOCIETY

Television has profound impact on our society. It has changed the life styles of the people and has become a major influence in our culture. Unlike printing, which took hundreds of years to influence the culture, TV's impact was almost instantaneous.

Television has occupied an important position in homes and therefore, it is bound to make an impact on the individuals and the society Television, as a technology has changed the complexion and manner of conveying ideas to people and therefore, there is a need to examine the individual's relationship with the television.

Explaining the importance of television, Joseph aptly mentions, "Having earned a niche for itself in ways that are inimitable and unprecedented, TV has worked its way as an indispensable member of hundreds of millions of families across the world. To say that it merely educates, informs and entertains is an understatement. For in the seven decades since its invention by John Baird, the fascinating minutiae of how the medium works and influences has put it in a class of its own. From an apparently innocuous box it has metamorphosed into the protagonist, altering the very character of human transactions and shaping the way human beings think and behave. This has opened a Pandora's box and fulled a stormy debate on the role of television in human society".

In view of the fact that television in India is fast developing as a major source of mass enlightenment, leisure and pleasure, it is essential that it's impact in various areas is analysed. This can go a long way in providing guidelines for future developmental programmes of television in India. In terms of critics, comments and reviews no other medium, print, radio, cinema, caught the fancy of the analysts as television has.

Deodhar strongly feels that television has made contributions to the lives of people of India. Traditional media people consistently underestimate television's culture changing effects, mainly because they overlook certain characteristics that are so obvious that one takes them for granted. The most important feature of television is it's ability to deliver simultaneously into the intimate environment of millions of homes, touching lines of the entire household, ideas mingled with powerful drama.

Television has brought a revolutionary change in the way people receive information and understand the world by shifting them from direct experience of life and environment to the second hand or contrived experiences, which make people feel that they are directly experiencing the events or different places.

Research studies have pointed out that perceptions of the television messages, images and ideas shape the entire social system. The present out reach of television has created awareness and appreciation of the socio-cultural ethos of our different regions. Television has contributed to breaking the social barriers and inculcation of the scientific temper in our masses. Studies have shown that exposure to media leads to the appreciation of social and cultural ethos. For any social change to take place flow of information is of prime importance. It increases the understanding of the people regarding the issue and develops common feeling for the need for social change. Information bridges the gap of understanding between the people and helps them to unite for the cause. Television has done this job by contributing to the information explosion. Saxena also points out "Today's information explosion has opened the" floodgates of knowledge and curiosity. This is being attributed to the vast television exposure. A majority of our people live in remote villages, cut off from, what is Known as, modernity. Till late, they led a life submerged in age old conservatism. But now they are able to see and appreciate what is going around, adding to their information gain".

In United States of America television created a great impact on homogenization of a heterogeneous society. It played an important role in providing a common denominator to multi-lingual, multi racial American society which led to certain uniformity in societal reaction to situations or events, in developing common response in personal and social communication, in better appreciation of people with diverse beliefs and life styles. Nationwide television thus, could provide a platform for cultural meeting.

Television has made far reaching impact on various groups of people as well as in certain areas of our life, which are discussed here.

Children. Extensive communication research on the use of Indian Television for development purposes, has been conducted under SITE and KCP, but in-depth studies on impact of television on family life are few. However, television's impact on children has been the area of interest for social scientists.

The effect of television on home and family and particularly on children has become a matter of concern for behavioural science researchers.

Looking at the 'influence, it seems television has become like a member of the family. Studies have shown that it has upset the tone, tenor and stability of household activity and atmosphere, drew children away from their assigned and imperative tasks and discipline in growing up. It has strongly affected their attitudes and emotions. Thus it holds dangerous potential for damage of children's personalities.

Children watch the programmes with undue sex, violence and adult themes and glorified affluent lifestyles. This raises undue expectations among children and thereby pressures on the family. There are no programmes left on television schedule which could be exclusively called children's programmes, except channels like cartoon's, which again take children in to fantasy world.

Children and even housewives sit glued to TV regardless of time.

Various studies have been conducted regarding the impact of television on children. The observations of these studies have been:

1. Television provides children with thrill. The thrill syndrome results in behaviour abnormalities.
2. Television viewing has led children to under exposure to print.

A study by Media Advocacy Group (1980) observed that across all income and sex groups, parents have a problem with unrestricted viewing by children. They felt helpless in controlling the TV viewing by children. Inspite of its entertaining nature, television violence develops among viewers the sense of fear, victimization, mistrust, insecurity and dependence. The study suggested that the violence terror scenario may have several consequences which include the cultivation of aggressive tendencies, the accommodation to violence, the personalisation and isolation of offenders, the sporadic triggering of violent acts, and the levels of vulnerability and dependence felt by different groups living with the images of a mean and dangerous world.

Trivedi (1991) investigated the impact of TV on children. The study revealed that:

(1) Their activities of play outside home had decreased, they had given up playing indigenous games and their interests in cricket and other costly games had increased.

(2) Mischievous nature of children had calmed down after the introduction of TV in the house. Children had stopped wondering outside the house during TV programmes.

(3) TV advertisements created an adverse impact on the demands among children for new goods and items to be purchased for them and household. The demand for items of the daily use, such as fancy soap, etc. normally not used by the members of the households, have increased more. These tendencies were more in middle class and posh class.

(4) The overall impact of TV on education of children was not reported to be adverse.

Television takes away children's play time which causes negative effects on children' s development. Thus, their physical and cognitive development get adversely affected. Watching television for extended period of time impacts upon the availability of time for their other activities such as playing, reading, visiting friends or relatives. It limits the time for homework and other forms of learning and thus contributes to lower academic performance.

Research has also indicated that children do not distinguish between programmes and advertisements. Children under 8 cannot appreciate commercial's 'selling' intent and they do not have the defenses against commercial appeals that adults have.

There are also positive effects of television on children. It fosters prosocial behaviour in children, for example, interaction with family members and friends, mannerisms, ways of greeting people and so on. TV viewing enhanced children's selection of materials used in spontaneous play.

There is growing sense of unease at what has been happening in the world of television and the manner in which ideas conveyed by television.

The television explosion has been experienced by western countries, which has drawn people's attention to the fact that:

* The more TV a child watches, the greater the influence it has on the child.
* Television promotes violation and/or aggressive behaviour.
* Watching TV for long hours adversely affects reading and writing skills.
* Television as a passive activity takes children away from other, more direct, experiences.
* Television may encourage and influence early sexual activity, drug and alcohol abuse.
* The passivity induced by watching too much TV can lead to obesity.

Maniar (1994) studied the influence of television viewing on adolescents, which threw light on the positive side of television. The findings revealed high influence on development of civic competence and moderate influence on other development tasks such as body image, sex roles, independence, future roles, preparation for family life and preparation for career. Adolescents reported that the programme related to health such as Gharelu Nuskhe, Yoga, Head over Heels, Aerobics, Das Kadam etc. made them curious of health and body and helped them to adopt good health practices and made them figure conscious. Television viewing facilitated their discussions on sex matters and understanding of the changes occurring in their body.

Television made adolescents aware of social issues like dowry and adoption of child. They became informed about various career opportunities through the serials like Aur Bhi Hai Rahen. They also reported that their civic competence increased and feeling of patriotism developed in them after viewing programmes and documentaries or conservation of resources, environmental degradation, political discussions and analysis, and serials like Saudaa, Bharat Ke Shahid, Mashaal etc. They also became aware of consumer rights and laws, women and law, through programmes like Rajni, Apake Adhikar, Nari Tu Narayani and so on. They also learnt about the cultures of various states of India as well as other countries.

Family. Apart from children as a specific group, family as a whole has also been under the profound impact of television.

The rich and middle class families rushed to purchase television sets shortly after the medium entered the popular culture. Many lower class people went into debt to own this luxury item which gradually has become the necessity. Many family activities, which were cherished earlier, such as after dinner conversations among family members, parents, reading bedtime stories to the children, praying or reading religious books at night were replaced by TV watching.

Television has been reported to be giving a feeling of importance and relaxation from closed environment and monotonous living conditions. male members of the family have started spending more time at home. People have shown increase in the knowledge of political, social and economic issues of the country through the programmes such as talks and discussions.

It has been reported that there was marginal saving on account of TV in comparison to earlier expenditure on entertainment. It did not show any impact on the aged and old in the family except that they found it easy to spend their time. In case of entertainment, many viewers of TV have expressed that they get more entertainment and great satisfaction of its utility by watching sports and games on TV rather than sitting in the stadium or viewing film in a theatre. They enjoy watching film or sports programmes in relaxed, cosy and comfortable way. This affected the film industry and it did face serious challenge in eighties due to decrease in revenue. It is trying to face the challenge competently by excelling in technical aspect and its music and sound system.

Advertisements on TV have helped people to make their choice and selection of goods of household use. It has boosted consumerism among the people and raised aspirations of the people and their standard of living. It has resulted into westernized life style and widened the gap between information rich and the information poor.

Socially, it has been observed and reported that the frequency of visits to relatives and friends which helped in maintaining affectionate and intimate social relationships have been considerably reduced after the television invasion of homes.

A study by Trivedi (1991) showed that religious activities of the families were disturbed due to TV. Religious serials and programmes on TV were looked upon by people as adding sanctity to their house.

Politics. Television has contributed to political education of the masses. It gives extensive visual coverage to the political events of the country because of which people have become familiar with the day to day political programmes of TV and have become familiar with the national and international political figures. It has made many people interested in politics who found it a boring subject in non-TV days.

Indian Television has been criticized for over highlighting the activities of the ruling party and programmes taken up by it, which often raises doubts about the reliability of such broadcasts. It is observed that television has been effective in creating some kind of political awareness even among children and illiterates. Such as names of the prime minister., chief minister, importance of voting, how to vote, which party has won in the election, etc. To some extent, TV has familiarized rural masses with international political personalities also.

A study was conducted in ten villages of Ranga Reddy District of Andhra Pradesh to assess the impact of television on rural folk and to see how far the present political programmes on television are useful to the masses in creating political consciousness among them. The study revealed that television created interest in knowing further about politics, parties, increased knowledge about the prevailing situation in the society, and value of voting. Persons watching news in only Telugu 'were politically less aware as compared to those watching in Hindi and English in addition to Telugu. There was small increase in the political awareness of the people watching for longer hours.

Consumerism. Television expanded the consumer culture and made it a mass culture by providing new outlet for selling the products. It became a major medium of advertising. The commercialisation of Indian television intensified the nation wide policy debate about television's role. Those favouring commercialisation claim that it provides funds for improving production of TV programmes, while the detractors of the policy argue that such TV programme quality comes at a high price.

It encourages competition among advertisers for larger audiences. Moreover advertiser cater to urban masses and the needs of poor are neglected. Teleshopping networks have developed all over the country. It is another method of selling consumer goods. It is designed to stimulate instant sales. This has further boosted the consumerism.

A study conducted by ORG revealed that majority of the viewers under the study purchased ommercial products after seeing them advertised in television. Younger viewers, heavy viewers and those with higher levels of mass media exposure showed higher levels of consumerism.

Education. The educational network of Doordarshan kept on expanding as the Television Service developed, adding newer areas and dimensions. Today, most of the programme originating Kendras of Doordarshan run regular programmes, bearing on education whether formal or informal or both. Television programmes are now regularly available from primary classes to university level.

Besides Doordarshan, organisations like IGNOU, UGC, NCERT and Education Department of State Governments are fully involved today in the use of television as a medium of education.

Recently, IGNOU conducted a two-way-audio and one way video experiment by linking up the experts in Delhi TV studio and the audience in the studios in the far off cities. Here audience could ask questions and get instantaneous replies from the experts on television. This provides the opportunity for audience to participate and give feed back in the communication process.

Doordarshan puts out programmes for various age groups. Some of its centres telecast programmes on 'Adult Education'. Bombay Doordarshan's programme entitled 'Gyandeep' was the most successful one by Doordarshan in the area of Adult Education. It was considered very effective in educating the adult audience, in whose life the gap was created due to illiteracy or failure to continue schooling. The similar programme by Delhi Doordarshan did not gain the popularity.

Television has imparted non formal education to people and made them better informed, aware and educated in the areas like consumer education, vocational education, education to industrial workers, civic education, safety, health, legal education, and so on. Such efforts are sporadic and therefore do not create boosting impact. Most of them lack messages of general interest.

Vedantam, an education correspondent of the 'Deccan Herald' felt that at present 10 percent of TV time set aside for education is not enough, if we want the next generation to become something good. Doordarshan has failed to create an entertainment channel which educates at the same time. UGC programmes on TV are highly academicised in nature, catering to those, who already have access to that kind of education. She felt that Doordarshan has not been able to deliver the goods. Perhaps, it is unable to cope with its multifarious responsibilities. It has lack of direction especially in its educational thrust. So, if this area of responsibility at least is shifted to another organisation, where specialists in the field could devote their complete attention, we may be able to look forward to a more constructive, balanced and really useful TV education. Something on the lines of the BBC open university programmes.

Very few studies on impact of these programmes have been carried out so as to draw any conclusions or generalisations.

Non Formal Education. With the launching of National Literacy Mission, the emphasis was laid on the utilisation of television for adult education and the programmes of general interest and social awareness were broadcasted. The impact studies of these programmes revealed that adults watching television had become better sources of information, males discussed television programmes more and females gained more knowledge in the areas of health and nutrition innovations, family planning and social problems. Television helped adult in developing favourable opinion regarding adults education.

Cherian (1986) studied the impact of the selected Health and hygiene, nutrition and family planning programmes of PIJ Television (Under Kheda Communication Project) on the rural people of the Kheda District. The findings revealed that there was significant gain in knowledge in the experimental groups about the importance of green leafy vegetables, polio vaccination and laproscopy.

Many studies have highlighted the fact that the deprived sections remained unreached by the television medium.

The broad content of rural programmes included areas like agriculture, animal husbandary, employment schemes, agricultural institutions, interviews with progressive farmers, documentaries on villages, cooperation and marketing, social education, healthcare and cultural programmes.

A study to examine the status and role performance of television *vis-a-vis* other media in villages threw light on the following points.

* About 30 percent of the villagers remained completely unexposed to television. The non-participation among females was to the extent of 53 percent, while it was about 23 percent among the males.

* Illiteracy had been found to be an important barrier to television exposure and this was contrary to the general presumption that TV can effectively communicate with the illiterate audience.

* These having exposure to other media like print, radio, etc. maintained greater interaction with Television.

* The community TV sets exist only in better-off villages.

* The interior villages mostly depended upon traditional channels like the weekly market, kin groups, mends, local leaders and to a fairly large extent the radio.

To summarise, television has had some influence and undoubtedly on the social, cultural, political environment of the urban and rural masses. In-depth studies need to be taken up to find out the impact of television in various age groups. Although television has contributed to development of a nation, it's potential for development has not been fully tapped.

However, the major satellite and cable television companies in the world view India as one of the top five TV markets in the 21st century. And now with the supreme court judgement on freeing airwaves from government monopoly, and private broadcasters, TV programme is poised to break new grounds in a big way as never before.

Originally television was a novelty, but now it has become medium. It is diffusing rapidly in India and intensifying the debate about it's socio-culture impact on Indian society.

Advantages of Television

Television has the intimacy of radio and the believability of personal participation. It has intimate approach due to which it becomes more appealing and attracts the attention and interest of the people. As it combines all the elements, namely, sight, sound and motion it becomes possible to show variety of indoor and outdoor situations, scenes and places effectively. Thus, it is very effective in stimulating and inspiring new insights, discoveries and inventions.

Television breaks the barrier of illiteracy, as due to its combination of sight, sound and motion, understanding of the message becomes easier, whereas, with the print media like newspapers and magazines, readers have to put a lot of efforts on reading and understanding the message which may not be possible for illiterates. It provides entertainment, informs, educates and persuades and thus performs all functions of mass media.

It makes news releases and features action oriented and colorful for greater impact. The visual experience of watching TV is more dynamic and meaningful due to the movement and sound associated with it. Thus it becomes most exciting and efficient means of mass communication.

Television can bring the live programmes right into the living room of the audiences. This provides the vicarious experience of participating in the event.

Limitations of Television

Television requires a fully developed Television network and electrical supply for broadcasting the programmes. Therefore, inspite of 85 percent of area covered by television network in India, people in remote as well as rural areas are not able to take advantage of television due to lack or absence of electrical supply.

Television is an expensive mass medium compared to other mass media, because not only the television sets are expensive but both production of television programmes and their utilisation are expensive unless they are used extensively. Moreover, TV programme production requires trained personnels.

There is a need to learn about the beneficial and harmful effects of television, exploit it's positive potential and prevent the damage it can do to the various groups of people.

FOLK FORMS AS MASS MEDIA

In the recent years educationists, media experts and development practitioners have realized the tremendous potential of folk art forms as means of communication with people. Folk media are primarily concerned with appealing to emotions, and include strong dimension of communication of message. They constitute an integral part of the culture and tradition of the people and they have instant mass appeal. They function within the cultural framework of the society, which appeals to the audience and thus folk media acquire credibility among masses.

Folk media provide for face to face communication. Thus they envisage an audio visual impact as well as maximum audience participation and instant feed back. These media have three major objectives.

1. Aesthetic expression

2. Expressional

3. Communicational

These objectives are realised during performance with simultaneous audience involvement creating a live and direct dialogue with the audience.

Folk media convey developmental and educational messages through entertainment, colour, costume, dance and music remain the heart of the folk theatre. The initial aim of the folk theatre is to give the first impact with sound and sight and then slowly open the audiences mental eye for the message on morality. Thus, on one hand it gives expression to the life style and values of the people in spoken word and song, rhythm and spontaneous choreography, on the other hand it acts as a most persuasive communicator and an effective corrective force.

As folk media constitute an integral part of the culture, the audience is able to identify itself with the experience provided by folk media. They provide the audience with emotional, intellectual and subconscious level of experience through music, melody, fantasy, humour and intelligible information. Moreover, repetition of ideas by repeating dialogues or lines of songs ensure understanding of the messages. Such repetitions through modem media would require huge budgets.

Due to the informality and simplicity of the folk media, they allow for prompt improvisation by the intelligent and imaginative performers and thus become immediately relevant and responsive to the environment or situation. Generally they are informal and unscripted and do not fall in the category of works of high art. They are spontaneous manifestation of the art and due to their informal nature it provides unlimited scope for improvisation in song, speech, dance and gesture.

The flexibility of folk media is mainly responsible for their immense potentiality as message carriers. They are also adaptable to modern mass media. Thus they remain nearer to masses than classical forms. Folk forms are larger than life and melodramatic. Gestures, movements and speech are more simple and down to earth than the of rigidity of classical theatre and the abstractions of modern theatre.

Folk media have simplified realism and suggestivity to rural symbols which mass audiences can easily relate, for example, dress, dialects, folk songs, are taken from the existing culture of the region only. Comments by Sutradhar, Vidushak or Jester provide for comments on the contemporary issues in a satire form, which is most liked by the public because the main plot of the folk drama is well known.

Folk media are the most appropriate for bringing about changes in attitude or for popularizing new practices in a traditional society.

For example, Bhavai on use of unconventional sources of energy, treatment to lower caste people, importance of exercising vote etc. can convey the messages very effectively. Thus, they could play role in framing, structuring and patterning our national ethos.

Folk media have capacity to change and adapt to socio political situations. The cause for this change is clearly the demand of the audience. It can be seen in many of our folk forms. For example, the dances in Nautanki are derived from classical Kathak and Gayaki is based on pure ragas. Nowadays, we find light, 'filmy' kind of dance and music replacing these earlier traditions of folk dance and music.

Urban audience also respond to folk theatre favourably if one brings in a few sophistications. For example, messages related to urban environment and population can be conveyed effectively through Bhavai or Nautanki or Street play.

In India folk forms have special significance as mass media. People in remote rural and tribal areas do not have an access to the modern media. Studies have shown that the messages sent through modern media do not reach these target groups. Here folk forms of communication can help immensely in dissemination of the messages emitted by the electronic media. These groups have low level of media literacy due to lack of experience to modern media, which are not close to their culture and values.

In short, folk media are the tools of communication having special characteristics. They remain alive through oral and functional sources. They can work as the most effective channels for expressing socio-cultural, religious, moral and emotional needs of the people of the society to which they belong.

Kwnar strongly feels that trom a countrywide perspective the folk and traditional media are still the only 'mass' media, in the sense that they have their roots in the tradition and experience of a large majority of the population, and also that they have a reach much more extensive than any of the modern traditional media. It can be noted, however, that the numerous religious, caste and linguistic groups across the 22 states of the country have their own distinctive folk and traditional media, though there has been some interaction among them.

Indian Folk Forms

Folk arts have been identified in three categories on the basis of their form, content and performance situation: Ritual, traditional and functional. It is learnt from experience that the first category of ritual arts like tribal dances and religious acts, should best be left untouched in relation to a communication strategy on themes of contemporary significance, as they are rigid and reject the new message as a 'foreign body'. The traditional ones which draw themes from the much regarded classics and ancient fore, do permit their flexible characters like the jester (Vidushak) and narrator manager (Sootradhara) to absorb and reflect new messages despite the rigid story frame. These arts could be judiciously employed as message carriers to the audience through a face-to-face situation, which makes rural communication meaningful and convincing. The third category of functional or folk songs, acts and narration has been found to be ideally suited for development communication, with a judicious exploitation of their inherent flexibility to absorb contemporary messages.

Folk arts are also categorized on the basis of their form of communication such as, verbal, verbal-musical, musical and visual folk art.

Folk drama encompasses the entire inner personality of the villager. It seeks to meet all his intellectual, emotional and aesthetic needs. Unlike urban and modern drama, it freely uses songs, dances and instrumental music, besides dialogues. This multiple approach results in a form that is self contained and complete entertainment for the audience to whom it is directed. It is more than an entertainment, it is a complete emotional experience and aims at creating an environment or receptivity in which verbal communication of ideas is an effortless process.

Some of the most eminent folk dramas in India, have been used for social awakening since independence. In the hands of Mukund

Das and Utpal Dutt, Bengal's traditional Jaatra became a powerful tool of social and political education. 'Tamaasha' of Maharashtra was raised to the status of national theatre. Habib Tanvir in Madhya Pradesh gave a new dimension to the rural drama as a powerful interpreter of new and provocative ideas. Other forms such as, Bhavai of Gujarat, Burrakatha of Andhra Pradesh, Yakshagana of Karnataka came to the fame as dependable and persuasive change agents in the rural context.

The ballads like Lavni and Pawada of Maharashtra, Garba of Gujarat, Gee-Gee of Karnataka, Kabigaun of West-Bengal and Villupatta of Tamilnadu also came in forefront and played roles in altering the rural mind to the importance of social or political themes like social welfare, national unity, status of women and so on. The original content of these ballads is replaced by new messages to suit the needs of time and place. This has given them contemporanity and functional relevance.

Folk drama has grown as an entertainment form. All forms of folk dramas have their origin in different regional cultures and languages. Some of the popular types of folk dramas are discussed here.

Jatra. Jatra is a robust folk theatre of eastern India. Folk theatre is currently attracting a lot of attention as a vehicle of nonformal education in developing countries. As entertainment, it has the potentiality to hold the interest of large members of people in the remote villages. As a public social activity, it brings a community together and creates the context for co-operative thinking and action.

In the beginning, the Oriya folk drama was in the form of an opera. Ramlila, Krishnalila and Rasa were very popular in ancient times. Subsequently, they were developed and came to be known as Jatras. The good and bad results of good and evil actions were clearly shown in Jatra which served to educate the masses.

The Jatra contains stock characters. They are generally the attendants (Dwari or Dwarapala) or the sweeper and his wife or gypsies meant to create humour and to unfold the play further.

Mostly written in Satire, the Jatra songs are lively and full of fun. The jester could be rehearsed to make hilarious gags. He has the unique chance to comment on specific attitudes which are resisted by the masses. The huge drums, cymbals, trumpets and bugles are used as musical instruments. Artificially prepared figures representing life size elephants and terrible looking demon and dragons carry a strong mass appeal for the Jatra.

Tamasha. Tamasha has been the folk theatre and popular entertainment of Maharashtra. It is extremely lively. It has female artist who sings the favourite songs of the patrons. The form had originally no religious or social message to convey except those of refined type which raised philosophical and moral questions. Tamasha starts with prayer called Gana to Ganesh, followed by gaulan, a milkmaid scene. Next comes the story (vag), which is told in the form of dialogue, song and dance and is based on stories derived from myth and folk-lore and satirical comments are made. Vag begins with a chorus chanted at a high pitch to introduce the audience to the plot. In between Lavni (harvest song) and powada—a folk ballad of Maharashtra are also woven. It does not require elaborate stage and the actors wear traditional Maharashtrian costume.

Puppets. Puppetry is a distinct form of folk medium. It is a dramatic expression with the help of little creatures called puppets, having varying degree of freedom of movement. It was mostly considered a play activity. Nowadays, it is finding popularity as a means of educational communication. It is the oldest form of folk theatre in India. Ramayana and Mahabharata were the two frequent themes, used by most of the puppet plays in India and neighbouring Asian countries.

A marionette show is very popular among the masses, both urban and rural. There are also shadow puppets, popularly called Chhaya Puttali. They are made of single piece tanned skin with dyes, when illuminated from behind, they throw black and white shadow over the screen.

Glove puppets are worn on hand and are manipulated with the help of first finger fitted in to hollow head and thumb and middle finger fitted into hollow hands of puppets. These can be handled easily evenly children and untrained persons. Puppetry is low cost medium, easy to adopt and handle and can make impact providing scope for participation of local people and use of local dialect.

Nautanki. The Nautanki is a folk theatre of north India. It uses open stage. It has simple dramatic structure comprising small units linked by a Ranga or Sutradhar, the narrator. The themes are derived from the ancient epics and form folklore like the tale of Laila and Majnu or the heroic deeds of some rulers and decoits. Music provides the pace and tempo to Nautanki. Dholak and Makkara (Kettle drum) are mainly used for music. The dialogues are sung to popular folk melodies and now, even to popular film tunes.

Yakshagana. It is a most popular folk drama of Karnataka. It is full of song and repartee. It's themes are from Bhagvata but with a lot of local flavour. The narrator here is known as the Bhagvata who sings verses and exchanges witty remarks with the players and handles the symbols and songs. Besides, there is a jester, Hanumanayaka, as also kings, villains and demons all elaborately made up. Dr. Shivaram Karanth, who died recently, was largely responsible for injecting new life into this dying drama form by setting up his own troupes, and taking them for performances all over the country.

Bhavai. Bhavai is the colorful and vigorous form of folk drama native to North Gujarat. In its original form, Bhavai was a purely religious and developmental folk dance drama, performed before the Goddess Ambaji, for the eradication of darkness and illusion. With the passage of time Bhavai has acquired many secular elements. Bhavai represents 3 categories. Pauranic (based on old Hindu religious books), historical, social. It usually presented mythological and historical romances and aimed at poking fun at the hypocrisy of the society. Ills of the society such as the marriage of an old man to a young girl, wasteful expenditure of the marriage and death ceremonies or the hypocrisy of the social and political leaders were exposed. It uses satire as a medium.

Bhavai has three main characters - Nayak, Ranglo and Rangli. Nayak is a 'Sutradhar' or manager. He is a singer, vocalist, narrator director combined. 'Ranglo' is the jester of clown, while 'Rangli' is a helpmate of 'Ranglo', to checks that he remains on the track. Ranglo makes satirical remarks and exposes social and political evils.

Street Play. A street play is of a recent origin. It is also called a 'Street theatre'. It provides link between the highly sophisticated drama and the improvised street theatre. In cities it is performed either in the streets or at the important key places of a city such as main road-crossings, city square, near a busy market place and so on.

The origin of a street play is more political rather than traditional. In 1944, Bijor Bhattacharya, a founder of Indian People's Theatre Association (IPTA) staged perhaps the first street play called 'Nibanna' about the exploitations of peasants by Bengali landlords. Street plays are closer to the literary dramatic piece. They have pre written scripts, practiced well by the actors for the performance on the streets. In street plays, no specitic costumes are worn by the actors. The message of a play is conveyed effectively through their rigorous actions, expressions and dialogues. They are characterized by vivid portrayal of real events, popular languages, dialects and minimal properties. They are culture specific, and employ folk theatre forms, local songs and dances and the local dialect. The striking difference between folk drama and street play is that the street play uses folk darnes, songs etc. for communication but it is more educative, less traditional and performed by educated persons. The themes mainly deal with current social problems. Nowadays, it has become a medium of communication for agricultural extension workers, health workers, women activists, student activists and so on.

Folk Songs. These are musical form of communication. There are folk songs of every region. These folk songs are sung on the specific occassions and festivals. They can absorb a new message. For example, folk songs relating to harvest can carry the new themes like improved methods of cultivation, use of fertilizer and preservation of food grains. Revival and popularization of such traditional singing strengthens the sense of social democracy and help in fostering the mutual understanding among the regional language groups.

Parmar says, ''the folk music makes the most sense to the people who use it as a part of their behavioural and ritualistic activities". According to Panigrahy, "Attitudes, which have been inherited as part of tradition and are unamendable to change, could be modified by pressing into service the folk songs of the region".

Apart from the various forms discussed here there are popular folklore tales, ballad singing , Harikatha and many other oral communication forms are practiced in our country for communicating with various groups especially rural and tribal. Ballad and Harikatha are verbal musical forms of communication.

Folk art in the form of drawings and paintings also visually communicate the culture of the region. These arts are the basis for many of the arts and designs in vogue today especially on cards, decorative pieces, wall hangings, textile and so on. These arts have made impact on the artistic and aesthetic taste of urban people.

Folk music supplements the oral communication. In part folk music styles were used by poets, patriots and village singers to motivate the people for some action, such as, rising against the existing rule.

Riddles, sayings, proverbs also convey innumerable messages reflecting the social relationship and the experiences of the people and when used while communicating, they not only perform the persuasive function but create desired impact.

Folk and Electronic Media Blending

The adaptation of the folk media to mass media like radio and television has been the subject of much discussion. Folk media have also been presented over radio and television to relatively anonymous audiences. Here, they do not readily lend themselves to spontaneous adaptation, they are still found to be effective in making an impact. AIR integrated folk media in it's rural broadcasts all over the country in the form of folk songs and plays. The formats of radio play and folk play are similar as both are free from the dramatic unities of space and time and do not require any physical setting and both are close to the audience.

In a paper presented at the UNESCO Seminar in New Delhi, Khanna, pointed out the advantages that would accrue from a fusion of the two media. In terms of technique, at least some of the mass communication media could greatly amplify, augment and intensify the effect usually created by traditional media. For example, the aural quality of the radio liberates the mind of the listener from the traditional concept of time and space, and leaves his imagination free to add other dimensions drawn from subjective improvisation. This additive factor for free imagination constitutes the main strength of the medium of radio. In TV, the close up can convey much more with greater emotional impact, largely by isolating the non-essential and focussing the viewers attention on only essentials tremendously enhancing the evocative power of human face or gesture. The film too achieves similar results by breaking away from time and space, and using the element of mobility and flex to great advantage. Television as a medium can be used for such folk media which involve visuals and broadcasting can be used for those having only oral information. However, TV and broadcasting can not substitute live performances. They can supplement live programmes.

In theory it is true that the use of traditional and folk forms, with suitable adaptation, over the electronic media will give them a much wider reach than can be achieved through live performances. But wide rural reach can in fact be achieved only when a large number of local radio and local TV stations are established at district level with adequate provision for community access.

It may sound contradictory that the very modernity which has been considered as one of the causes for the decline of the folk media, is in some cases partly or wholly responsible for reviewing, revitalising, preserving and disseminating the traditional media. For example, radio devotes 3.6 percent of it's broadcast time to folk music and 1.6 percent to tribal music, apart from Bhavai and Tamasha programmes. TV, though it has smaller reach as compared to radio, is doing a vital job with its multiple effect of reaching a large audience simultaneously and is capturing new audience. Thus TV and radio help to preserve the art forms.

Traditional media were integrated with mass media in the interest of multiplicity of programmes and simultaneous application to a far wider field. Traditional performing arts gained glamour through mass media, but there is every chance of their suffering in this blending, when they are not presented in their proper perspective. In order to transfuse them through mass media without loss of their charm and rural ruggedness, it is necessary to shoot the programmes in their native field rather than bringing the performers to the studio. The studio treatment of the folk media is so harsh as to cut the most delightful angularities and make it a tailor-made, devoid ofit's inherent culture.

Many media experts feel that it would be disastrous to allow science and technology dominate folk media as it is a living symbol that carries the light and delight of the grass roots culture of the past, through the present into the future.

❐